SELECT DOCUMENTS FOR
QUEEN ANNE'S REIGN
DOWN TO THE UNION WITH
SCOTLAND. 1702–7

SELECT DOCUMENTS FOR QUEEN ANNE'S REIGN

DOWN TO THE UNION WITH SCOTLAND. 1702–7

SELECTED
AND EDITED BY

G. M. TREVELYAN

*Regius Professor of Modern History
in the University of
Cambridge*

CAMBRIDGE
AT THE UNIVERSITY PRESS
1929

CAMBRIDGE UNIVERSITY PRESS
Cambridge, New York, Melbourne, Madrid, Cape Town, Singapore,
São Paulo, Delhi

Cambridge University Press
The Edinburgh Building, Cambridge CB2 8RU, UK

Published in the United States of America by
Cambridge University Press, New York

www.cambridge.org
Information on this title: www.cambridge.org/9780521103978

© Cambridge University Press 1929

First published 1929
This digitally printed version 2009

A catalogue record for this publication is available from the British Library

ISBN 978-0-521-06647-1 hardback
ISBN 978-0-521-10397-8 paperback

PREFACE

HAVING undertaken to lecture on the first years of Queen Anne's reign as a Special Subject for the Cambridge Historical Tripos, I was at once confronted with the fact that nearly all the contemporary authorities which it would be necessary for students to have in their hands, were either out of print, or were on the point of going out of print. Moreover they were widely scattered in a number of different books. The Cambridge University Press has overcome these difficulties by consenting to issue this book of Select Documents. A few transcripts, hitherto unpublished, from the British Museum MSS have been added.

I have made no selections from Burnet's *History of his own Time*, because it can be found in nearly every College or other Library of any pretension. Moreover, it should be read *in extenso* for the relative period, to obtain a general view of "how it appeared to a contemporary"; it is less valuable for detailed study as an authority for the facts of Queen Anne's reign. When possible it should be read in those nineteenth-century editions which reproduce at the foot of the page the comments of Dartmouth, Hardwicke, Onslow and Swift.

There is, I think, very little in this volume of selections of which the general drift and import will not be clear to any student of the period who has read such excellent introductions to the subject as Leadam's *Political History of England* (Longman), vol. IX, chaps. I–V; Atkinson's *Marlborough* (Heroes of Nations Series); Julian Corbett's *England in the Mediterranean*, vol. II, chaps. XXVII–XXXII; Hume Brown's *History of Scotland*, vol. III, chaps. II and III; and Keith Feiling's *History of the Tory Party*, chaps. XIII–XIV.

The six Sections into which I have divided the documents here printed, naturally keep the domestic history separate from the diplomatic and military-naval operations. But the intimate connection between home and foreign affairs is indicated in Section V, the Marlborough correspondence, which serves as a supplement to Section II (Home Politics) and Section IV (Blenheim).

Both the Marlborough correspondence here printed and the modern works which I have just mentioned make clear the dependence of the successful conduct of the war on the triumph of the "moderate" or "coalition" policy at home. Viewed in that light, the quarrel between Lords and Commons over the Occasional Conformity Bill appears something more than a passing phase of the ceaseless wrangle of Church and Dissent, Tory and Whig. And the departure of Rochester from office in 1703 and of Nottingham in 1704, leaving Marlborough supreme in the State, appears as something more important than an incident in the rivalry of ambitious noblemen. For on these things depended the carrying out of Marlborough's grand schemes of combined naval, military and diplomatic strategy, to wrest back the control of the world from Louis XIV and his grandson the King of Spain, and to restore the independence of the State system of Europe. For Rochester scarcely wished to see the war carried on with vigour anywhere on land, and Nottingham believed that we should concentrate our military efforts on Spain.

So too the Scottish Union, immensely important and beneficial as it proved to be to both countries in the course of succeeding generations, was passed primarily as a war measure. The immediate object in view was to remove the grave possibility of Scotland declaring the Pretender as King on the death of Anne, even if the demise of the crown should occur in the middle of the war with France.

The struggle to reduce "the exorbitant power of France" was involved in the struggle to maintain the Protestant Succession in the person of Anne, and after her, in the House of Hanover designated to the succession by the Act of Settlement of 1701. Louis XIV, by acknowledging the Pretender as King of England on the death of his father James II in September 1701, had made the English dynastic question one of the issues of the war. Another issue was the right of the English merchants to trade with South America, and with the States of the Mediterranean basin which the new Franco-Spanish Alliance was closing to us. A third was the independence and safety of the Low Countries in particular, and of Europe in general, when the French troops were in actual occupation not only of Spain but of Flanders, Italy and Bavaria. A "universal monarchy" seemed on the very point of being set up.

Indeed when Anne came to the throne in 1702 the situation seemed almost desperate. The independence of Europe seemed already lost, and the independence of England, symbolized by the Protestant Succession, did not seem likely to survive. It was saved by the genius of Marlborough and the good sense displayed by Queen Anne and by the English people. The turning-point in the struggle was Blenheim. That battle saved Vienna and central Europe from falling under French control, and broke the prestige of the French arms. The work was completed two years later when Flanders was reconquered at Ramillies, and Italy at Turin, and when the Treaty of Union with Scotland secured the unity of the island on the basis of the Protestant Succession. Simultaneously, the establishment of English sea power in the Mediterranean, symbolized first by the capture and then by the heroic defence of Gibraltar, was a further proof that the young eighteenth century was destined to be controlled by other forces than a supreme French despotic system.

The credit for effecting this great work of deliverance between 1702 and 1706 rests with the "moderates" of English politics—Anne herself, Harley as Parliamentary manager behind the scenes, Godolphin as paymaster, Marlborough as the great executant. It is perhaps good upon the whole that England should be governed by the alternating supremacy of two rival parties. At least it has been found the line of least resistance for carrying on Parliamentary government in normal times. But there are great exceptional cases, as for instance in the crisis of a dangerous foreign war. And such a case was found in the opening of Anne's reign.

The "moderate" domestic policy of the Marlborough Ministry, bent only on winning the war, had more unqualified support in the House of Lords than in the House of Commons, at least till the general election of 1705. One of the most interesting and most hotly contested constitutional issues of the time was the degree to which the House of Lords could act as a brake upon the House of Commons. In the Lords

PREFACE

parties were evenly balanced, and on several occasions in the
reigns of William, Anne and George I, the Lords checked the
partisan action of the Lower House which was alternately
strong Whig and strong Tory. This restraining action of the
House of Lords came into play early in Anne's reign on the
question of the Occasional Conformity Bill (Section II below).
At any other time the measure might have been passed, as indeed
it was passed in 1711. But in 1702–4 it was felt by many who
did not disapprove of the principle of the Bill that it was inimical
to national unity to do anything to alienate the Dissenters and
the city of London at the most dangerous crisis of the war. For
that reason the moderate Tories came to join with the Whigs
against the strongest provisions of the Bill. And it was in the
House of Lords that the "moderates" found their stronghold.

The action of the House of Lords in this and other matters
was of great assistance to the Queen and her Ministers early
in the reign, when they were endeavouring to lay the restless
spirit of faction in order to conduct the war with vigour and
success. After the war had been substantially won at the end
of the year 1706, the tendency of English Parliamentary life
towards the two-party system reasserted itself, and first the
Whigs and then the Tories took charge of the later fortunes
of Queen Anne. It can hardly be said by the most ardent
partisans that either the Whig Ministers of 1708–10 or the
Tory Ministers of 1710–14 did so well by the country as the
"Marlborough group" between 1702 and 1706.

I acknowledge the kindness of Lord Crawford and of the
family of the late Charles Butler in expressing their willingness
that I should reprint from the Roxburghe Club text the large
quotation from the *Memoirs* of Sir John Clerk of Penicuik. I am
similarly grateful to the goodwill of Mr Craster and of the
English Historical Review in the matter of Lord Orkney's
Letter on Ramillies; and to the Secretary and Council of the
Royal Historical Society in the matter of the Torrington
Memoirs on the capture of Gibraltar.

[Students will note the difference between the New Style
[N.S.] and Old Style [O.S.] of reckoning dates. Until 1752

viii

the English at home always used the Old Style, eleven days behind the New Style of Gregory XIII's Calendar which was current in all continental countries except European Russia. Our soldiers in Flanders and Germany sometimes used the Old Style, more often the New. Our sailors on service at sea, as for instance at the taking of Gibraltar, often used the Old Style familiar at home. The clearest method was to use both, and to say that the battle of Blenheim was won on Aug. 2/13 or Aug. 2–13.]

G. M. TREVELYAN

CONTENTS

xi

CONTENTS

SECTION III

GIBRALTAR

SECTION IV

BLENHEIM AND RAMILLIES

CONTENTS

SECTION V

MARLBOROUGH PAPERS

SECTION VI

SCOTLAND AND THE UNION

LISTS

SKETCH MAPS

I
FOREIGN TREATIES OF ALLIANCE

FOREIGN TREATIES OF ALLIANCE

THE TREATY of Grand Alliance, made in the last year of William III's reign, represents the reply of England, Holland and Austria to the acceptance by Louis XIV of Charles II of Spain's will; that will left the whole Spanish empire to Louis' grandson, Philip V of Spain. It will be observed that the Treaty of Grand Alliance of September 1701 does not bind the allies to recover Spain and Spanish America from Philip, but only to obtain security and compensation for his kingship. The allies bind themselves to secure English trade with Spain, Spanish America, and the Mediterranean; a barrier for the Dutch in the Netherlands; and territorial compensation in Italy for Austria, in return for her forgoing her claims to the whole Spanish inheritance. The additional clause, added in May 1703, further binds the allies to force Louis to acknowledge the Protestant Succession in Britain. This clause was rendered necessary when Louis acknowledged the Pretender as King of England a few days after the first draft of the Grand Alliance had been signed. It was Sir Edward Seymour, a leading Tory, who moved to have this vindication of the national honour inserted in the Treaty of Alliance.

The Treaties with Prussia and Brunswick-Lüneburg are typical of many such treaties with other allied States, particularly in Germany. It was in this way that the English and Dutch Governments paid many of the allies to fight for them. It was in effect the famous "subsidy system" which financed all English alliances against France down to the Napoleonic wars.

The Treaty with Portugal of 1703 is not merely another such "subsidy" treaty. It marks also the opening of a great new theatre of war—the Iberian Peninsula. It represents the effective opening of the Mediterranean basin to our fleets. For without Lisbon as a naval base we could have done nothing in the Mediterranean; we could not even have held

Gibraltar, which we were only able to defend in the siege of 1704–5 because we had Lisbon as a naval base. It will also be observed that this treaty with Portugal alters the basis of the Grand Alliance; it substitutes the attempt to win Spain and Spanish America on behalf of the Austrian candidate "Charles III," for the original basis of the Grand Alliance of two years before, which had been security and compensation for the admitted fact of Philip V's kingship.

In the text of these Treaties I have preserved *the grammar and the spelling* of names and words as they are found in de Lamberty and the *House of Commons Journals* respectively.

TABLE OF THE SPANISH SUCCESSION

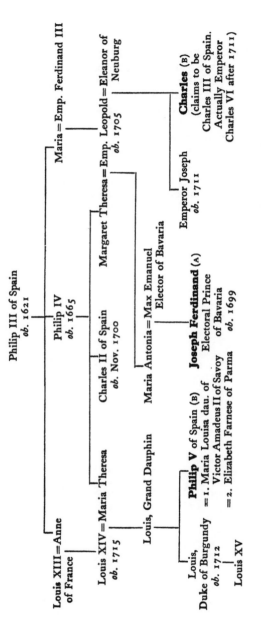

Philip III of Spain
ob. 1621

Maria = Emp. Ferdinand III

Philip IV
ob. 1665

Louis XIII = Anne of France

Charles II of Spain
ob. Nov. 1700

Margaret Theresa = Emp. Leopold = Eleanor of Neuburg
ob. 1705

Louis XIV = Maria Theresa
ob. 1715

Maria Antonia = Max Emanuel Elector of Bavaria

Emperor Joseph
ob. 1711

Charles (B)
(claims to be
Charles III of Spain.
Actually Emperor
Charles VI after 1711)

Louis, Grand Dauphin

Joseph Ferdinand (A)
Electoral Prince
of Bavaria
ob. 1699

Philip V of Spain (B)
= 1. Maria Louisa dau. of
    Victor Amadeus II of Savoy
= 2. Elizabeth Farnese of Parma

Louis,
Duke of Burgundy
ob. 1712

Louis XV

(A) Recognised as heir by Charles II; chief beneficiary of the First Treaty of Partition.

(B) Rival claimants of Spain after Charles II, the elder brother of each resigning his pretensions.

I. *Treaty of Grand Alliance*

7 September 1701

(de Lamberty, *Mémoires*, 1735, I, 620–628.)

D'Autant que le Roi d'Efpagne CHARLES II. de glorieufe memoire, étant mort fans Enfans, Sa Sacrée Majefté Imperiale a affûré que la Succeffion des Roiaumes & Provinces du Roi defunt appartiennent legitimement à fon Augufte Maifon, & que le Roi T. C. defirant avoir la même Succeffion pour le Duc d'ANJOU fon Petit-Fils, & alleguant qu'elle lui vient de Droit en vertu d'un certain Teftament du Roi defunt, il s'eft d'abord mis en poffeffion de tout l'Heritage ou Monarchie d'Efpagne pour le fufdit Duc d'ANJOU, & s'eft emparé à main armée des Provinces du Païs-Bas Efpagnol, & du Duché de Milan, & qu'il tient une Flotte dans le Port de Cadix, toute prête à faire voile, & qu'il a envoié plufieurs Vaiffeaux de Guerre aux Indes qui font foûmifes à l'Efpagne, & que par ce moien & plufieurs autres, les Roiaumes de France & d'Efpagne font fi étroitement unis, qu'il femble qu'ils ne doivent plus être regardez à l'avenir, que comme un feul & même Roiaume, tellement que fi on n'y prend garde, il y a bien de l'apparence que Sa Majefté Imperiale ne doit plus efperer d'avoir jamais aucune fatisfaction de fa pretention; Que l'Empire Romain perdra tous fes Droits fur les Fiefs qui font en Italie, & dans le Païs-Bas Efpagnol, de même que les Anglois & Hollandois perdront la liberté de leur Navigation & de leur Commerce dans la Mer Mediterranée, aux Indes, & ailleurs; Et que les Provinces-Unies feront privées de la fûreté qu'elles avoient par l'interpofition entr'elles & la France des Provinces du Païs-Bas Efpagnol, appellées communement *la Barriere*; Et qu'enfin les François & les Efpagnols étant ainfi unis deviendroient en peu de tems fi formidables qu'ils pourroient aifement foûmettre toute l'Europe à leur obéïffance & empire. Or comme cette conduite du Roi T. C. a mis Sa Majefté Imperiale dans la neceffité d'envoier une Armée en Italie, tant pour la confervation de fes Droits particuliers, que pour celle des Fiefs de l'Empire; de même, le Roi de la Grande-Bretagne a jugé qu'il étoit neceffaire d'envoier fes Troupes auxiliaires aux Provinces-Unies, dont les Affaires font dans le même état, que fi on en étoit deja venu à une Guerre ouverte, & les Seigneurs Etats Generaux, dont les Frontieres font prefque de toutes parts ouvertes, par la rupture de la Barriere qui empêchoit le voifinage des François, font contraints de faire, pour la fûreté & pour la confervation de leur Republique, tout ce qu'ils auroient dû & pû faire, s'ils étoient effectivement attaquez par une Guerre ouverte. Et comme un état fi douteux & fi incertain en toutes chofes, eft plus dangereux que la Guerre même, & que la France & l'Efpagne s'en prevalent pour s'unir de plus en plus, afin d'opprimer la Liberté de l'Europe, & ruïner le Commerce accoûtumé; Toutes ces raifons ont porté Sa Sacrée Majefté Imperiale, Sa Sacrée Roiale Majefté de la Grande-Bretagne, & les Hauts & Puiffans Seigneurs Etats Generaux des Provinces-Unies, d'aller au devant de tous les maux qui en proviendroient; & defirant d'y apporter remede felon leurs forces, ils ont jugé qu'il étoit neceffaire de faire entr'eux une étroite Alliance & Confederation pour éloigner le grand & commun danger. Pour cet effet ils ont donné leurs Ordres & Inftructions.

* * * * * *

1. Qu'il y ait dès à prefent & à l'avenir, une conftante, perpetuelle, & inviolable Amitié, entre Sa Sacrée Majefté Imperiale, Sa Sacrée Roiale Majefté de la Grande-Bretagne, & les Seigneurs Etats Generaux des Provinces-Unies, & qu'ils foient tenus reciproquement de procurer ce qui leur fera avantageux, & d'éloigner ce qui leur feroit nuifible & dommageable.

2. Sa Sacrée Majefté Imperiale, Sa Sacrée Roiale Majefté de la Grande-Bretagne, & les Seigneurs Etats Generaux des Provinces-Unies, n'aiant rien tant à cœur que la Paix & la tranquillité de toute l'Europe, ont jugé qu'il ne pouvoit rien y avoir de plus efficace pour l'affermir, que de procurer à Sa Majefté Imperiale une fatisfaction jufte & raifonnable, touchant fes pretentions à la Succeffion d'Efpagne, & que le Roi de la Grande-Bretagne, & les Seigneurs Etats Generaux obtiennent une fûreté particuliere & fuffifante, pour leurs Roiaumes, Provinces, Terres, & Païs de leur obéïffance, & pour la Navigation & le Commerce de leurs Sujets.

6

3. Pour cet effet les Alliez mettront premierement en ufage tous les moiens poffibles, & tout ce qui dependra d'eux, pour obtenir amiablement, & par une Tranfaction ferme & folide, une fatisfaction jufte & raifonnable pour Sa Majefté Imperiale, au fujet de ladite Succeffion, & la fûreté dont il a été fait mention ci-deffus, pour Sa Majefté Britannique, & pour les Seigneurs Etats des Provinces-Unies; Et à cette fin, ils emploieront tous leurs foins & offices pendant deux mois, à compter du jour de l'échange des Ratifications de ce prefent Traité.

4. Mais fi dans ce tems-là les Alliez viennent à être fruftrez de leur efperance & de leurs defirs, tellement que l'on ne puiffe pas tranfiger dans le terme fixé, en ce cas ils promettent & s'engagent reciproquement de s'aider de toutes leurs forces, felon ce qui fera reglé par une convention particuliere, pour obtenir la fatisfaction & fûreté fufdite.

5. Et afin de procurer cette fatisfaction & cette fûreté, les Alliez feront entr'autres chofes leurs plus grands efforts pour reprendre & conquerir les Provinces du Païs-Bas Efpagnol, dans l'intention qu'elles fervent de Digue, de Rempart, & de Barriere pour feparer & éloigner la France des Provinces-Unies, comme par le paffé, lefdites Provinces du Païs-Bas Efpagnol aiant fait la fûreté des Seigneurs Etats Generaux jufques à ce que depuis peu Sa Majefté Très-Chrêtienne s'en eft emparée, & les a fait occuper par fes Troupes. Pareillement les Alliez feront tous les efforts pour conquerir le Duché de Milan avec toutes fes dependances, comme étant un Fief de l'Empire fervant pour la fûreté des Provinces Hereditaires de Sa Majefté Imperiale, & pour conquerir les Roiaumes de Naples & de Sicile, & les Ifles de la Mer Mediterranée, avec les Terres dependantes de l'Efpagne le long de la Côte de Tofcane, qui peuvent fervir à la même fin & être utiles pour la Navigation & le Commerce des Sujets de Sa Majefté Britannique & des Provinces-Unies.

6. Pourront le Roi de la Grande-Bretagne, & les Seigneurs Etats Generaux, conquerir à force d'Armes, felon qu'ils auront concerté entr'eux, pour l'utilité & la commodité de la Navigation & du Commerce de leurs Sujets, les Païs & les Villes que les Efpagnols ont dans les Indes, & tout ce qu'ils pourront y prendre fera pour eux, & leur demeurera.

7. Que si les Alliez se trouvent obligez à entrer en Guerre pour obtenir ladite satisfaction à S. M. Imperiale, & ladite sûreté à Sa Majesté Britannique, & aux Seigneurs Etats Generaux, ils se communiqueront fidellement les avis & resolutions des Conseils qui se tiendront pour toutes les entreprises de Guerre, ou expeditions militaires, & generalement tout ce qui concernera cette affaire commune.

8. La Guerre étant une fois commencée, aucun des Alliez ne pourra traiter de Paix avec l'Ennemi, si ce n'est conjointement avec la participation & le conseil des autres Parties. Et ladite Paix ne pourra être concluë, sans avoir obtenu pour Sa Majesté Imperiale une satisfaction juste & raisonnable; & pour le Roi de la Grande-Bretagne, & les Seigneurs Etats Generaux la sûreté particuliere de leurs Roiaumes, Provinces, Terres, & Païs de leur obéïssance, Navigation & Commerce; ni sans avoir pris auparavant de justes mesures, pour empêcher que les Roiaumes de France & d'Espagne, soient jamais unis sous un même Empire, ou qu'un seul & même Roi en devint le Souverain; & specialement que jamais les François se rendent maîtres des Indes Espagnoles, ou qu'ils y envoient des Vaisseaux pour y exercer le Commerce, directement ou indirectement, sous quelque pretexte que ce soit. Enfin ladite Paix ne pourra être concluë sans avoir obtenu pour les Sujets de Sa Majesté Britannique & pour ceux des Provinces-Unies, une pleine & entiere faculté, usage & jouïssance de tous les mêmes Privileges, Droits, Immunitez, & Libertez de Commerce tant par Terre que par Mer, en Espagne & sur la Mer Mediterranée, dont ils usoient & jouïssoient pendant la vie du feu Roi d'Espagne dans tous les Païs qu'il possedoit tant en Europe qu'ailleurs, & dont ils pouvoient de Droit user & jouir en commun ou en particulier, par les Traitez, Conventions, & Coûtumes, ou de quelque autre maniere que ce puisse être.

9. Lors que ladite Transaction, ou Traité de Paix se fera, les Alliez conviendront entr'eux de tout ce qui sera necessaire pour établir le Commerce & la Navigation des Sujets de Sa Majesté Britannique, & des Seigneurs Etats Generaux, dans les Païs & lieux que l'on doit acquerir, & que le feu Roi d'Espagne possedoit. Ils conviendront pareillement des moiens

propres à mettre en fûreté les Seigneurs Etats Generaux par la Barriere fufmentionnée.

10. Et d'autant qu'il pourroit naître quelque controverfe au fujet de la Religion dans les lieux que les Alliez efperent de conquerir, ils conviendront entr'eux de fon exercice, au tems fufdit de la Paix.

11. Les Alliez feront obligez de s'entr'aider & fecourir de toutes leurs forces, au cas que le Roi de France, ou quelque autre que ce foit, vint à attaquer l'un d'entr'eux à caufe du prefent Traité.

12. Soit que l'on puiffe maintenant tranfiger fur ladite fatisfaction & fûreté, ou foit que la Paix fe faffe après que l'on aura entrepris une Guerre neceffaire, il y aura & demeurera toûjours entre les Parties contractantes une Alliance defenfive, pour la Garantie de ladite Tranfaction, ou de ladite Paix.

13. Tous les Rois, Princes, & Etats, qui ont la Paix à cœur, & qui voudront entrer dans la prefente Alliance, y feront admis. Et parce qu'il eft particulierement de l'interêt du Saint Empire Romain, de conferver la Paix publique, & qu'il s'agit ici entr'autres chofes de recouvrer les Fiefs de l'Empire, on invitera fpecialement ledit Empire d'entrer dans la prefente Alliance. Outre quoi tous les Alliez enfemble, & chacun d'eux en particulier, pourront y inviter ceux qu'ils verront bon être.

14. Ce Traité d'Alliance & Confederation fera ratifié par tous les Alliez dans l'efpace de fix femaines, & plûtôt fi faire fe peut.

En foi de quoi, nous Plenipotentiaires fufnommez avons figné le prefent Traité de nos mains, & l'avons muni de nos Sceaux & Cachets. A la Haie le feptieme du mois de Septembre de l'an mil fept cens un.

Etoit figné en chacun des Inftrumens feparez; fçavoir, de la part de Sa Majefté Imperiale, *Pierre Comte de Goës*; & *Jean Wenceflaus Comte de Wratiflau & Mitrowitz*. De la part de Sa Majefté le Roi de la Grande-Bretagne, *Marlborough*. Et de la part des Seigneurs Etats Generaux des Provinces-Unies, *D. Eck van Panteleon, Hr. van Gent. F. B. van Rheede. A. Heynfius. W. de Naffau. E. de Weede. W. van Haren. B. J. van Welvelde. W. Wickers.*

Additional article of the Grand Alliance—
"Vienna clause"

(Klopp, *Fall des Hauses Stuart*, IX, 500.)

16 May 1703

Puisque depuis que le traité entre Sa Majesté Imperiale, Sa Majesté Britannique et Mss. les Etats Generaux des Provinces Unies des Pays Bas fut conclu et signé à La Haye, le 7 septembre 1701, le Roy de France s'est resolu de reconnoistre et proclamer le pretendu Prince de Galles pour Roy d'Angleterre, d'Ecosse et d'Irlande, et que par là il a fait un grand tort à Sa dite Majesté Britannique et à toute la nation anglaise, les dits Hauts Alliez, Sa Majesté Imperiale, Sa Majesté Britannique, et Mss. les Etats Generaux des Provinces Unies des Pays Bas sont convenus par cet article (qui aura la même force, nature et effect comme s'il avoit été inséré dès le commencement dans le dit traité) qu'on ne fera point de paix avec la France avant que réparation ne soit faite à Sa Majesté Britannique du dit très grand tort.

II. *Treaty with Prussia*, December 1701

(de Lamberty, *Mémoires*, 1735, I, 710.)

Comme Sa Majesté le Roi de Prusse a offert à Sa Majesté le Roi de la Grande-Bretagne, & à Leurs Hautes Puissances les Etats Generaux des Provinces-Unies, de leur remettre un corps de cinq mille hommes de bonnes & vieilles Troupes, & cette offre aiant été bien reçûë, on est convenu de part & d'autre des conditions suivantes:

I. Le Corps consistera en deux Regimens de Cavalerie, faisant ensemble, avec l'Etat Major & primes planes, 874. hommes, & en cinq Regimens d'Infanterie, chacun de douze Compagnies, faisant ensemble avec l'Etat Major, & primes planes 4255. hommes; & le total en Cavalerie & Infanterie 5129. hommes.

II. Les Troupes seront bien habillées & bien armées, & la Cavalerie sera fournie de bon chevaux; & Elles seront en tout traitées & paiées sur le pied que l'Etat traite les siennes propres.

III. Lefdites Troupes feront paiées, moitié de la part de Sa Majefté le Roi de la Grande-Bretagne, & l'autre moitié de celle de Leurs Hautes Puiffances. Ce päiement fera auffi prompt & fur le pied des Troupes de Sa Majefté le Roi de Pruffe, qui ont été au fervice de Leurs Hautes Puiffances durant la derniere Guerre.

IV. On fera paier à ce Corps un mois de gage pour fon tranfport, dès qu'il fe mettra effectivement en marche.

V. Sa Majefté le Roi de Pruffe fera fortir des quartiers, & mettre en marche, ledit Corps de Troupes, quinze jours après la fignature de ce Traité, & plûtôt s'il eft poffible.

VI. La folde de ces Troupes ne commencera que du jour qu'elles feront entrées dans les limites des Etats de Leurs Hautes Puiffances. C'eft alors qu'on en fera la revûë par les Commiffaires de Sa Majefté Britannique & de Leurs Hautes Puiffances & que lefdites Troupes prêteront ferment au Roi de la Grande-Bretagne & à l'Etat.

VII. A l'égard des revûës defdites Troupes on en ufera fur le pied que Leurs Hautes Puiffances feront avec les leurs propres. Et d'ailleurs on laiffera de part & d'autre auxdites Troupes la liberté de faire leurs recruës, où il leur fera le plus convenable, auffi-bien dans les Etats de Sa Majefté le Roi de Pruffe que dans ceux de Leurs Hautes Puiffances.

VIII. En tems de Guerre on fera paier à ces mêmes Troupes en argent pour chariots & autres équipages, ce qu'on paie de la part de Leurs Hautes Puiffances à leurs propres Troupes; & au refte on traitera lefdites Troupes en tout également à ce qui fe pratique envers celles de Leurs Hautes Puiffances.

IX. Au cas qu'après un Accommodement ou Paix faite avec les Couronnes de France & d'Efpagne, Sa Majefté le Roi de la Grande-Bretagne, & Leurs Hautes Puiffances veuillent renvoier ledit Corps de Troupes, Sa Majefté le Roi de Pruffe fera avertie deux mois avant qu'il fe mette en marche pour s'en retourner.

X. Si Sa Majefté le Roi de Pruffe venoit à être attaquée dans fes propres Etats, éloignez du Rhin, & feroit obligé de redemander là-deffus lefdites Troupes, on les lui renvoiera inceffamment, fans aucune contradiction.

XI. Quand Sa Majefté de la Grande-Bretagne & Leurs Hautes Puiffances renvoieront ledit Corps de Troupes, en ce cas, il lui fera paié un mois de gage pour le retour & tranfport; mais au cas que Sa Majefté le Roi de Pruffe le rapelle, on ne lui paiera que le refte du mois de gage, dans lequel le apel fe fait.

XII. Au cas de rapel ou de renvoi de ces Troupes, Sa Majefté le Roi de la Grande-Bretagne & Leurs Hautes Puiffances ne paieront ni remplaceront point les fimples Soldats qui pourroient alors y manquer; & ce fera aux Officiers dudit Corps d'en repondre à Sa Majefté le Roi de Pruffe.

XIII. Audit cas de renvoi ou de rapel defdites Troupes, ce qui fe trouvera alors leur être dû, fera paié promptement & autant qu'il fera poffible, avant qu'elles fe mettent en marche pour leur retour.

XIV. La prefente Convention fera ratifiée, & les Ratifications feront échangées de part & d'autre dans l'efpace de fix femaines à compter du jour de la fignature.

III. *Treaty with Brunswick Lüneburg*
November 1703

A Copy of the Treaty for Troops of *Lunebourg*, for the Year 1704. (*H. of C. Journals*, xiv, 222.)

LA Convention, conclu entre fa Majefté la Reine de la Grande Bretagne, et leurs Alteffes Electorale et Sereniffime de Brunfwic Lunebourg, le 16me du Mois de Novembre, 1702, pour un Secours de Dix mille Hommes, allant expirer, on eft convenu de part et d'autre de la Continuation du dit Traité pour toute l'Année prochaine, aux Conditions fuivants:

I

Sa Majefté continuera à faire payer et entretenir les Troupes de leurs Alteffes Electorale et Sereniffime, qui reftent dans fon Service pour l'Année prochaine 1704, a raifon, de Sept cent Chevaux, en deux Regiments de Cavallerie, et de Huit mille Cinq cent Vingt et cinq Fantaffins, en onze

Regiments d'Infanterie, felon l'Etat cy joint, fur le Pied des
Troupes, que leurs Alteffes Electorale et Sereniffime ont aus
Service des Seigneurs Etats Generaux des Provinces Unies,
tant pour les Gages ordinaires, que pour les Emolumens
Extraordinaires, ce qui fera, par un long Mois de Six Semaines,
ou de quarante deux Jours (y compris les Mille et Cinquante
Florins, que fa Majefté donne par Mois pour le Frais des
Hopitaux fuivant le fufdit Etat joint à cette Convention) la
Somme de Cent nonante et deux mille Sept cent foixante et
deux Francs Quatre Sols Monoye d'Hollande; qui fera payée
à Rotterdam regulierement de quinze Jours en quinze Jours.
Et comme le Payement, reglé par la premiere Convention cy
deffus allegué, finit avec cette Année felon le nouveau Stile,
le Payement de cette nouvelle Convention commencera avec
le premier Jour de l'Année prochaine 1704, et continuera à
couler jufqu'au dernier; et ces Troupes jouiront auffi dans
tout le refte, fans Exception, des memes Avantages, Benefices,
Douceurs, et Comodités, que l'Etat donne à fes propres
Troupes.

2

Sa Majefté ne payant le Cavallerie, fuivant l'Article 4me,
que fur le Pied de deux Regiments de Sept cent Chevaux, non
obftant qu'il y en a un beaucoup plus grand Nombre, qui ne
paffe dans le Paye que pour de l'Infanterie, on eft convenu de
part et d'autre, que leurs Alteffes Electorale et Sereniffime
pourront, quand il leur plaira, changer contre de l'Infanterie,
ce qu'il y a en Cavallerie dans ce Corps au deffus des dits deux
Regiments qui font les Sept cent Chavaux enfemble. Et on
ne feparera point le corps de ces Troupes en Campagne,
pour fervir en diverfes Armées; ni on ne les logera, ni ne les
mettra en Garnifon non plus dans la Flandre, ou autre Lieux
Maritimes.

3

Leurs Alteffes Electorale et Sereniffime fe refervant la
Liberté de retirer ces Troupes, ou toutes ou en partie, en cas
qu'ils feront attaques, ou dans un Danger evident de l'eftre,
dans les Etats qu'ils poffedent: Et fa Majefté confent à cette
Refervation; et, pour faciliter leur Retraite dans des Cas

femblables, on les aloignera le moins qu'il fera poffible du Bas Rhin.

4

Les Deferteurs pourront étre reclamés reciproquement, et feront rendus de bonne foy, fans aucune Reftitution de Frais ou Depenfes. Et comme il arrive fouvent, qu'on difpute, fi les Gens reclamés peuvent etre reputés Deferteurs, ou non, on n'aura pour cela befoin d'autres Preuves ou Forme de Procés, que de trouver ces Sortes des Gens dans d'autres Corps, fans Congé par ecrit de leurs Commandants.

5

Cette Convention n'etant faite que pour la feule Année prochaine, on travaillera de bonne heure à fa Prolongation; mais fi cela n'arrivoit pas, les Troupes feront renvoyées au 15 Novembre, fans rien retrancher de l'Entretien ftipulé pour toute l'Année par la premier Article, à fin que ce qui en refte puiffe fervir pour les Frais de leur Marche pour retourner; et pour cela la Reine fera payer content le dit refte avant leur depart.

6

Les Ratifications de la prefente Convention feront echangées en quatre Semaines, au plutot, s'il fe peut. Fait et figné par le Duc de Marlborough, Ambaffadeur Extraordinaire et Plenipotentiaire, &c. de fa Majefté la Reine de la Grande Bretagne, à Londres ce $\frac{9}{20}$ Novembre, 1703, et par le Baron de Bothmer, Plenipotentiaire de leurs Alteffes Electorale et Sereniffime à la Haye.

(L. S.) LE DUC DE MARLBOROUGH

IV. *Treaty with Portugal*

1703

The Tranflation of the Treaty of an Offenfive Alliance, concluded between the Emperor, the Queen, and the States General, on one Side, and the King of *Portugal* on the other, at *Lifbon, May* the 16th, 1703. (*H. of C. Journals*, XIV, 224.)

1ft Article

THE Three Confederate Potentates above-mentioned fhall contribute their Endeavours unanimoufly, that the moft Serene Archduke *Charles*, Second Son of his Imperial Majefty, be put into the Poffeffion of all *Spain*, as the Catholick King, *Charles* the Second, did poffefs it; with this however, that his facred royal Majefty of *Portugal* be not bound to make an Offenfive War, except in *Spain* itfelf.

2

For making this Offenfive War in *Spain*, his facred royal Majefty of *Portugal* fhall not be bound to have and maintain, at his own Charge, above Twelve thoufand Foot, and Three thoufand Horfe, which he is to bring into the Field.

3

Befides, his facred royal Majefty of *Portugal* fhall raife Thirteen thoufand *Portuguefe* Soldiers, that, in the Whole, the Forces of *Portugal* may be Twenty-eight thoufand Men; whereof Five thoufand fhall be Horfe, and Twenty-three thoufand Foot.

4

Of thefe 13,000 Soldiers, *viz.* Eleven thoufand Foot, Two thoufand Horfe, thofe 11,000 Foot fhall be armed with proper Arms, which, for that Purpofe, the Confederates are to furnifh, and over and above, as an Addition, Two thoufand Arms for thofe Soldiers.

5

The Confederates shall be bound to give to his sacred royal Majesty of *Portugal* Ten hundred Thousand Silver *Philips*, *Spanish* Money, or, as commonly called, a Million of Pattacoons each Year while the War lasts, for the Charge of the said 13,000 Soldiers, as well for their Pay, as for all other Expences, whereof they shall stand in need, as well in Quarters as in the Field.

6

The Payment of these Ten hundred thousand Silver *Philips*, *Spanish* Money, or, as commonly called, a Million of Pattacoons, shall be made by equal Parts, devised through all the Months of the Year; *viz.* that Part which relates to the Pay of the 13,000 Men, shall begin from the Exchange of the Ratifications, in Proportion to the Number of Men which shall then be raised, and as they shall afterwards be raised; but as to that Part of this Million, which belongs to the extraordinary Expences of the Army, marched out of their Quarters, the Payment thereof shall begin from the Day the Forces shall march out of their Quarters: But it is agreed, that, for the Payment of the first Part of this Million, there shall be always ready at *Lisbon* Two Months Pay; and, for the Payment of the Second Part of this Million, as soon as the Army shall march out of their Quarters, Two Months Pay shall be advanced; which shall not be placed to Account, unless for the Two last Months of the Year.

7

But if it shall happen, that his sacred royal Majesty of *Portugal* shall not have raised all the said 13,000 Soldiers, there shall be deducted out of this Million of Pattacoons, that Part of the Pay, which [may*] belong to that Number of Soldiers who shall [not*] effectively be raised.

8

Besides the said 1,000,000 Silver *Philips*, *Spanish* Money, or Million of Pattacoons, which the Confederates are to give every Year for the Payment of the 13,000 *Portuguese* Soldiers,

* This Word is supplied from the Translation of this Treaty, presented to the House.

as abovefaid, they fhall be bound further to give to his facred
royal Majefty of *Portugal* Five hundred thoufand Silver
Philips, or Five hundred thoufand Pattacoons, for his Preparations of the Army, and what elfe is neceffary this Firft
Year; and they fhall deliver this Sum of Money at the Time
of the Ratification of this Treaty.

9

The Confederates fhall furnifh, and fhall always have ready
every Year, during the War, Twelve thoufand foreign
Veteran Soldiers, *viz.* Ten thoufand Foot, One thoufand
Horfe, and One thoufand Dragoons; which Twelve thoufand
Soldiers they fhall not only recruit from time to time, at their
own Expence, as it fhall be neceffary, but they fhall alfo arm
and pay them, with their own Money, what fhall be needful
for them, both for their Pay, whether in their Quarters or out
of them, and alfo for the Ammunition Bread for the Soldiers,
Straw and Barley for the Horfes; which Bread, Straw, and
Barley, fhall be furnifhed to them at the fame Prices as they
are to his facred royal Majefty of *Portugal*'s Arms, and that
by the Miniftry and Care of his General, Queftors, and
Officers; fo that his facred royal Majefty of *Portugal* fhall not
be at any Charge at all for the faid foreign Forces, nor furnifh
them any Thing, except Hofpitals and Carriages, and what
belongs to the Hofpitals and Carriages.

10

His royal Majefty of *Portugal* fhall furnifh Two thoufand
Horfes in *Portugal*, to be bought by the Confederates for their
foreign Forces, in fuch Manner, that for each Horfe to the
private Soldiers they fhall pay 40,000 Rials, *Portuguefe* Money,
or as they are called, Forty Millrees, and, for the Officers
Horfes, 60,000 Rials of the fame Money, or Sixty Millrees;
at which Prices the faid King fhall furnifh all the other Horfes
which the Confederates fhall defire, according to what the
Kingdom fhall be able to do for the augmenting of the Horfe.

*   *   *   *   *   *

17

The Maritime Potentates fhall be bound to have, and maintain, on the maritime Coaft of *Portugal*, and in the Havens
thereof, a competent Number of Ships of War for defending
fafely the Coaft and Havens, and alfo the Trade and Fleets
of Merchant Ships, againft any hoftile Force; fo as that it
being found, or even underftood, that the Havens themfelves,
and the faid Fleets, may be invaded by a greater hoftile Force,
the faid Confederates fhall be bound, before the Cafe of that
Invafion happens, to fend into *Portugal* that Number of Ships
of War, which may be equal, and even fuperior, to the Ships
and Forces of the Enemies, who fhall defign to invade the
Havens and Fleets aforefaid. Againft any fudden Accidents
that may happen, upon the Departure of the Ships of the faid
Confederates from the Coaft and Havens of *Portugal*, the
Confederates fhall be bound to order it fo, that in thefe Seas,
or in thefe Havens, thofe Ships remain, whereof his facred
royal Majefty of *Portugal* fhall judge that there is need.

* * * * * *

21

Neither Peace, nor Truce, fhall be made, but by mutual
Confent of all the Confederates; and they fhall not be made
at any time while the moft Chriftian King's Grandfon, the
Dauphin's fecond Son, or any other Prince of the Houfe of
France, remains in *Spain*; nor yet, unlefs that the Crown of
Portugal do intirely poffefs, and reign over, all Lands, Kingdoms, Iflands, States, Dominions, Caftles, Towns, Villages,
and their Territories and Appurtenances, which it now
poffeffes, as well in, as out of, *Spain*.

22

In the fame Manner Peace fhall not be made with the moft
Chriftian King, unlefs he yield all the Right which he pre-
tends to have unto the Countries reaching to *Cape de Norte*,
and appertaining to the Dominion of the State of *Maranon*,
and lying between the River of the *Amazons* and that of
Vincent Pinfon, notwithftanding any Treaty, either pro-

18

vifional or decifive, made between his facred royal Majefty of
Portugal, and the moft Chriftian King, about the Poffeffion
and Right of the faid Countries.

*   *   *   *   *   *

24

The moft ferene Archduke *Charles* fhall come hither into
Portugal, and fhall land in it with all the Succours, which the
Confederates are to fend, as is covenanted in this Treaty; and
his facred royal Majefty of *Portugal* fhall not be bound to
make War, till the moft ferene Archduke be landed in
Portugal, and the Succours, both of Men and Ships, are
arrived there.

25

But, as foon as the moft ferene Archduke fhall be come into
Portugal, his facred royal Majefty of *Portugal* fhall acknowledge him, and own him, for King of *Spain*, as the King
Charles the Second did poffefs it; yet fo, that it do before
juridically appear to his facred royal Majefty of *Portugal*, that
the Right whereby he is King of *Spain*, is in a legal Manner
yielded and transferred to him.

26

At the fame time that his facred royal Majefty of *Portugal*
fhall make War, the maritime Potentates fhall be bound to
invade the Coaft of *Spain* with a ftrong Fleet, and to infeft it
as they are able; that the Enemies Forces may be divided,
and fo the Sum of the Expedition be rendered more eafy.

27

For the fame Reafons, the Confederates fhall be bound
vigoroufly to make War, as well in the *Low Countries* and the
Upper *Rhine*, as in *Italy*, at the fame time that *Portugal* fhall
carry its Arms into *Spain*; and this fhall thenceforth be continued in the fame Manner, during the other Years, while
the War fhall laft.

II
HOME POLITICS

SECTION TWO

HOME POLITICS

I. *The Abjuration Oath*

THE action of Louis XIV in acknowledging the Old
Pretender as King of England, on his father James II's
death in September 1701, contrary to the terms of the
Treaty of Ryswick four years before, aroused the indignation
of all parties in England except the extreme Jacobites. It
caused the passage of an Act in the last days of William's
reign, requiring Members of both Houses of Parliament,
office-holders and clergymen to take an oath abjuring the
claims of the Pretender. Hitherto it had been possible to
swear allegiance to William without stating whether he was
regarded by the swearer as King *de jure* or only *de facto*. By
the terms of the new Oath of Abjuration this was no longer
possible. Therefore at the beginning of Anne's reign the
extreme High Churchmen and High Tories were vexed by
being required to make a more unequivocal declaration of
Revolution principles under Anne than had been required of
them under William. The new oath probably retarded the
reconciliation of some of the Non-juring clergymen to the
Established Church, and somewhat reduced the satisfaction
of the High Tories in the accession of James II's daughter to
the throne. The pamphlet here quoted from is an argument
directed to such hesitating persons, as to the legitimacy of
taking the new oath.

THE
CASE
OF THE
𝕬𝕭𝕵𝖚𝖗𝖆𝖙𝖎𝖔𝖓 𝕺𝖆𝖙𝖍,

Endeavoured to be cleared to the Satisfaction of those who are Required to take it.

Q. GOOD morrow Sir, I was desired by a Kinsman of mine, of a certain *House* you know, to enquire (under-hand as it were) whether you intended to take the *Abjuration-Oath*, or no: and I am glad I have met you, to know your mind in that matter.

    *   *   *   *   *   *

    A. .... And since I now speak to a Man, who believes the P. P. of *Wales* to be the only Son of the late King *James*, and yet *has* taken the Oath of Allegiance to the late King *William* and Queen *Mary*, and *will* to her Present Majesty— I desire to know upon what grounds he can do this, which will not also bear the excluding the P. P. of *Wales*, for ever? If the Parliament had Power to set by the Right and Title of the P. P. of *Wales*, during the Government of King *William*, and of Her *present Majesty*, why not for twenty Reigns longer, why not for ever? But you your self have acknowledged this Power, by submitting, and swearing Allegiance twice, to the defeating the Right and Title (as you believe) of the P. P. why may you not do so, if you should live a hundred years longer? If you are satisfied with what you have already done, why may you not continue to do the like.

    Q. Why, being told by Learned Men, and Learned Books, that the Laws of the Land requir'd, and would bear out, the Subjects taking the Oath of Allegiance to a King Elected, Crown'd, and Acknowledg'd King by the States of the Realm,

23

I have done it hitherto with a very honeſt mind, without diſclaiming any ones Right or Title, which I am now requir'd to do; which is a new thing, and therefore is ſomething more than I have been doing all this while.

A. 'Tis *ſaying* ſomething more, but *doing* the ſame: You have, for 13 Years paſt, excluded, defeated, renounc'd, and refus'd, the Right of King *James* to your Allegiance and Obedience, becauſe you have actually transferr'd them to another Perſon; and when he has by Declaration reclaim'd you as a Subject, you attended not to him, but told him you owed him no Service or Allegiance, but were the true Subject of the King in *Poſſeſſion*. Was this to own his Right and Title? Doubtleſs he thought not ſo himſelf. I ſpeak not thus, to blame you for what you did, for you did what you ought, as a true Subject, to do; but only to ſhew you, that you have actually, virtually, and effectually, and to all Intents and Purpoſes, for 13 Years ſpace, excluded and renounc'd to the Right of King *James*, and of his Son (ſo thought by you,) altho' you have never done it in *Words* and *Form:* ...

II. *The Occasional Conformity Bill Proceedings*
Printed by Lords February 1702–3

THIS PAMPHLET *was published by Order of the House of Lords. It shows the original text of the Occasional Conformity Bill, as sent up by the Tory House of Commons in December* 1702, *the amendments made by the Lords, those which the Commons accepted, those which they refused to accept, and the arguments used by both sides in the conferences that ensued.*

As agreement could not be reached, the Bill was lost, to the secret satisfaction of the Qyeen's moderate Tory Ministers, who were anxious to "get on with the war," and to unite the country for that purpose (see Preface, p. vi, above).

Die Mercurii, 24 Febr. 1702

IT *is Ordered by the Lords Spiritual and Temporal in Parliament Aſſembled, That the Bill, Intituled,* An Act for Preventing Occaſional Conformity, *and the Proceedings thereupon, ſhall be forthwith Printed ana Publiſhed.*

Math. Johnſon,
Cleric' Parliamentor'

*Die Mercurii,
2 Decemb.* 1702.
A Meffage from the Houfe of Commons, by Mr. *Bromley,* and others, who brought up a Bill, Intituled, *An Act for Preventing Occasional Conformity*; to which they defire the Concurrence of this Houfe.

Hodie prima vice lecta eft Billa, Intituled, An Act for Preventing Occasional Conformity.

AS nothing is more contrary to the Profeffion of the Chriftian Religion, and particularly to the Doctrine of the Church of *England,* than Perfecution for Confcience only; in due Confideration whereof an Act paffed in the Firft Year of the Reign of the late King *William* and Queen *Mary* Intituled, *An Act for Exempting Their Majefties Proteftant Subjects, Diffenting from the Church of* England, *from the Penal-*

Agreed to by the Commons.

The Amendments made by the Lords to the Bill for Preventing Occafional Conformity.

After [*Mary*] add [*of Glorious Memory*]

ties of certain Laws, which Act ought inviolably to be Obferved, and Eafe given to all Confciences truly Scrupulous; Nevertheleſs, whereas the Laws do Provide that every Perfon to be Admitted into any Office or Imployment ſhould be Conformable to the Church, as it is by Law Eſtabliſhed, by Enacting, That every fuch Perfon, fo to be Admitted, ſhould Receive the Sacrament of the Lords Supper, according to the Rites and Uſage of the Church of *England*; Yet ſeveral Perfons Diſſenting from the Church, as it is by Law Eſtabliſhed, do joyn with the Members thereof in Receiving the Sacrament of the Lords Supper, to Qualifie themſelves to Have and Enjoy fuch Offices and Imployments, and do afterwards Reſort to Conventicles or Meetings for the Exerciſe of Religion in other manner than according to the Liturgy

Difagreed to by the Commons.
Difagreed to by the Commons.

Difagreed to by the Commons.

After [*Scrupulous*] add [*but*]
Leave out from [*whereas*] to [*ſeveral*]

Leave out [*ſuch*]

27

and Practice of the
Church of *England*,
which is contrary to
the Intent and Mean-
ing of the Laws al-
ready made: Be it
therefore Enacted by
the Queens moſt Ex-
cellent Majeſty, by
and with the Advice
and Conſent of the
Lords Spiritual and
Temporal,   and
Commons in Parlia-
ment Aſſembled, and
by Authority of the
ſame, That if any
Perſon or Perſons
after the Firſt Day of
March, which ſhall
be in the Year of our
Lord, One thouſand
ſeven hundred and
two, either Peers or
Commoners,   who
have or ſhall have
any Office or Offices,
Civil or Military, or
Receive any Pay,
Salary,   Fee,   or
Wages, by reaſon of
any Patent or Grant
from Her Majeſty,
or ſhall have any
Command or Place
of Truſt from or un-
der Her Majeſty, or
from any of Her Ma-
jeſties Predeceſſors,
or by Her or Their
Authority, or by Au-
thority derived from

28

Her or Them, within the Kingdom of *England,* Dominion of *Wales,* or Town of *Berwick* upon *Tweed,* or in Her Majefties Navy, or in the feveral Iflands of *Jerfey* and *Guernfey,* or fhall be Admitted into any Service or Imployment in Her Majefties Houfhold or Family; Or if any Mayor, Alderman, Recorder, Bayliff, Town Clerk, Common Council Man, or other Perfon bearing any Office of Magiftracy or Place of Truft, or other Imployment relating to or concerning the Government of the refpective Cities, Corporations, Boroughs, Cinque Ports, and their Members, and other Port Towns within the Kingdom of *England,* Dominion of *Wales,* and Town of *Berwick* upon *Tweed,* who by the Laws are Obliged to Receive the Sacrament of the Lords Supper according to the Rites and Ufage of the Church of *England,* fhall at

Difagreed to by the Commons.

Leave out from [*Family*] to [*fhall*]

Agreed to by the Commons.

any time after their Admiffion into their refpective Offices or Imployments, or after having fuch Grant, as aforefaid, during his or their Continuance in fuch Office or Offices, Imployment or Imployments, or the Injoyment of any Profit or Advantage from the fame, fhall Refort to or be prefent at any Conventicle, Affembly or Meeting, under Colour or Pretence of any Exercife of Religion, in other manner than according to the Liturgy and Practice of the Church of *England*, in any Place within the Kingdom of *England*, Dominion of *Wales*, and Town of *Berwick* upon *Tweed*, at which Conventicle, Affembly or Meeting there fhall be Five Perfons or more Affembled together, over and befides thofe of the fame Houfhold, if it be in any Houfe where there is a Family Inhabiting, or if it be in an Houfe or Place where there is

Leave out [*fhall*] and read [*knowingly and willingly*]

Agreed to by the Commons with the Amendments following, *viz.*

After [*aforefaid*] add [*or at any Meeting where the Liturgy is ufed, and where*

30

1. After the word [or] add [shall knowingly & willingly be present]

After the word [any] add [such]

After the word [Meeting] leave out [where] and insert [in such house or place, as aforesaid, altho']

After [Liturgy] leave out [is] and insert [be there]

After [used] leave out [and where] and insert [in case]

After [Majesty] add [whom God long preserve, Catherine the Queen Dowager]

After [Sophia] add [or such others as shall from time to time be lawfully appointed to be prayed for]

After [be] add [there]

2. To which Addition of the Lords (to the Amendments made by the Commons to the Lords Amendment) as Entred on the other side, the Commons agreed.

no Family Inhabiting, then where any Five Persons or more are so Assembled, as aforesaid, shall Forfeit

Her Majesty and the Princess Sophia shall not be prayed for in express words, according to the Liturgy of the Church of England]

1. To which Amendments of the Commons (to the Lords Amendment) as Entred on the other side, the Lords Agreed, with the Addition following:

2. After the words [prayed for] in the Commons Amendment, add [in pursuance of an Act Passed in the First Year of King William and Queen Mary, Intituled, An Act Declaring the Rights and Liberties of the Subject, and Settling the Succession of the Crown; and the Act Passed in the Twelfth and Thirteenth of King William the Third, Intituled, An Act for the further Limitation of the Crown, and better Securing the Rights and Liberties of the Subject.]

Disagreed to by the Commons.

the Sum of One hundred Pounds, and Five Pounds for every Day that any such Person or Persons shall continue in the Execution of such Office or Imployment after he or they shall have Resorted to or been present at any such Conventicle, Assembly or Meeting, as aforesaid, to be Recovered by him or them that shall Sue

Leave out [One hundred Pounds, and Five Pounds for every Day that such Person or Persons shall continue in the Execution of such Office or Imployment] and instead thereof insert [Twenty Pounds, to be divided into Three parts, whereof one Third Part to the Queen, one other to the Poor of the Parish where the Offence shall be for the fame, by any Action of Debt, Bill, Plaint or Information, in any of Her Majefties Courts at *Weftminfter*, wherein no Effoign, Protection or Wager of Law fhall be allowed, nor more than one Imparlance.

And be it further Enacted, That every Perfon Convicted in any Action to be brought, as aforefaid, or upon any information, Prefentment or Indictment in any of Her Majefties Courts at *Weftminfter*, or at the Affizes, fhall be difabled from thenceforth to hold fuch Office or Offices, Imployment or Imployments, or to receive any Profit or Advantage by reafon of them, or of any Grant, as aforefaid, and fhall be Adjudged incapable to bear any Office or Imployment whatfoever, within the Kingdom of *England*, Dominion of *Wales*, or Town of *Berwick* upon *Tweed*.

Provided always, and be it further En-

Committed, and one Third Part to the Informer.]

Leave out from [*aforefaid*] to the end of the Bill.

And add the Claufes A, B, C, D, E.

[A] *Provided, That no Perfon fhall fuffer*

Difagreed to by the Commons.

Claufe [*A*]
Agreed to by the

32

Commons.

acted by the Authority aforesaid, That if any Person or Persons who shall have been convicted, as aforesaid, and thereby made Incapable to hold any Office or Imployment, shall after such Conviction Conform to the Church of *England* for the Space of One Year, without having been present at any Conventicle, Assembly or Meeting, as aforesaid, and Receive the Sacrament of the Lords Supper at least Three times in the Year, every such Person or Persons shall be Capable of a Grant of any Office or Imployment, or of being Elected into or holding of any the Offices or Imployments aforesaid.

Claufe [B]
Difagreed to by the
Commons.

Provided also, and be it Enacted, That every Person so Convicted, and afterwards Conforming in manner, as aforesaid, shall at the next Term after his Admiffion into any such Office or Imployment, make Oath in

any Punishment for any Offence committed against this Act, unless Oath be made of such Offence before some Judge or Justice of the Peace (who is hereby Impowered and Required to take the said Oath) within Ten Days after the said Offence Committed, and unless the said Offender be Profecuted for the same within Three Months after the said Offence Committed; nor shall any Person be Convicted for any such Offence, unless upon the Oath of Two Credible Witnesses at the least.

[B] *Provided always, and be it Enacted, That from and after the said First Day of* March, *no Protestant Diffenter shall be Compelled or Compellable to take, serve, hold or bear any Office or Place whatsoever, for the Taking, Serving or Holding whereof he cannot be duly Qualified by Law, without Receiving the Holy Sacrament according to the Usage of the*

Writing in any of Her Majesties Courts at *Westminster*, in Publick and Open Court, between the Hours of Nine of the Clock and Twelve in the Forenoon, or at the next Quarter Seffions for that County or Place where he shall reside, That he has Conformed to the Church of *England* for the Space of One Year before such his Admission, without having been present at any Conventicle, Affembly or Meeting, as aforesaid, and that he has Received the Sacrament of the Lords Supper at least Three times in the Year, which Oath shall be there Inrolled and kept upon Record.

Provided also, and be it further Enacted by the Authority aforesaid, That if any Person after such his Admission, as aforesaid, into any Office or Imployment, shall a second time Offend, in manner aforesaid, and shall be thereof Lawfully Convicted,

Church of England, *and also Making and Subscribing the Declaration mentioned in the Statute, made* 25 Car. 2. *Intituled,* An Act for Preventing Dangers which may happen from Popish Recufants, *any Statute, Law, Ufage, or other thing to the contrary notwithstanding.*

[C] *Provided nevertheless, That this Act shall not extend to the University Churches in the Universities of this Realm, or either of them, when, or at such times as any Sermon or Lecture is Preached or Read in the same Churches, or any of them, for, or as the Publick University Sermon or Lecture, but that the same Sermons and Lectures may be Preached or Read, in such sort or manner, as the same have been heretofore Preached or Read; This Act, or any thing therein contained to the contrary, in any wife notwithstanding.*

[D] *Provided, That no Person shall Incur any the Penalties in*

Claufe [*C*]
Disagreed to by the Commons.

Claufe [*D*]
Disagreed to by the Commons.

he fhall for fuch Offence incur Double the Penalties before mentioned, to be Recovered in manner, as aforefaid, and fhall Forfeit fuch Office or Imployment, and fhall not be Capable of having any Office or Imployment, until he fhall have Conformed for the Space of Three Years, in manner aforefaid, whereof Oath fhall be made in Writing in One of Her Majefties Courts at *Weftminfter*, or at the Quarter Seffions of the County where he Refides.

Claufe [E] Difagreed to by the Commons.

this *Act, by Reforting to, or being Prefent at the Religious Exercifes ufed in the* Dutch *and* French *Languages, in Churches Eftablifhed in this Realm, in the Reigns of* King Edward *the 6th, or of* Queen Elizabeth, *or of any other King or Queen of this Realm.*

[E] *Provided always, and be it Enacted by the Authority aforefaid, That nothing in this Act fhall extend, or be Conftrued to extend to any Governor or Governors of any Hofpital or Hofpitals, or to any Affiftants of any Corporation or Corporations, Work-houfe or Work-houfes, Conftituted, Erected or Imployed for the Relief, and Setting of the Poor on Work, and for Punifhing of Vagrants and Beggars; all which faid Perfons, and every of them, fhall be, and are hereby Exempted from all the Penalties mentioned in this Act, and are hereby Adjudged and Declared not to be fubject or liable to any of the Penalties or Forfeitures mentioned in one Act of Parliament made in the 25th Year of the Reign of* King Charles *the Second,* For Preventing Dangers which may happen from Popifh Recufants, *for or by reafon of any of the aforefaid Offices or Imployments.*

Ordered, That the faid Bill fhall be Read a fecond time to Morrow, at One a Clock, and all the Lords Summoned.

*   *   *   *   *   *

35   3-2

1. The Lords do not go about to take away the Force of the Corporation Act, or to leffen any Security the Church of *England* has by it, but cannot Agree to Extend the Penalties of this Bill.

* * * * * *

2. They Conceive the Penalty of One hundred Pounds, and Five Pounds a day for every day after the Offence Committed, to be Exceffive; and the whole being given to the Informer, would prove a dangerous Temptation to Perjury, and a pernicious Encouragement to Informers, the moft odious Sort of Perfons, which would be a Blemifh on the beft Reign.

Their Lordfhips have given a fufficient Proof of their Willingnefs, to make this Bill as Effectual as will Confift with Reafon, by agreeing to fuch a Pecuniary Penalty (befides the lofs of Office) as may be a proper Encouragement to Informers to Swear the Truth, tho' not perhaps a fufficient Temptation to go further.

* * * * * *

3. The Lords think, that an *Englifh* Man cannot be reduced to a more unhappy Condition, than to be put by Law under an Incapacity of Serving his Prince and Country, and therefore nothing but a Crime of the moft Deteftable Nature, ought to put him under fuch a Difability, they who think the being Prefent at a Meeting to be fo High a Crime, can hardly think, that a Toleration of fuch Meetings ought to Continue long, and yet the Bill fays, The Act of Toleration ought to be kept Inviolable.

The Lords do not think it at all Neceffary, to make any increafe of Punifhment for a Second Offence, becaufe the Firft Offence is made Forfeiture of Office, and when the Office is gone, the Perfon may go to a Meeting without Breach of any Law while the Act of Toleration Continues; and if he fhall afterwards get another Office, he will Forfeit the fame, and incur the Penalties in this Act, if he fhall ever after be Prefent at a Conventicle, which their Lordfhips think Sufficient Punifhment for a Second Offence.

* * * * * *

The Lords infift on the Claufe (*B*).

Becaufe to leave Proteftant Diffenters fubjeƈt to Penalties, if they do not Accept of Offices, and at the fame Time to Reftrain them, if they Accept of them upon the Penalties of this Bill, from doing what they think themfelves Obliged to in Confcience, is perfecution for Confcience, and does not agree with what is fet forth in the Preamble of the Bill.

* * * * * *

The Managers for the Lords at the Free Conference, were the Duke of *Devonfhire*, Lord Steward, the Earl of *Peterborough*, the Lord Bifhop of *Salisbury*, the Lord *Sommers*, and the Lord *Halifax*.

The Lords of this Houfe who were commanded to Manage the Free Conference with the Commons, on *Saturday* the 16th of *January*, did meet the Commons, and the Free Conference was begun by the Managers for the Commons, who were Mr. *Bromley*, Mr. *St. John*, Mr. *Finch*, Mr. Solicitor General, and Sir *Thomas Powis*.

They acquainted the Managers for the Lords, that the Commons had agreed to the addition of words their Lordfhips had made to the Commons Amendments to the Lords Amendment in the 2d Skin, l. 33. but infifted on their Difagreement to the Lords other Amendments, and to their Lordfhips Claufes Marked *B, C, D,* & *E*, and therefore had defired this Free Conference with the Lords, in order to preferve a good Correfpondence between the two Houfes.

* * * * * *

That the Commons were incapable of having any Defigns they were afhamed to own: That they defigned nothing but the prefervation of the Church of *England*, and the Monarchy, and doubted not to meet with a ready Concurrence from the Lords in their defigns.

That an Eftablifhed Religion, and a National Church, are abfolutely neceffary, when fo many ill Men pretend to Infpiration, and when there are fo many weak Men to follow them.

That if a National Church be neceffary, the only effeƈtual way to preferve it, is, by keeping the Civil Power in the Hands of thofe whofe Praƈtices and Principles are Conformable to it.

37

That when the Corporation Act was made, the Parliament had fresh in their Minds the Confusions and Calamities that had been brought upon the Nation, by such as pretended to be at the same time in the true Interest of Religion and their Countrey: That the Parliament by that Act, and afterwards by the Test Act, thought they had Secured our Establishment both in Church and State, and that they had provided a sufficient Barrier to Defeat and Disappoint any Attempts against them, by Enacting, That all in Offices should Receive the Sacrament of the Lords Supper, according to the Rites and Usage of the Church of *England*, and never imagined a Set of Men would, at any time, rise up, whose Consciences were too tender to obey the Laws, but hardned enough to break thro' any.

* * * * * *

That by Occasional Conformity the Dissenters may let themselves into the Government of all the Corporations, and 'tis obvious how far that would influence the Government of the Kingdom.

That to separate from a Church which has nothing in it against a Mans Conscience to Conform to, is Schism.

That Schism is certainly a Spiritual Sin, without the super-adding of a Temporal Law to make it an Offence.

That Occasional Conformity Declares a Mans Conscience will let him Conform, and in such a Man Non Conformity is a wilful Sin, and why should Occasional Conformity be allowed in Corporations? when the Lords Agree, That out of Corporations it ought not to be allowed.

* * * * * *

That the Lords did equally desire a good Correspondence betwixt the two Houses, and were so satisfied of the necessity of Union at this time, that they thought all Measures fatal that might create any Divisions amongst Protestants at home, or give any Check to the necessary Union amongst our Allies abroad, of the Reformed Religion.

For which Reasons, in a time of War they thought Altera-tions unnecessary, and dangerous, and were unwilling to bring any real hardships upon the Dissenters at this time, or give them any cause of Jealousies or Fears.

That the Toleration hath had such visible and good effects, hath contributed so much to the Security and Reputation of the Church of *England*, and produced so good a temper amongst the Dissenters, that the Lords are unwilling to give the least discredit to that Act; being sensible that Liberty of Conscience, and gentle Measures are most proper, and have been found most effectual toward increasing the Church, and diminishing the number of Dissenters.

That the Lords apprehend that some parts of this Bill by them amended, have an Air of Severity improper for this Season; that tho' there may be some things to be found fault with, yet a proper time ought to be taken to apply Remedies; that the attempting too hasty Cures, have often proved fatal.

* * * * * *

The Church has no Reason to Complain of the Effects of the Toleration, for as the Numbers of those who Divide from us do visibly Abate all over the Nation, so the Heat and Firmentation which was Raised by those Divisions is almost entirely laid, and we cannot but look on that as a Happy Step towards the Healing of our Wounds.

But what may we not look for under the Reign of such a Queen! Whose Example, whose Virtues and Zeal give us Reason to Hope for a Happy State of Matters in the Church, if undue Severities do not again Raise new Flames, and set a new Edge on Mens Spirits, which may Blast these Hopes, and Defeat the Success that we might otherwise Expect under such an Auspicious Reign.

* * * * * *

As for this Occasional Conformity, the Lords do not go about to Excuse, or to Defend it; but they who have observed the Progress of those Matters, and have born a large share in these Controversies, must acquaint the Commons, that it is no New Practice invented to Evade a Law: It has been both the Principle and Practice of some of the most Eminent among the Dissenters ever since St. *Bartholomews* in the Year, 1662. It is known, that *Baxter* and *Bates* did still Maintain it, and that several Books have been writ about it: And as the fiercest of the Dissenters, who intended to keep up a Wall of Partition

between them and the Church, have oppofed it much; fo the
Party of all the Diffenters that came neareft the Church, and
of whom the greateft Numbers have come over to it, were
thofe that Pleaded for it. Nor is it a certain Inference, that
becaufe a Man Receives the Sacrament in the Church, he can
therefore Conform in every other Particular; The Office of
the Communion, is certainly One of the Brighteft and Beft
Compofed of any that ever was in the Church of God: The
little Exceptions that lay to the Pofture, were fo fully cleared
by the Rubrick that is added, that it is indeed a wonder how
any Perfon fhould except to any thing in the whole Office.
But it does not neceffarily follow, that therefore every Man
who is fatisfied with this, fhould be likewife fatisfied with
every other Part of Conformity. There was a very Learned
and Famous Man that lived at *Salifbury*, Mr. *Tombs*, who was
a very Zealous Conformift in all Points but in One, Infant
Baptifm; fo that the receiving the Sacrament, does not neceffarily Import an entire Conformity in every other Particular;
no more than a Man who can fubfcribe to the two Firft
Articles of Our Religion, that are indeed the Main Ones, and
contain the Doctrine of the Trinity, and the Incarnation and
Satisfaction of Chrift, is by that concluded to Affent to the reft
of the Thirty Nine; The Diffenters agree to the Firft, but
refufe fome of the Laft: This is likewife to be Remembred, .
That after St. *Bartholomew* in 1662. Occafional Conformity
was a ftep that carried many much further; from Occafional
Conformity it grew to a Conftant Conformity, if not in the
Perfons themfelves, yet in their Children; fo the Lords now
fee fome defcended from Occafional Conformifts, efpoufe the
Caufe of the Church with much Zeal.

For thefe Reafons the Lords do Conceive the Penalties in
this Bill to be exceffive, and unreafonable.

III. *Defoe on the Occasional Conformity Bill*

D EFOE, *though a Non-conformist, disapproved of the practice of occasional conformity, at least when attendance at church was resorted to merely in order to qualify for office. But while disapproving of the interested practice of occasional conformity, he resented the violence of the High Church attack on Non-conformists, the spirit evoked in support of the Bill, more than he objected to the Bill itself.*

(a) *An Enquiry into Occasional Conformity* (Defoe)

THE subject I am upon needs no introduction, the history is in every man's knowledge; the parliament are upon a bill to prevent occasional conformity, and about that bill the press swarms with pamphlets; the pulpit sounds with exaltations on one hand, and deprecations on the other. Every one speak their opinions, some their hopes, some their fears, and so it should have been to the end of the chapter, if I could have found but one middle sort, that, free from prejudice of parties, could have discerned the native state of the case as it really is discovered from the passions and follies of men.

About their act of parliament, I affirm most of the people I have met with are mistaken; and, that I may be as explicit as I can, I shall inquire more particularly who are mistaken, how, and then I doubt not the sequel of this paper shall make it appear that the fact is true.

1st. All those people who designed the act as a blow to the dissenting interest in England are mistaken.—2ndly. All those who take it as a prelude or introduction to the further suppressing of the dissenters, and a step to repealing the Toleration, or intend it as such, are mistaken.—3rdly. All those who think the dissenters at all concerned in it, or have designed to mortify them by it, are mistaken.—4thly. All those Hotspurs of divinity who prophesy destruction from the pulpit, and from this step pretend to foretell that the time of plundering their brethren is at hand, are mistaken.—5thly. All those phlegmatic dissenters who fancy themselves undone, and that persecution and desolation are at the door again, are mistaken.—6thly. All those dissenters who are really at all

41

disturbed at it, either as an advantage gained by their enemies, or as a real disaster upon themselves, are mistaken.—7thly. All those dissenters who deprecate it as a judgment, or would vote against it if it were in their power, are mistaken.—8thly. That all those who begun or promoted this bill with a design to ruin, weaken, and destroy the interest or body of the dissenters in England, are mistaken.

Not that I hereby suppose the parliament, or the persons originally concerned in moving this bill, did it in mere kindness to the dissenters, in order to refine and purge them from the scandals which some people had brought upon them; that it was an action of Christian charity to the dissenters, to prevent and detect frauds and hypocrisy in religion, and to clear their reputation.

I never yet saw or read of a division of parties in any nation, but the hotheads of both parties were always for inflaming the reckoning. If the hot men of the dissenters have done any mischief, I am sorry for it; but let us examine a little what other hot men would be now adoing.

No sooner was Queen Anne settled upon the throne of England, and had declared that the Church of England should be the men of her favour, as being the church she had been educated in, and ever constant to, but these hot men fly out upon their brethren with all the excesses of their furious temper.

Nothing would serve them but this Queen and parliament must, root and branch, blast the dissenters with their breath, blow up their interest in the nation, and we should be all one church and one people of a sudden; it was to be done with a blow, all at once, and so certainly, that no possible doubt could be made of it.

But her Majesty was pleased to let these people know from her own mouth, that, forasmuch as concerned her, they were mistaken; in that, upon the address of the dissenters to her, she gave them her royal word for her protection, and whenever she breaks it, we shall all be mistaken.

Upon this the pulpit, that drum ecclesiastic, began the war, and Mr Sachavrel, in his sermon at Oxford, dooms all the dissenters to destruction, without either bell, book, or candle;

not regarding common decency, not respecting his good manners to the Queen, nor his deference to the parliament; but tells them it is their duty, if they will be true members of the Church of England, to lift up a standard against the fanatics, and the like, as much as to say, Madam, whatever your Majesty has promised, you must break your word; and gentlemen of the House of Commons, we will have you do it.

Now all these gentlemen have lived to see themselves mistaken; and if they retain any expectations of seeing it fulfilled, they must exercise their faith upon it as a thing *in futuro*, and believe that some time or other her Majesty will break her word; but as yet there is no great probability, for hitherto we have seen they are all mistaken.

But to revive their expectations, comes a bill into the house for preventing occasional conformity. This has been matter of great triumph to some gentlemen, who upon this act revive their common discourse, and are pleased to treat the dissenters in this manner: Well, gentlemen, now down you go. The parliament are a beginning with you, and they do not use to do business by halves; they have taken the insulted Church into consideration; they will reduce you, and this is the first step: you shall soon see some more on it. We have got a Church parliament now, and down ye go. This bill will effectually ruin your interest, and bring all your great men off from you.

This brings us close to the point; and it is no small matter for any one to show these gentlemen how they are mistaken.

First: It is time for these gentlemen to tell us what the parliament will do when they either know it, or the house has declared their intentions; and till they have, it is a presumption some houses would have taken notice of, for any people to pretend to lead them to their business; and therefore when they tell us this is a taste of the rest they are preparing for us, I must say, either they are too well acquainted with the mind of the house, or they are all mistaken; and as to the blow, this bill is to the dissenters' interest in England.

As far as I may be allowed to give my judgment, and as the nature of the thing seems to speak itself, it is plain this bill is no damage at all to the dissenters in England, and we hope the house did not intend it as such.

I cannot imagine that so great a spirit of enmity and contempt can be entertained in the breast of a nation against their neighbours, their brethren, people born in the same climate, submitting to the same government, professing the same God, and in most fundamental points of religion agreeing, people linked together in the same common interest, by intermarriages continually mixed in relation, concerned in the same trade, making war with the same enemies, and allied with the same friends; were it not that these people, called dissenters, are represented to them under some strange and untrue character, or that under the name of dissenter some ill persons, shrouded and disguised, who deserve to be thus treated.

Wherefore, in order to set the dissenters right in the eyes of their brethren, and that they may have common justice at least, if they can have nothing of courtesy, that peace may be where there is no occasion for war, and quietness and good manners preserved, it will be needful to set the matter in a true light, and examine who this dissenter is, what the people dissenters are, and what they have done, for which they are treated after so infamous a manner by scurrilous preachers, and scandalous pamphleteers, and other ignorant people, not a few.

The dissenter is an Englishman, that being something desirous of going to heaven, having heard his Church of England father and schoolmaster, and the minister of the parish, talk much of it, begins seriously to inquire about the way thither; and to that purpose, consulting his bible and his conscience, he finds that in his opinion there are some things in the established way of worship which do not seem to correspond with the rule he has found out in the scripture.

Now I shall not examine here whether the man thus scrupulous be in the right, or whether the church be in the right; it does not at all belong to the case in hand.

But the man being fully convinced that he ought to worship God in that way, exclusive of all others, which is most agreeable to the will of God revealed in the scripture; and being on mature consideration also, and after sincere endeavours to be otherwise satisfied, fully convinced that this established way is not so near to that rule as it ought to be, ventures the displeasure of the civil magistrate in dissenting, in pure obedience to the commands of his conscience, and of that rule which bids him obey God rather than man; firmly believing that it is his duty so to do, and that the compass and extent of human laws do not reach to bind him in matters of conscience; at the same time living in charity with all the rest of the world whose consciences do not require the same restriction, and peaceably submitting to the laws and government he lives under, as far as either his right as an Englishman, or his duty as a Christian, can require.

This is the English Protestant dissenter which I have been speaking of, and concerning whom I have ventured to say so many men, so much wiser than I, are mistaken.

If there are crept into his company state dissenters, politic dissenters, or any that give no reason or other, or less reasons, for their dissenting than these, they are not of them, and we wish they would go out from them.

I see no act of parliament a-making to the prejudice of this dissenter; and let hot men preach, print, and say what they please, it is impossible it should ever enter into the breast of an English Protestant parliament, or an English Protestant Queen, either to oppress or suppress such a dissenter.

It is for the protection of this honest, well-meaning dissenter, that in the late reign the king and parliament, finding their number great, thought it was meet for the quiet of the nation, and as an acknowledgment of the superiority of conscience to all human laws, to settle their liberty in an act of parliament; the same undisputed authority on which all our civil as well as religious rights are established.

This is the dissenter to which her Majesty has promised her protection, and this act of parliament is the toleration to tender consciences for which her Majesty openly declared herself, even to the hazard of her royal person.

These are the dissenters who never gave her Majesty any reason to believe they did not merit her protection, and I firmly believe never will.

From these the Church of England has nothing to fear, unless their exemplary lives and unquestioned piety should prevail to weaken her numbers, and we heartily wish all the strife were reduced to this, viz., who should live best and who should preach best.

If there are among them vicious youths or grown hypocrites —if there are crept in errors, heresies, and enthusiasts, are not the same among the church? If there are among these dissenters quakers, antinomians, sweet-singers, muggletonians, and the like, the church has also her socinians, deists, antitrinitarians, sceptics, asgilites, and the like. There can be no advantage pleaded against heresy and damnable heterodox opinions from one side more than another.

If we regard the matters of state, the dissenters and the Church of England have small advantage of the argument one against another; and I may without arrogance challenge the hot churchmen, who can treat them with nothing but the odious name of disturbers of the peace, enemies of monarchy, and authors of confusion, to bring the loyalty of the Church of England, so much boasted of in the world, to the test with the loyalty of the dissenter; and it has lately been done to my hand. It is easy to prove that the dissenter has been equally loyal to princes, equally true to the government and constitution of England as the church; and the church has been equally disloyal, and has as often resisted, and took arms against the lawful established power and prince as the dissenter, and let them enter into this dispute whenever they please.

But what is all this to the present case? What we do as Englishmen is one thing, and what we do as Christians and dissenters is another.

It is also foreign to our purpose to examine or reply to Mr Stubbs, or the multitude of pamphleteers who place themselves at the forlorn hope of the church, and begin the war in hopes of drawing on that whole body to an engagement: when they can make it out that the dissenter and the church are as far asunder in religion as God and Baal, I may possibly think they merit what they so much covet, viz., to be replied to.

Whole reams of paper are spoiled since that to prove that this act of parliament is needful, because it is fit the church should be established; to which I answer with a question, asked once with much less reason in another case, "What need all this waste?"

Gentlemen, establish your church with all the precaution you can, build a fence of impregnable laws about it, you are welcome; we never did, nor do we now, disturb you; leave but us, your poor brethren, liberty to serve God according to our consciences; do not bind us to do as you can do whether we can or no; take your places, and pensions, and profits, and deserve them of the nation if you can, we ask nothing but our right, and what is now become so by law; if you claim the civil power as your own, you consequently take us into your protection, and let us see how generous you will be.

As to those among us who can conform to your church for a place, for a salary, you are also welcome to take them among you, and let them be a part of yourselves; all the converts you can make by the mammon of unrighteousness are your own; all you can buy off, or bribe off, or fright off, let them go; we readily grant that whoever among us can, with satisfaction to his conscience, conform, ought to conform, and we heartily wish you would make some small steps, by way of condescension to your brethren, such as might open your door for us all to conform to you, and then you should dissent from principles of obstinacy and ill-nature, or from a mere necessity of conscience; you should then see whether the dissenters in England were schismatics by nature and heterodox by inclination; or whether their objections are grounded upon scripture, and their dissenting from you an act of an enlightened conscience; you would then try the spirits whether they be of God.

But since you are of the opinion that you are capable of no amendment, that you cannot reform farther, and therefore will not condescend one step, though it would bring over half a million of souls to you, an eminent instance of the charity of your church, all we have to say in the case is, let us have the protection of the government and the liberty the laws allow us, and we are content.

Upon this score it is that we say the act against occasional conformity does not concern us; they who can conform for one reason may conform without two, and ought to conform, and we are therefore content to be distinguished who cannot conform at all; and if we might offer so boldly to you who

47

have any interest in the House of Commons, we would humbly propose to have the title of the act altered, and to have it entitled 'An Act for the better Uniting the Protestant Dissenters, by preventing Occasional Conformity to the Church of England,' and when that is done let it pass with all our hearts; and though we can easily see what the design is, viz., that no dissenter shall be employed in a place of trust or profit in the government, yet since it must be so, we hope, gentlemen, you will be content to take all the miscarriages of the government on you too; we shall acquiesce. Let us alone in our religion, let us worship God as we believe he has directed us, and all the rest is your own.

But before we part let us have leave to remind you, that although you are willing to quit all our civil right to the honours, as well as the advantages of serving our country when we are chosen to it by a fair majority, rather than not enjoy our religion and the profession we make with peace and liberty, yet it is no less an oppression upon us, and the hardships are such as can never be defended by reason or equity.

We would be glad we had no cause to think ourselves injured, and to such of the Church of England who can judge without prejudice, we would appeal whether it is not very hard?

First. That the dissenter shall be excluded from all places of profit, trust, and honour, and at the same time shall not be excused from those which are attended with charge, trouble, and loss of his time.

Secondly. That a dissenter shall be pressed as a sailor to fight at sea, enlisted as a soldier to fight on shore, and let his merit be never so much above his fellows, shall never be capable of preferment, no, not a lieutenant at sea, or so much as a halbert in the army.

Thirdly. That we must maintain our own clergy and your clergy, our own poor and your poor; pay equal taxes and equal duties, and not be thought worthy to be trusted to set a drunkard in the stocks.

We wonder, gentlemen, you will accept our money on your deficient funds, our stocks to help carry on your wars, our loans and credits to your victualling office and navy office.

If you would go on to distinguish us, get a law made we

shall buy no lands, that we may not be freeholders, and see if you could find money to buy us out.

Transplant us into towns and bodies, and let us trade by ourselves, let us card, spin, knit, and work with and for one another, and see how you will maintain your own poor without us.

Let us freight our ships apart, keep our money out of your bank, accept none of our bills, and separate yourselves as absolutely from us in civil matters as we do from you in religious, and see how you can go on without us.

If you are not willing to do this, but we must live among you, trade, work, receive and pay together, why may we not do it in peace, with love and unity, without daily reproach? If we have any knaves among us, take them; if we have any hypocrites, any who can conform and do not, we are free to part with them, that the remainder may be all such as agree with the character here given; and when you have garbled us to your heart's desire and ours, you need never fear your church as to her politic interest in the world; pray, then, let us be quiet.

What have we to do with your distinctions of Whig and Tory? No farther that I know of than this, that when, distinct from our religious concerns, we come to talk of our liberties, properties, and English privileges, we are not for having them destroyed by absolute authority, dispensing power, and the like; and if this be to be Whigs, ye are Whigs.

As to kings and rulers, we are of the opinion that when they degenerate into tyrants, oppress their people, destroy the laws, with all the et ceteras of arbitrary power, it is lawful for the injured people to reduce them to reason, and to seek protection and powerful help from anybody, to assist them to recover their undoubted rights and liberties; if this be to be traitors, why then, gentlemen of the Church of England, hold up your hands; how say you, are you guilty or not guilty?

As to oaths, with which, gentlemen, ye were the men that loaded your allegiance farther than you had any occasion, we are of the opinion that they can bind the subject no longer than the sovereign continues the protection of the executive power; and that the late king, by his deserting the throne, absolved all his subjects from the bond of their allegiance, and on this foot we made no scruple to swear to the government as it now stands, on the foot of the late revolution; and if you have sworn with us, and yet do not believe so, you may get off of the perjury if you can.

And what need is there now of running down the dissenters with a full cry, as if this act a coming out was a machine to blow them all up? we see no harm in it at all, other than the hardships we mentioned before, most of which we suffered before, and are like only to have them the faster entailed on our posterity.

All those gentlemen, therefore, who think this act will weaken the dissenters, or wish it would, are manifestly mistaken, it may distinguish them better, and I am persuaded will fortify them in their honest profession; it will teach them that if they will hold fast the truth, they must learn to live like people under the power of those who hate them and despitefully use them.

The dissenters, too, are strangely mistaken in their apprehensions of the ill consequences of this act.

To such I would say, I cannot imagine what they have to fear from it, or why they should be uneasy with the honour; they are also rid of the incumbrance of being mayors, aldermen, jurats, and sheriffs of the towns and corporations; and let them but reflect what was the gain that all the dissenters in England have made by places and pensions from the government since the late revolution, I am persuaded it will not all amount to the sum that one churchman will be found to have cheated the nation of.

The church are willing to engross all the knaves to themselves, and let them do it and welcome, though they get all the money into the bargain; if they would but come to a fair account with us now, and repay all the dissenters' money the nation has been cheated of by church knaves, I dare undertake the dissenters shall repay all that can be charged on their knaves out of the balance.

The foundation of the dissenters' safety is lodged by God's especial providence in the queen's veracity; while the queen esteems her word sacred, as she has assured us she will, we have no occasion to be concerned at all.

The safety of the dissenters consists in their own honesty and integrity; while they do nothing to offend either her majesty or the laws, if it were possible to have a parliament of church bigots or of pulpit Sachaverells, there will be no fear of their liberty.

As to the present act, I doubt not but they will live to see cause to be thankful for the making it, when the miscarriages of all people in public offices and employments are so eminently fixed upon a party, and so openly and fairly taken off from them.

They are mistaken, too, in the sense of the present parliament, and they may be assured, had not their enemies seen that an English Protestant parliament, as this is, is not to be prevailed upon to overthrow so substantial a part of the nation's liberty as is settled in the act of toleration, they had not rested so long, but before now had attempted it.

They have tried it in the pulpit, scattered it in scandalous pamphlets from the press, affirmed that toleration is destructive of the churches as well as the nation's safety; they have endeavoured, by calumny and reproach, to blacken the dissenters with crimes never committed, and, which they would never own before, are at last come to represent them as a formidable party.

And yet all this could never bring so much as one member of the house to be so blind to his country's interest as to make a motion against the act of toleration.

Being thus disappointed, and willing to play at small game rather than stand out, they fly to the sanctuary of this bill, and feign themselves gratified by it more than ever the bill or the house itself intended, for in all their arguments for the bill it is supposed to be a means to reduce, humble, and mortify the dissenters; *ridiculus mus!* is this all? Why, really, gentlemen, had it been in our power, you should have had all this without an act of parliament; this will strengthen, not reduce us— it will please, not mortify or humble us; and thus you find yourselves all mistaken, mistaken in the House of Commons themselves, in thinking the representatives of a Protestant nation will repeal the act of toleration, upon which the tranquillity of their native country so much depends; but above all mistaken in their expectation of the queen, to whom their behaviour is preposterous and unmannerly.

No, gentlemen, we do not tell you we like that part of the bill which excludes us from the native honours and preferments of our country, which are our due, our birthright, equally with our neighbours, and to which we should be called by the suffrage of the people; and we cannot but think it a hardship beyond the power of reason to justify, and still believe it will never pass upon us. But since this right must be clogged with so many inconveniences, that we must mortgage our consciences to enjoy them, no man can have any charity left for us, but must presently conclude we shall freely forego such trifles for our consciences, or else that we may have no consciences at all.

Therefore it is no feint; we are so content with the suppressing the grievance of this scandalous *ambo-dexter* conformity, that we think the hardships put upon us with it not worth naming. We doubt not the parliament will one time or other see cause to do us justice, and to restore to us the privileges of our ancestors, and which we have done nothing to forfeit.

(b) *The Shortest Way with the Dissenters*

I T *would have been well for Defoe if he had confined his remarks on the Occasional Conformity Bill to the* Enquiry *quoted above. But his indignation at the abuse being showered on his co-religionists by the High Church Party led him to indulge in a very questionable piece of irony, a pamphlet entitled* The Shortest Way with Dissenters, *purporting to be an extreme High-Church attack on Dissenters. It was not at once perceived that it was a parody, and was at first taken for the real article. When the truth became apparent, the indignation of the High Churchmen was naturally great. Defoe, discovered to be the author, was imprisoned, after having been made first to stand in the pillory in London, where, however, the crowd instead of pelting him gave him an ovation. His subsequent imprisonment was a more serious matter for him.*

IT was a great argument some people used against suppressing the old money, that it was a time of war, and it was too great a risk for the nation to run, if we should not master it we should be undone; and yet the sequel proved the hazard was not so great but it might be mastered, and the success was answerable. The suppressing the dissenters is not a harder work, nor a work of less necessity to the public; we can never enjoy a settled, uninterrupted union and tranquillity in this nation, till the spirit of Whiggism, faction, and schism is melted down like the old money.

To talk of the difficulty is to frighten ourselves with chimeras and notions of a powerful party, which are indeed a party without power; difficulties often appear greater at a distance than when they are searched into with judgment and distinguished from the vapours and shadows that attend them.

We are not to be frightened with it, this age is wiser than that by all our own experience and theirs too; King Charles the First had early suppressed this party if he had taken more deliberate measures. In short, it is not worth arguing to talk of their arms, their Monmouths, and Shaftesburys, and Argyles are gone, their Dutch sanctuary is at an end, heaven has made way for their destruction, and if we do not close with the divine occasion we are to blame ourselves, and may remember that we had once an opportunity to serve the Church of England by extirpating her implacable enemies, and having let slip the minute that heaven presented, may experimentally complain, *Post est occasio calva.*

Here are some popular objections in the way.

As first, the Queen has promised them, to continue them in their tolerated liberty; and has told us she will be a religious observer of her word.

What her majesty will do we cannot help, but what, as the head of the church, she ought to do, is another case: her majesty has promised to protect and defend the Church of England, and if she cannot effectually do that without the destruction of the dissenters, she must of course dispense with one promise to comply with another. But to answer this cavil more effectually: her majesty did never promise to maintain the toleration to the destruction of the church; but it is upon supposition that it may be compatible with the well-being and safety of the church which she had declared she would take especial care of; now if these two interests clash, it is plain her majesty's intentions are to uphold, protect, defend, and establish the church, and this we conceive is impossible.

Perhaps it may be said, that the church is in no immediate danger from the dissenters, and therefore it is time enough: but this is a weak answer.

For first, if a danger be real, the distance of it is no argument against, but rather a spur to quicken us to prevention, lest it be too late hereafter.

And secondly, here is the opportunity, and the only one perhaps that ever the church had to secure herself and destroy her enemies.

The representatives of the nation have now an opportunity, the time is come which all good men have wished for, that the gentlemen of England may serve the Church of England, now they are protected and encouraged by a Church of England Queen.

What will you do for your sister in the day that she shall be spoken for?

If ever you will establish the best Christian Church in the world.

If ever you will suppress the spirit of enthusiasm.

If ever you will free the nation from the viperous brood that have so long sucked the blood of their mother.

If ever you will leave your posterity free from faction and rebellion, this is the time.

This is the time to pull up this heretical weed of sedition, that has so long disturbed the peace of our church, and poisoned the good corn.

But, says another hot and cold objector, this is renewing fire and faggot, reviving the act *De Heret. Comburendo:* this will be cruelty in its nature and barbarous to all the world.

I answer, it is cruelty to kill a snake or a toad in cold blood, but the poison of their nature makes it a charity to our neighbours to destroy those creatures, not for any personal injury received, but for prevention; not for the evil they have done, but the evil they may do.

Serpents, toads, vipers, &c. are noxious to the body, and poison the sensitive life; these poison the soul, corrupt our posterity, ensnare our children, destroy the vitals of our happiness, our future felicity, and contaminate the whole mass.

Shall any law be given to such wild creatures? Some beasts are for sport, and the huntsmen give them advantages of ground; but some are knocked on the head by all possible ways of violence and surprise.

I do not prescribe fire and faggot, but as Scipio said of Carthage, *Delenda est Carthago*, they are to be rooted out of this nation, if ever we will live in peace, serve God, or enjoy our own. As for the manner, I leave it to those hands who have a right to execute God's justice on the nation's and the church's enemies.

(c) Defoe's *Explanation of the Shortest Way with the Dissenters*

THE Author professes he thought, when he wrote the book, he should never need to come to an explanation, and wonders to find there should be any reason for it.

If any man takes the pains seriously to reflect upon the contents, the nature of the thing, and the manner of the style, it seems impossible to imagine it should pass for anything but a banter upon the high-flying churchmen.

That it is free from any seditious design, either of stirring up the dissenters to any evil practice by way of prevention, much less of animating others to their destruction, will be plain, I think, to any man that understands the present constitution of England, and the nature of our government.

But since ignorance or prejudice has led most men to a hasty censure of the book, and some people are like to come under the displeasure of the government for it, in justice to those who are in danger to suffer for it; in submission to the parliament and council, who may be offended at it; and in courtesy to all mistaken people, who it seems have not penetrated into the real design, the author presents the world with the native genuine meaning and design of the paper, which he hopes may allay the anger of the government, or at least satisfy the minds of such as imagine a design to inflame and divide us.

The paper, without the least retrospect to or concern in the public bills in parliament now depending, or any other proceedings of either house, or of the government, relating to the dissenters, whose occasional conformity the author has constantly opposed, has its immediate original from the virulent spirits of some men who have thought fit to express themselves to the same effect in their printed books, though not in words so plain, and at length, and by an irony not unusual, stands as a fair answer to several books published in this liberty of the press; which, if they had been handed to the government with the same temper as this has, would no question have found the same treatment.

The sermon preached at Oxford, 'The New Association,' 'The Poetical Observator,' with numberless others, have said the same thing, in terms very little darker, and this book stands fair to let those gentlemen know that what they design can no further take with mankind than as their real meaning stands disguised by artifice of words; but that when the persecution and destruction of the dissenters, the very thing they drive at, is put into plain English, the whole nation will start at the notion, and condemn the author to be hanged for his impudence.

The author humbly hopes he shall find no harder treatment for plain English, without design, than those gentlemen for their plain design, in duller and darker English.

Any gentlemen who have patience to peruse the author of 'The New Association,' will find gallows, galleys, persecution, and destruction of the dissenters are directly pointed at, as fairly intended and designed, as in this 'Shortest Way,' had it been real, can be pretended; there is as much virulence against a union with Scotland, against King William's government, and against the line of Hanover, there is as much noise and pains taken in Mr S—ll's sermon to blacken the dissenters, and thereby to qualify them for the abhorrence of all mankind, as is possible.

The meaning, then, of this paper is, in short, to tell these gentlemen:

1. That it is nonsense to go round about and tell us of the crimes of the dissenters, to prepare the world to believe they are not fit to live in a humane society, that they are enemies to

the government and law, to the queen and the public peace, and the like; the shortest way, and the soonest, would be to tell us plainly that they would have them all hanged, banished, and destroyed.

2. But withal to acquaint those gentlemen who fancy the time is come to bring it to pass that they are mistaken, for that when the thing they mean is put into plain English, the whole nation replies with the Assyrian captain, "Is thy servant a dog, that he should do these things?" The gentlemen are mistaken in every particular; it will not go down; the queen, the council, the parliament are all offended, to have it so much as suggested that such a thing was possible to come into their minds; and not a man, but a learned mercer, not far from the corner of Fenchurch street, has been found to approve it.

Thus a poor author has ventured to have all mankind call him villain and traitor to his country and friends, for making other people's thoughts speak in his words.

From this declaration of his real design he humbly hopes the lords of her majesty's council, or the house of parliament, will be no longer offended, and that the poor people in trouble on this account shall be pardoned or excused.

He also desires that all men who have taken offence at the book, mistaking the author's design, will suffer themselves to think again, and withhold their censure till they find themselves qualified to make a venture like this for the good of their native country.

As to expressions which seem to reflect upon persons or nations, he declares them to be only the cant of the nonjuring party exposed, and thinks it very necessary to let the world know that it is their usual language, with which they treat the late king, the Scotch union, and the line of Hanover.

It is hard, after all, that this should not be perceived by all the town, that not one man can see it, either churchman or dissenter.

That not the dissenters themselves can see that this was the only way to satisfy them, that whatever the parliament might think fit to do to restrain occasional communion, persecution and destruction was never in their intention, and that therefore they have nothing to do but to be quiet and easy.

For anything in the manner of the paper which may offend either the government or private persons the author begs their pardon, and protesting the honesty of his intention, resolves, if the people now in trouble may be excused, to throw himself upon the favour of the government, rather than others shall be ruined for his mistakes.

IV, V. Swift and Addison

THESE famous pieces of Swift and Addison, from *The Examiner* of 1711 and *The Freeholder* of 1715 are a decade later in date than the early years of Queen Anne, but they represent very perfectly the feeling of the Tories about the Whigs and Dissenters throughout the reign, and the corresponding feelings of the Whigs about the Tory "fox-hunting" squires. The accusation made by Swift in No. 37 of *The Examiner* (pp. 64–66 below) against the Dissenters of having joined with James II to ruin the Church of England is the exact opposite of the truth of history.

IV. Swift. *The Examiner* NUMB. 36

FROM THURSDAY MARCH 29, TO THURSDAY APRIL 5, 1711

What the Tories thought of the Whigs and Dissenters

I HAVE been considering the old constitution of this kingdom, comparing it with the monarchies and republics whereof we meet so many accounts in ancient story, and with those at present in most parts of Europe: I have considered our religion, established here by the legislature soon after the Reformation: I have likewise examined the genius and disposition of the people, under that reasonable freedom they possess: Then I have turned my reflections upon those two great divisions of Whig and Tory, (which, some way or other, take in the whole kingdom) with the principles they both profess, as well as those wherewith they reproach one another.

From all this, I endeavour to determine, from which side her present M[ajest]y may reasonably hope for most security to her person and government, and to which she ought, in prudence, to trust the administration of her affairs. If these two rivals were really no more than *parties*, according to the common acceptation of the word, I should agree with those politicians who think, a prince descends from his dignity by putting himself at the head of either; and that his wisest course is, to keep them in a balance; raising or depressing either as it best suited with his designs. But when the visible interest of his crown and kingdom lies on one side, and when the other is but a faction, raised and strengthened by incidents and intrigues, and by deceiving the people with false representations of things; he ought, in prudence, to take the first opportunity of opening his subjects' eyes, and declaring himself in favour of those, who are for preserving the civil and religious rights of the nation, wherewith his own are so interwoven.

This was certainly our case: for I do not take the heads, advocates, and followers of the Whigs, to make up, strictly speaking, a national party; being patched up of heterogeneous, inconsistent parts, whom nothing served to unite but the common interest of sharing in the spoil and plunder of the people; the present dread of their adversaries, by whom they apprehended to be called to an account; and that general conspiracy, of endeavouring to overturn the Church and State; which, however, if they could have compassed, they would certainly have fallen out among themselves, and broke in pieces, as *their predecessors* did, after they destroyed the monarchy and religion. For, how could a Whig, who is against all discipline, agree with a Presbyterian, that carries it higher than the Papists themselves? How could a Socinian adjust his models to either? Or how could any of these cement with a Deist or Freethinker, when they came to consult upon settling points of faith? Neither would they have agreed better in their systems of government, where some would have been for a king, under the limitations of a Duke of Venice; others for a Dutch republic; a third party for an aristocracy, and most of them all for some new fabric of their own contriving.

But however, let us consider them as a party, and under those general tenets wherein they agreed, and which they publicly owned, without charging them with any that they pretend to deny. Then let us *Examine* those principles of the Tories, which their adversaries allow them to profess, and do not pretend to tax them with any actions contrary to those professions: after which, let the reader judge from which of these two parties a prince hath most to fear; and whether her M[ajest]y did not consider the ease, the safety and dignity of her person, the security of her crown, and the transmission of monarchy to her Protestant successors, when she put her affairs into the present hands.

Suppose the matter were now entire; the Qu[een] to make her choice, and for that end, should order the principles on both sides to be fairly laid before her. First, I conceive the Whigs would grant, that they have naturally no very great veneration for crowned heads; that they allow, the person of the prince may, upon many occasions, be resisted by arms; and that they do not condemn the war raised against King Charles the First, or own it to be a rebellion, though they would be thought to blame his murder. They do not think the prerogative to be yet sufficiently limited, and have therefore taken care (as a particular mark of their veneration for the illustrious house of Hanover) to clip it closer against next reign; which, consequently, they would be glad to see done in the present: not to mention, that the majority of them, if it were put to the vote, would allow, that they prefer a commonwealth before a monarchy. As to religion; their universal, undisputed maxim is, that it ought to make no distinction at all among Protestants; and in the word Protestant they include every body who is not a Papist, and who will, by an oath, give security to the government. Union in discipline and doctrine, the offensive sin of schism, the notion of a Church and a hierarchy, they laugh at as foppery, cant and priestcraft. They see no necessity at all that there should be a national faith; and what we usually call by that name, they only style the "religion of the magistrate." Since the Dissenters and we agree in the main, why should the difference of a few speculative points, or modes of dress, incapacitate them from serving their

prince and country, in a juncture when we ought to have all
hands up against the common enemy? And why should they
be forced to take the sacrament from our clergy's hands, and
in our posture, or indeed why compelled to receive it at all,
when they take an employment which has nothing to do with
religion?

These are the notions which most of that party avow, and
which they do not endeavour to disguise or set off with false
colours, or complain of being misrepresented about. I have
here placed them on purpose, in the same light which themselves do, in the very apologies they make for what we accuse
them of; and how inviting even these doctrines are, for such
a monarch to close with, as our law, both statute and common,
understands a King of England to be, let others decide. But
then, if to these we should add other opinions, which most of
their own writers justify, and which their universal practice
has given a sanction to, they are no more than what a prince
might reasonably expect, as the natural consequence of those
avowed principles. For when such persons are at the head of
affairs, the low opinion they have of princes, will certainly
tempt them to violate that respect they ought to bear; and at
the same time, their own want of duty to their sovereign is
largely made up, by exacting greater submissions to themselves
from their fellow-subjects: it being indisputably true, that the
same principle of pride and ambition makes a man treat his
equals with insolence, in the same proportion as he affronts
his superiors; as both Prince and people have sufficiently felt
from the late m[inist]ry.

Then from their confessed notions of religion, as above
related, I see no reason to wonder, why they countenanced
not only all sorts of Dissenters, but the several gradations of
freethinkers among us (all which were openly enrolled in their
party); nor why they were so very averse from the present
established form of worship, which by prescribing obedience
to princes from the topic of conscience, would be sure to
thwart all their schemes of innovation.

One thing I might add, as another acknowledged maxim
in that party, and in my opinion, as dangerous to the constitution as any I have mentioned; I mean, that of preferring, on

all occasions, the moneyed interest before the landed; which they were so far from denying, that they would gravely debate the reasonableness and justice of it; and at the rate they went on, might in a little time have found a majority of representatives, fitly qualified to lay those heavy burthens on the rest of the nation, which themselves would not touch with one of their fingers.

However, to deal impartially, there are some motives which might compel a prince, under the necessity of affairs, to deliver himself over to that party. They were *said* to possess the great bulk of cash, and consequently of credit in the nation, and the heads of them had the reputation of presiding over those societies who have the great direction of both: so that all applications for loans to the public service, upon any emergency, must be made through them; and it might prove highly dangerous to disoblige them, because in that case, it was not to be doubted, that they would be obstinate and malicious, ready to obstruct all affairs, not only by shutting their own purses, but by endeavouring to sink credit, though with some present imaginary loss to themselves, only to shew, it was a creature of their own.

From this summary of Whig-principles and dispositions, we find what a prince may reasonably fear and hope from that party. Let us now very briefly consider, the doctrines of the Tories, which their adversaries will not dispute. As they prefer a well-regulated monarchy before all other forms of government; so they think it next to impossible to alter that institution here, without involving our whole island in blood and desolation. They believe, that the prerogative of a sovereign ought, at least, to be held as sacred and inviolable as the rights of his people, if only for this reason, because without a due share of power, he will not be able to protect them. They think, that by many known laws of this realm, both statute and common, neither the person, nor lawful authority of the prince, ought, upon any pretence whatsoever, to be resisted or disobeyed. Their sentiments, in relation to the Church, are known enough, and will not be controverted, being just the reverse to what I have delivered as the doctrine and practice of the Whigs upon that article.

But here I must likewise deal impartially too, and add one principle as a characteristic of the Tories, which has much discouraged some princes from making use of them in affairs. Give the Whigs but power enough to insult their sovereign, engross his favours to themselves, and to oppress and plunder their fellow-subjects; they presently grow into good humour and good language towards the crown; profess they will stand by it with their lives and fortunes; and whatever rudenesses they may be guilty of in private, yet they assure the world, that there never was so gracious a monarch. But to the shame of the Tories, it must be confessed, that nothing of all this hath been ever observed in them; in or out of favour, you see no alteration, further than a little cheerfulness or cloud in their countenances; the highest employments can add nothing to their loyalty, but their behaviour to their prince, as well as their expressions of love and duty, are, in all conditions, exactly the same.

Having thus impartially stated the avowed principles of Whig and Tory; let the reader determine, as he pleases, to which of these two a wise prince may, with most safety to himself and the public, trust his person and his affairs; and whether it were rashness or prudence in her M[ajest]y to make those changes in the ministry, which have been so highly extolled by some, and condemned by others.

Numb. 37

FROM THURSDAY APRIL 5, TO THURSDAY APRIL 12, 1711

I WRITE this paper for the sake of the Dissenters, whom I take to be the most spreading branch of the Whig party, that professeth Christianity, and the only one that seems to be zealous for any particular system of it; the bulk of those we call the Low Church, being generally indifferent, and undetermined in that point; and the other subdivisions having not yet taken either the Old or New Testament into their scheme. By the Dissenters therefore, it will easily be understood, that I mean the Presbyterians, as they include the sects of

Anabaptists, Independents, and others, which have been melted down into them since the Restoration. This sect, in order to make itself national, having gone so far as to raise a Rebellion, murder their king, destroy monarchy and the Church, was afterwards broken in pieces by its own divisions; which made way for the king's return from his exile. However, the zealous among them did still entertain hopes of recovering the "dominion of grace"; whereof I have read a remarkable passage, in a book published about the year 1661 and written by one of their own side. As one of the regicides was going to his execution, a friend asked him, whether he thought the cause would revive? He answered, "The cause is in the bosom of Christ, and as sure as Christ rose from the dead, so sure will the cause revive also." And therefore the Nonconformists were strictly watched and restrained by penal laws, during the reign of King Charles the Second; the court and kingdom looking on them as a faction, ready to join in any design against the government in Church or State: And surely this was reasonable enough, while so many continued alive, who had voted, and fought, and preached against both, and gave no proof that they had changed their principles. The Nonconformists were then exactly upon the same foot with our Nonjurors now, whom we double tax, forbid their conventicles, and keep under hatches; without thinking ourselves possessed with a persecuting spirit, because we know they want nothing but the power to ruin us. This, in my opinion, should altogether silence the Dissenters' complaints of persecution under King Charles the Second; or make them shew us wherein they differed, at that time, from what our Jacobites are now.

Their inclinations to the Church were soon discovered, when King James the Second succeeded to the crown, with whom they unanimously joined in its ruin, to revenge themselves for that restraint they had most justly suffered in the foregoing reign; not from the persecuting temper of the clergy, as their clamours would suggest, but the prudence and caution of the legislature. The same indulgence against law, was made use of by them and the Papists, and they amicably employed their power, as in defence of one common interest.

But the Revolution happening soon after, served to wash

away the memory of the rebellion; upon which, the run
against Popery, was, no doubt, as just and seasonable as that
of fanaticism, after the Restoration: and the dread of Popery,
being then our latest danger, and consequently the most fresh
upon our spirits, all mouths were open against that; the Dissenters were rewarded with an indulgence by law; the rebellion and king's murder were now no longer a reproach;
the former was only a civil war, and whoever durst call it a
rebellion, was a Jacobite, and friend to France. This was the
more unexpected, because the Revolution being wholly brought
about by Church of England hands, they hoped one good
consequence of it, would be the relieving us from the encroachments of Dissenters, as well as those of Papists, since
both had equally confederated towards our ruin; and therefore, when the crown was new settled, it was hoped at least
that the rest of the constitution would be restored. But this
affair took a very different turn; the Dissenters had just made
a shift to save a tide, and joined with the Prince of Orange,
when they found all was desperate with their protector King
James. And observing a party, then forming against the old
principles in Church and State, under the name of Whigs and
Low-Churchmen, they listed themselves of it, where they
have ever since continued.

It is therefore, upon the foot they now are, that I would
apply myself to them, and desire they would consider the
different circumstances at present, from what they were
under, when they began their designs against the Church and
monarchy, about seventy years ago. At that juncture they
made up the body of the party, and whosoever joined with
them from principles of revenge, discontent, ambition, or love
of change, were all forced to shelter under their denomination;
united heartily in the pretences of a further and purer Reformation in religion, and of advancing the "great work" (as
the cant was then) "that God was about to do in these nations,"
received the systems of doctrine and discipline prescribed by
the Scots, and readily took the Covenant; so that there appeared no division among them, till after the common enemy
was subdued.

But now their case is quite otherwise, and I can hardly

think it worth being of a party, upon the terms they have been received of late years; for suppose the whole faction should at length succeed in their design of destroying the Church; are they so weak to imagine, that the new modelling of religion, would be put into their hands? Would their brethren, the Low-Churchmen and Freethinkers, submit to their discipline, their synods or their classes, and divide the lands of bishops, or deans and chapters, among them? How can they help observing that their allies, instead of pretending more sanctity than other men, are some of them for levelling all religion, and the rest for abolishing it? Is it not manifest, that they have been treated by their confederates, exactly after the same manner, as they were by King James the Second, made instruments to ruin the Church, not for their sakes, but under a pretended project of universal freedom in opinion, to advance the dark designs of those who employ them? For, excepting the anti-monarchical principle, and a few false notions about liberty, I see but little agreement betwixt them; and even in these, I believe, it would be impossible to contrive a frame of government, that would please them all, if they had it now in their power to try. But however, to be sure, the Presbyterian institution would never obtain. For, suppose they should, in imitation of their predecessors, propose to have no King but our Saviour Christ, the whole clan of Freethinkers would immediately object, and refuse His authority. Neither would their Low-Church brethren use them better, as well knowing what enemies they are to that doctrine of unlimited toleration, wherever they are suffered to preside. So that upon the whole, I do not see, as their present circumstances stand, where the Dissenters can find better quarter, than from the Church of England.

Besides, I leave it to their consideration, whether, with all their zeal against the Church, they ought not to shew a little decency, and how far it consists with their reputation, to act in concert with such confederates. It was reckoned a very infamous proceeding in the present most Christian king, to assist the Turk against the Emperor: policy, and reasons of state, were not allowed sufficient excuses, for taking part with an infidel against a believer. It is one of the Dissenters' quarrels against the Church, that she is not enough reformed from Popery; yet they boldly entered into a league with Papists and a popish prince, to destroy her. They profess much sanctity, and object against the wicked lives of some of our members; yet they have been long, and still continue, in strict combination with libertines and atheists, to contrive our ruin. What if the Jews should multiply, and become a formidable party among us? Would the Dissenters join in alliance with them likewise, because they agree already in some general principles, and because the Jews are allowed to be a "stiff-necked and rebellious people"?

It is the part of wise men to conceal their passions, when they are not in circumstances of exerting them to purpose: the arts of getting power, and preserving indulgence, are very different. For the former, the reasonable hopes of the Dissenters, seem to be at an end; their comrades, the Whigs and Freethinkers, are just in a condition proper to be forsaken; and the Parliament, as well as the body of the people, will be deluded no longer. Besides, it sometimes happens for a cause to be exhausted and worn out, as that of the Whigs in general, seems at present to be: the nation has had enough of it. It is as vain to hope restoring that decayed interest, as for a man of sixty to talk of entering on a new scene of life, that is only proper for youth and vigour. New circumstances and new men must arise, as well as new occasions, which are not like to happen in our time. So that the Dissenters have no game left, at present, but to secure their indulgence: in order to which, I will be so bold to offer them some advice.

First, That until some late proceedings are a little forgot, they would take care not to provoke, by any violence of tongue or pen, so great a majority, as there is now against them, nor keep up any longer that combination with their broken allies, but disperse themselves, and lie dormant against some better opportunity: I have shewn, they could have got no advantage if the late party had prevailed; and they will certainly lose none by its fall, unless through their own fault. They pretend a mighty veneration for the Queen; let them give proof of it, by quitting the ruined interest of those who have used her so ill; and by a due respect to the persons she is pleased to trust at present with her affairs: When they can no longer hope to govern, when struggling can do them no good, and may possibly hurt them, what is left but to be silent and passive?

Secondly, Though there be no law (beside that of God Almighty) against *occasional conformity*, it would be prudence in the Dissenters to use it as tenderly as they can: for, besides the infamous hypocrisy of the thing itself, too frequent practice would perhaps make a remedy necessary. And after all they have said to justify themselves in this point, it still continues hard to conceive, how those consciences can pretend to be scrupulous, upon which an employment has more power than the love of unity.

In the last place, I am humbly of opinion, That the Dissenters would do well to drop that lesson they have learned from their directors, of affecting to be under horrible apprehensions, that the Tories are in the interests of the Pretender, and would be ready to embrace the first opportunity of inviting him over. It is with the worst grace in the world, that they offer to join in the cry upon this article: as if those, who alone stood in the gap against all the encroachments of Popery and arbitrary power, are not more likely to keep out both, than a set of schismatics, who to gratify their ambition and revenge, did, by the meanest compliances, encourage and spirit up that unfortunate prince, to fall upon such measures, as must, at last, have ended in the ruin of our liberty and religion.

V. Addison. "*The Freeholder*," Nos. 14 and 22

What the Whigs thought of the Tories

HAVING thus far confidered the political faith of the party as it regards matters of fact, let us in the next place take a view of it with refpect to thofe doctrines which it embraces, and which are the fundamental points whereby they are diftinguifhed from thofe, whom they ufed to reprefent as enemies to the conftitution in Church and State. How far their great articles of political faith, with refpect to our ecclefiaftical and civil government, are confiftent with themfelves and agreeable to reafon and truth, may be feen in the following paradoxes, which are the effentials of a Tory's creed, with relation to political matters. Under the Name of Tories, I do not here comprehend multitudes of well-defigning men, who were formerly included under that denomination, but are now in the intereft of his Majefty [George I, 1715] and the prefent government. Thefe have already feen the evil tendency of fuch principles, which are the Credenda of the party, as it is oppofite to that of the Whigs.

Article I

That the church of *England* will be always in danger, till it has a Popifh King for its Defender.

II

That for the fafety of the church, no fubject fhould be tolerated in any religion different from the eftablifhed; but that the Head of our church may be of that religion which is moft repugnant to it.

III

That the Proteftant intereft in this nation, and in all *Europe*, could not but flourifh under the protection of one, who thinks himfelf oblîged, on pain of damnation, to do all that lies in his power for the extirpation of it.

*   *   *   *   *   *

F or the honour of his Majefty, and the fafety of his Government, we cannot but obferve, that thofe, who have appeared the greateft enemies to both, are of that rank of men, who are commonly diftinguifhed by the title of Fox-hunters. As feveral of thefe have had no part of their education in cities, camps, or courts, it is doubtful whether they are of greater ornament or ufe to the nation in which they live. It would be an everlafting reproach to politicks, fhould fuch men be able to overturn an eftablifhment which has been formed by the wifeft laws, and is fupported by the ableft heads. The wrong notions and prejudices which cleave to many of thefe country-gentlemen, who have always lived out of the way of being better informed, are not eafy to be conceived by a perfon who has never converfed with him.

That I may give my readers an image of thefe rural ftatefmen, I fhall, without farther preface, fet down an account of a difcourfe I chanced to have with one of them fome time ago. I was travelling towards one of the remoteft parts of *England*, when about three o'clock in the afternoon, feeing a country gentleman trotting before me with a fpaniel by his horfe's fide, I made up to him. Our converfation opened, as ufual, upon the weather; in which we were very unanimous, having both agreed that it was too dry for the feafon of the Year. My fellow-traveller, upon this, obferved to me, there had been no good weather fince the Revolution. I was a little ftartled at fo extraordinary a remark, but would not interrupt him till he proceeded to tell me of the fine weather they ufed to have in King *Charles* the Second's reign. I only anfwered, that I did not fee how the badnefs of the weather could be the King's fault; and, without waiting for his reply, afked him, whofe houfe it was we faw upon a rifing ground at a little diftance from us. He told me it belonged to an old fanatical cur, Mr. Such-a-one, 'You muft have heard of him,' fays he, 'he is one 'of the rump.' I knew the gentleman's character upon hearing his name, but affured him, that to my knowledge he was a good churchman: ay! fays he with a kind of furprife, 'we are told in the country, that he fpoke twice in the Queen's 'time againft taking off the duties upon *French* claret.' This naturally led us into the proceedings of late Parliaments, upon

which occafion he affirmed roundly, that there had not been
one good law paffed fince King *William*'s acceffion to the
Throne, except the act for preferving the Game. I had a mind
to fee him out, and therefore did not care for contradicting
him. 'Is it not hard,' fays he, 'that honeft gentlemen fhould
'be taken into cuftody of meffengers to prevent them from
'acting according to their confciences? But,' fays he, 'what
'can we expect when a parcel of factious fons of whores'—
He was going on in great paffion, but chanced to mifs his dog,
who was amufing himfelf about a bufh that grew at fome
diftance behind us. We ftood ftill until he had whiftled him
up; when he fell into a long panegyrick upon his fpaniel, who
feemed indeed excellent in his kind: But I found the moft
remarkable adventure of his life was, that he had once like
to have worried a diffenting-teacher. The mafter could hardly
fit on his horfe for laughing all the while he was giving me the
particulars of this ftory, which I found had mightily endeared
his dog to him, and, as he himfelf told me, had made him a
great favourite among all the honeft gentlemen of the country.
We were at length diverted from this piece of mirth by a poft-
boy, who winding his horn at us, my companion gave him two
or three curfes, and left the way clear for him. 'I fancy,' faid
I, 'that poft brings news from *Scotland*. I fhall long to fee the
'next *Gazette*.' 'Sir,' fays he, 'I make it a rule never to believe
'any of your printed news. We never fee, Sir, how things go,
'except now and then in *Dyer*'s letter, and I read that more
'for the ftile than the news. The man has a clever pen it muft
'be owned. But is it not ftrange that we fhould be making war
'upon Church of *England* men, with *Dutch* and *Swifs* foldiers,
'men of antimonarchical principles? Thefe foreigners will
'never be loved in *England*, Sir; they have not that wit and
'good breeding that we have.' I muft confefs, I did not expect
to hear my new acquaintance value himfelf upon thefe quali-
fications; but finding him fuch a critick upon foreigners, I
afked him, if he had ever travelled? He told me, he did not
know what travelling was good for, but to teach a man to ride
the great horfe, to jabber *French*, and to talk againft paffive
obedience: To which he added, that he fcarce ever knew a
Traveller in his life who had not forfook his principles, and

loft his hunting-feat. 'For my part,' fays he, 'I and my father 'before me have always been for paffive-obedience, and fhall 'be always for oppofing a Prince who makes ufe of minifters 'that are of another opinion. But where do you intend to inn 'to night? (for we were now come in fight of the next town) 'I can help you to a very good landlord, if you will go along 'with me. He is a lufty jolly fellow, that lives well, at leaft 'three yards in the girth, and the beft Church of *England* man 'upon the road.' I had the curiofity to fee this high church inn-keeper, as well as to enjoy more of the converfation of my fellow-traveller, and therefore readily confented to fet our horfes together for that night. As we rode fide by fide through the town, I was let into the charaƈters of all the principal inhabitants whom we met in our way. One was a dog, another a whelp, another a cur, and another the fon of a bitch, under which feveral denominations were comprehended all that voted on the Whig fide in the laft eleƈtion of burgeffes. As for thofe of his own party, he diftinguifhed them by a nod of his head, and afking them, how they did by their Chriftian names. Upon our arrival at the inn, my companion fetched out the jolly landlord, who knew him by his whiftle. Many endearments and private whifpers paffed between them; though it was eafy to fee, by the landlord's fcratching his head, that things did not go to their wifhes. The landlord had fwelled his body to a prodigious fize, and worked up his complexion to a ftanding crimfon by his zeal for the profperity of the Church, which he expreffed every hour of the day, as his cuftomers dropped in, by repeated bumpers. He had not time to go to church himfelf, but, as my friend told me in my ear, had headed a mob at the pulling down of two or three meeting houfes. While fupper was preparing, he enlarged upon the happinefs of the neighbouring fhire; 'for,' fays he, 'there is 'fcarce a Prefbyterian in the whole county, except the 'Bifhop.' In fhort, I found by his difcourfe that he had learned a great deal of politicks, but not one word of religion, from the Parfon of his parifh; and indeed, that he had fcarce any other notion of religion, but that it confifted in hating Prefbyterians. I had a remarkable inftance of his notions in this particular. Upon feeing a poor decrepit old woman pafs under the window

where he fat, he defired me to take notice of her; and afterwards informed me, that fhe was generally reputed a witch by
the country people, but that, for his part, he was apt to believe,
fhe was a Prefbyterian.

Supper was no fooner ferved in, than he took occafion, from
a fhoulder of mutton that lay before us, to cry up the plenty of
England, which would be the happieft country in the world,
provided we would live within ourfelves. Upon which, he
expatiated upon the inconveniencies of trade, that carried from
us the commodities of our country, and made a parcel of up-
ftarts, as rich as men of the moft ancient families of *England*.
He then declared frankly, that he had always been againft all
treaties and alliances with foreigners. 'Our wooden walls,'
fays he, 'are our fecurity, and we may bid defiance to the whole
'world, efpecially, if they fhould attack us when the militia
'is out.' I ventured to reply, that I had as great an opinion
of the *Englifh* fleet as he had; but I could not fee how they
could be paid, and manned, and fitted out, unlefs we encouraged trade and navigation. He replied, with fome
vehemence, that he would undertake to prove trade would be
the ruin of the *Englifh* nation. I would fain have put him upon
it, but he contented himfelf with affirming it more eagerly, to
which he added two or three curfes upon the *London* Merchants, not forgetting the Directors of the *Bank*. After fupper,
he afked me, if I was an admirer of punch; and immediately
called for a fneaker. I took this occafion to infinuate the advantages of trade, by obferving to him, that water was the only
native of *England* that could be made ufe of on this occafion:
But that the lemons, the brandy, the fugar, and the nutmeg,
were all foreigners. This put him into fome confufion; but the
landlord, who overheard me, brought him off, by affirming,
that for conftant ufe there was no liquor like a cup of *Englifh*
water, provided it had malt enough in it. My fquire laughed
heartily at the conceit, and made the landlord fit down with us.
We fat pretty late over our punch; and amidft a great deal of
improving difcourfe, drank the healths of feveral perfons in the
country, whom I had never heard of, that, they both affured
me, were the ableft ftatefmen in the nation: And of fome
Londoners, whom they extolled to the fkies, for their wit, and

73

who, I knew, paſſed in town for ſilly fellows. It being now midnight, and my friend perceiving by his almanack, that the moon was up, he called for his horſes, and took a ſudden reſolution to go to his houſe, which was at three miles diſtance from the town, after having bethought himſelf, that he never ſlept well out of his own bed. He ſhook me very heartily by the hand at parting, and diſcovered a great air of ſatisfaction in his looks, that he had met with an opportunity of ſhewing his parts, and left me a much wiſer man than he found me.

VI. *"The Spectator"*

Sir Roger at Church and in the Hunting Field

ADDISON'S famous portrait of the country gentleman, Sir Roger de Coverley, appeared in *The Spectator* in 1711. It may be compared to his portrait of the "Fox-hunter" in the last piece, as representing another and a superior variation of the genus "squire." No. 112, Sir Roger at Church, is by Addison; No. 116, Sir Roger hunting, is by Addison's nephew Budgell, but probably helped by his uncle.

No. 112 [Addison] Monday, July 9

'Αθανάτους μὲν πρῶτα θεοὺς, νόμῳ ὡς διάκειται,
Τίμα. Pyth.

I AM always very well pleased with a Country *Sunday*; and think, if keeping holy the Seventh Day were only a human Institution, it would be the best Method that could have been thought of for the polishing and civilizing of Mankind. It is certain the Country-People would soon degenerate into a kind of Savages and Barbarians, were there not such frequent Returns of a stated Time, in which the whole Village meet together with their best Faces, and in their cleanliest Habits, to converse with one another upon indifferent Subjects, hear their Duties explained to them, and join together in Adoration of the supreme Being. *Sunday* clears away the

Rust of the whole Week, not only as it refreshes in their Minds the Notions of Religion, but as it puts both the Sexes upon appearing in their most agreeable Forms, and exerting all such Qualities as are apt to give them a Figure in the Eye of the Village. A Country-Fellow distinguishes himself as much in the *Church-yard*, as a Citizen does upon the *Change*; the whole Parish-Politicks being generally discuss'd in that Place either after Sermon or before the Bell rings.

My Friend Sir ROGER being a good Church-man, has beautified the Inside of his Church with several Texts of his own chusing: He has likewise given a handsome Pulpit-Cloth, and railed in the Communion-Table at his own Expence. He has often told me, that at his coming to his Estate he found his Parishioners very irregular; and that in order to make them kneel and join in the Responses, he gave every one of them a Hassock and a Common-prayer Book: and at the same Time employed an itinerant Singing-Master, who goes about the Country for that Purpose, to instruct them rightly in the Tunes of the Psalms; upon which they now very much value themselves, and indeed out-do most of the Country Churches that I have ever heard.

As Sir ROGER is Landlord to the whole Congregation, he keeps them in very good Order, and will suffer no Body to sleep in it besides himself; for if by Chance he has been sur-prized into a short Nap at Sermon, upon recovering out of it he stands up and looks about him, and if he sees any Body else nodding, either wakes them himself, or sends his Servants to them. Several other of the old Knight's Particularities break out upon these Occasions: Sometimes he will be lengthening out a Verse in the Singing-Psalms, half a Minute after the rest of the Congregation have done with it; sometimes, when he is pleased with the Matter of his Devotion, he pronounces *Amen* three or four times to the same Prayer; and sometimes stands up when every Body else is upon their Knees, to count the Congregation, or see if any of his Tenants are missing.

I was Yesterday very much surprized to hear my old Friend, in the Midst of the Service, calling out to one *John Matthews* to mind what he was about, and not disturb the Congregation. This *John Matthews* it seems is remarkable for being an idle

75

Fellow, and at that Time was kicking his Heels for his Diversion. This Authority of the Knight, though exerted in that odd Manner which accompanies him in all Circumstances of Life, has a very good Effect upon the Parish, who are not polite enough to see any thing ridiculous in his Behaviour; besides that, the general good Sense and Worthiness of his Character, make his Friends observe these little Singularities as Foils that rather set off than blemish his good Qualities.

As soon as the Sermon is finished, no Body presumes to stir till Sir ROGER is gone out of the Church. The Knight walks down from his Seat in the Chancel between a double Row of his Tenants, that stand bowing to him on each Side; and every now and then enquires how such an one's Wife, or Mother, or Son, or Father do whom he does not see at Church; which is understood as a secret Reprimand to the Person that is absent.

The Chaplain has often told me, that upon a Catechizing-day, when Sir ROGER has been pleased with a Boy that answers well, he has ordered a Bible to be given him next Day for his Encouragement; and sometimes accompanies it with a Flitch of Bacon to his Mother. Sir ROGER has likewise added five Pounds a Year to the Clerk's Place; and that he may encourage the young Fellows to make themselves perfect in the Church-Service, has promised upon the Death of the present Incumbent, who is very old, to bestow it according to Merit.

The fair Understanding between Sir ROGER and his Chaplain, and their mutual Concurrence in doing Good, is the more remarkable, because the very next Village is famous for the Differences and Contentions that rise between the Parson and the 'Squire, who live in a perpetual State of War. The Parson is always preaching at the 'Squire, and the 'Squire to be revenged on the Parson never comes to Church. The 'Squire has made all his Tenants Atheists and Tithe-Stealers; while the Parson instructs them every *Sunday* in the Dignity of his Order, and insinuates to them in almost every Sermon, that he is a better Man than his Patron. In short, Matters are come to such an Extremity, that the 'Squire has not said his Prayers either in publick or private this half Year; and that the Parson threatens him, if he does not mend his Manners, to pray for him in the Face of the whole Congregation.

Feuds of this Nature, though too frequent in the Country, are very fatal to the ordinary People; who are so used to be dazled with Riches, that they pay as much Deference to the Understanding of a Man of an Estate, as of a Man of Learning; and are very hardly brought to regard any Truth, how important soever it may be, that is preached to them, when they know there are several Men of five hundred a Year who do not believe it.

No. 116 [Budgell]   Friday, July 13

—— *Vocat ingenti clamore Cithaeron,*
Taygetique canes——   Virg.

AFTER what has been said, I need not inform my Readers, that Sir ROGER, with whose Character I hope they are at present pretty well acquainted, has in his Youth gone through the whole Course of those rural Diversions which the Country abounds in; and which seem to be extremely well suited to that laborious Industry a Man may observe here in a far greater Degree than in Towns and Cities. I have before hinted at some of my Friend's Exploits: He has in his youthful Days taken forty Coveys of Partridges in a Season; and tired many a Salmon with a Line consisting but of a single Hair. The constant Thanks and good Wishes of the Neighbourhood always attended him, on Account of his remarkable Enmity towards Foxes; having destroyed more of those Vermin in one Year, than it was thought the whole Country could have produced. Indeed the Knight does not scruple to own among his most intimate Friends, that in order to establish his Reputation this Way, he has secretly sent for great Numbers of them out of other Counties, which he used to turn loose about the Country by Night, that he might the better signalize himself in their Destruction the next Day. His Hunting-Horses were the finest and best managed in all these Parts: His Tenants are still full of the Praises of a grey Stone-horse that unhappily staked himself several Years since, and was buried with great Solemnity in the Orchard.

77

Sir ROGER, being at present too old for Fox-hunting; to keep himself in Action, has disposed of his Beagles and got a Pack of *Stop-Hounds*. What these want in Speed, he endeavours to make Amends for by the Deepness of their Mouths and the Variety of their Notes, which are suited in such Manner to each other, that the whole Cry makes up a compleat Consort. He is so nice in this Particular, that a Gentleman having made him a Present of a very fine Hound the other Day, the Knight return'd it by the Servant with a great many Expressions of Civility; but desired him to tell his Master, that the Dog he had sent was indeed a most excellent *Base*, but that at present he only wanted a *Counter-Tenor*. Could I believe my Friend had ever read *Shakespear*, I should certainly conclude he had taken the Hint from *Theseus* in *the Midsummer-Night's Dream*.

> *My Hounds are bred out of the* Spartan *Kind*,
> *So flu'd, so sanded; and their Heads are hung*
> *With Ears that sweep away the Morning Dew.*
> *Crook-Knee'd and dew-lap'd like* Thessalian *Bulls;*
> *Slow in Pursuit, but match'd in Mouths like Bells,*
> *Each under each: A Cry more tuneable*
> *Was never hallow'd to, nor chear'd with Horn.*

Sir ROGER is so keen at this Sport, that he has been out almost every Day since I came down; and upon the Chaplain's offering to lend me his easy Pad, I was prevail'd on Yesterday Morning to make one of the Company. I was extremely pleas'd, as we rid along, to observe the general Benevolence of all the Neighbourhood towards my Friend. The Farmers' Sons thought themselves happy if they could open a Gate for the good old Knight as he passed by; which he generally requited with a Nod or a Smile, and a kind Inquiry after their Fathers and Uncles.

After we had rid about a Mile from home, we came upon a large Heath, and the Sports-men began to beat. They had done so for some time, when, as I was at a little Distance from the rest of the Company, I saw a Hare pop out from a small Furze-brake almost under my Horse's Feet. I marked the Way she took, which I endeavoured to make the Company sensible of by extending my Arm; but to no purpose, till Sir ROGER, who knows that none of my extraordinary Motions are insignificant, rode up to me, and asked me *if Puss was gone that Way?* Upon my answering *Yes* he immediately call'd in the Dogs, and put them upon the Scent. As they were going off, I heard one of the Country-Fellows muttering to his Companion, *That 'twas a Wonder they had not lost all their Sport, for want of the silent Gentleman's crying STOLE AWAY.*

This, with my Aversion to leaping Hedges, made me withdraw to a rising Ground, from whence I could have the Pleasure of the whole Chase, without the Fatigue of keeping in with the Hounds. The Hare immediately threw them above a Mile behind her; but I was pleased to find, that instead of running straight forwards, or, in Hunter's Language, *Flying the Country,* as I was afraid she might have done, she wheeled about, and described a sort of Circle round the Hill where I had taken my Station, in such Manner as gave me a very distinct View of the Sport. I could see her first pass by, and the Dogs some Time afterwards unravelling the whole Track she had made, and following her thro' all her Doubles. I was at the same Time delighted in observing that Deference which the rest of the Pack paid to each particular Hound, according to the Character he had acquired amongst them: If they were at a Fault, and an old Hound of Reputation opened but once, he was immediately follow'd by the whole Cry; while a raw Dog, or one who was a noted *Liar*, might have yelped his Heart out, without being taken Notice of.

The Hare now, after having squatted two or three Times, and been put up again as often, came still nearer to the Place where she was at first started. The Dogs pursued her, and these were followed by the jolly Knight, who rode upon a white Gelding, encompassed by his Tenants and Servants, and chearing his Hounds with all the Gaiety of Five and Twenty. One of the Sports-men rode up to me, and told me that he was sure the Chase was almost at an End, because the old Dogs, which had hitherto lain behind, now headed the Pack. The Fellow was in the Right. Our Hare took a large Field just under us, follow'd by the full Cry *in View.* I must confess the Brightness of the Weather, the Chearfulness of every thing around me, the *Chiding* of the Hounds, which was returned upon us in a double Eccho from two neighbouring Hills, with

79

the Hollowing of the Sports-men, and the Sounding of the Horn, lifted my Spirits into a most lively Pleasure, which I freely indulged because I was sure it was *innocent*. If I was under any Concern, it was on the Account of the poor Hare, that was now quite spent, and almost within the Reach of her Enemies; when the Hunts-man getting forward, threw down his Pole before the Dogs. They were now within eight Yards of that Game which they had been pursuing for almost as many Hours; yet on the Signal before-mentioned they all made a sudden Stand, and tho' they continued opening as much as before, durst not once attempt to pass beyond the Pole. At the same Time Sir ROGER rode forward, and alighting, took up the Hare in his Arms; which he soon after delivered to one of his Servants, with an Order, if she could be kept alive, to let her go in his great Orchard, where, it seems, he has several of these Prisoners of War, who live together in a very comfortable Captivity. I was highly pleased to see the Discipline of the Pack, and the Good-nature of the Knight, who could not find in his Heart to murder a Creature that had given him so much Diversion.

III
GIBRALTAR

SECTION THREE

GIBRALTAR

THESE accounts of the capture of Gibraltar in August
1704 and its heroic defence in the following winter and
spring against the efforts of the French and Spanish to
recover it, should be studied with chapters xxxi and xxxii of
Julian Corbett's *England in the Mediterranean*, where the
whole affair is admirably told in relation to the political and
naval strategy of the war in that region. The capture and
retention of Gibraltar was an outcome of the Treaty with
Portugal in 1703 and the consequent securing of Lisbon as a
naval base for our fleets.

The first document (Add. MSS. 28058) from the Godolphin MSS. in the British Museum, is an anonymous report
on the value of Gibraltar sent probably to Godolphin shortly
before its capture was attempted. It is to be noted that the
writer declares Gibraltar to be a more suitable object of
attack than Cadiz, because the interest of English and Dutch
merchants in the Cadiz trade is so great. A very feeble
attempt to take Cadiz had been made by Sir George Rooke
and the English and Dutch fleets in 1702. This is referred to
in the second document printed here, the letter of August 18,
1704, from Methuen, the British Ambassador to Portugal,
commenting on the capture of Gibraltar. Methuen, who
thoroughly understood the situation, "sollicits earnestly" the
proper garrisoning of the newly taken place.

The English seamen in close touch with home use the Old
Style of dating, eleven days behind the New Style of the
Continent, used by Marlborough writing from Flanders and
Germany.

I. *Godolphin Papers*

(B.M. Add. MSS. 28058, f. 31)

A Report on Gibraltar

GIBRALTAR and Ceuta make the very mouth of the Mediterranean, the first, viz. Gibraltar may be taken and afterwards
kept easier than Cadiz, for it is but badly fortifyed and may

82

quickly be made an island; and Ceuta must soon fall for want of provisions from Spain. The Bay of Gibraltar is capable of holding as many, and as big ships as that of Cadiz, and being in the very passage may much better hinder ships and galleys passing into and out of the Straits than at so great a distance as Cadiz is. Besides the bombing or pretending to take Cadiz will fright the commerce to Sevilla, to the prejudice of all other natives [nationals], especially English and Dutch, because of the freedom of the port and the great conveniency there is of shipping off gold and silver in time of peace. For if the commerce is once removed it won't easily be returned. And the people of Spain in general will be more affected by the loss of Gibraltar than Cadiz, this [Cadiz] being envied for the many strangers residing in it, and the other [Gibraltar] esteemed the key of the Kdom.

II. *Godolphin Papers*

(B.M. Add. MSS. 28056, f. 145)

Methuen to *Godolphin* on the taking of *Gibraltar*

THE news of the attacking of Gibraltar was beyond my expectation, but not the taking it when they attempted it. The account Sir G. Rooke gives of the force in it agrees with what I have always wrote, and if credit can be given to all sorts of people of all sorts of nations Cadiz had as little force and wld have surrendered as soon. I find the place is thought tenable and may facilitate the taking of Cadiz, and therefore I sollicit earnestly the sending a garrison to it. I hear every Spaniard hath left the place and am afraid care could not be taken to hinder the plundering.

III. *Torrington Memoirs. Taking of Gibraltar*

I T *will be seen from the following first-hand account of the capture of Gibraltar, from the* Memoirs relating to Lord Torrington, *edited by J. K. Laughton for the Camden Society,* 1889, *that the taking of the place was a comparatively easy affair, in the absence of any adequate garrison. The chief obstacle was the initial difficulty of inducing the somewhat unenterprising*

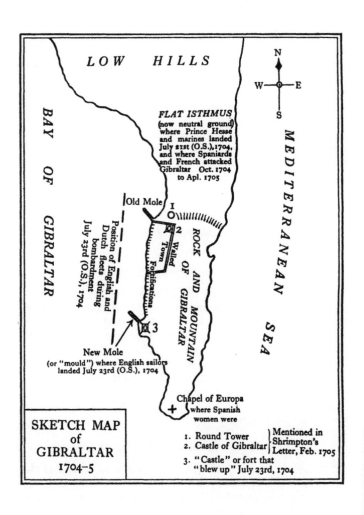

LOW HILLS

N
W — E
S

BAY OF GIBRALTAR

MEDITERRANEAN SEA

FLAT ISTHMUS
(now neutral ground)
where Prince Hesse
and marines landed
July 21st (O.S.),1704,
and where Spaniards
and French attacked
Gibraltar Oct. 1704
to Apl. 1705

Old Mole

1

Position of English and
Dutch fleets during
bombardment
July 23rd (O.S.), 1704

Walled Town

2

ROCK AND MOUNTAIN OF GIBRALTAR

Fortifications

3

New Mole
(or "mould") where English sailors
landed July 23rd (O.S.), 1704

Chapel of Europa
where Spanish
women were

SKETCH MAP
of
GIBRALTAR
1704–5

1. Round Tower
2. Castle of Gibraltar
3. "Castle" or fort that
   "blew up" July 23rd, 1704

Mentioned in
Shrimpton's
Letter, Feb. 1705

British admiral to make the attempt. The "rock" does not come
into the story, for the town with its old Spanish and Moorish
fortifications lay along the shore at the foot of the rock between
the two moles (or "moulds"); there were then no effective
batteries in the rock itself. In the whole operation resulting in
the capture of Gibraltar no one went up on to the mountain and
rock behind the town.

The dates in the margin of this narrative are the Old Style
then generally used by the English. Add eleven days to obtain
the usual European Calendar.

...and as he [Sir George Rooke] was plying under the Barbary coast, he received letters from Mr. Methuen, the English
ambassador at Lisbon, of the 10 and 17 of July, with the proposals made by the Kings of Spain and Portugal for attempting
Cadiz; as also letters from the Prince of Hesse. Upon which July 17.
he called a council of war of the admiralls of the fleet, where, [O.S.]
they being considered, it was concluded that to attempt Cadiz
with any prospect of success, without an army to cooperate
with the fleet, was impracticable. But, that the fleet might
not remain unactive, the attacking of Gibraltar was proposed;
which was lightly thought of by many at the council; of which
number was Admirall Byng. But Sir George Rooke replyed,
that place shoud not only be besieged, but that he shoud
comand the attack; to which Admirall Byng replied in a manner consistant with a soldier on whom he bestowed a mark of
his favour; tho' it is thought Sir George meant as he spoke
it in a pique. Then they came to a resolution to land the
English and Dutch marines in the Bay of Gibraltar under the
comand of the Prince of Hesse, to cut of any communication
of that town with the main; and at the same time bombard and
cannonade the place from the ships, and use their endeavours to
reduce it to the King of Spain's obedience.

* * * * * *

The fleet was now in Tetuan Bay on the Barbary coast, July 19.
when Sir George Rooke sent Admirall Byng orders to take
with him a squadron of 11 English and 6 Dutch ships under
Rear-admirall Vanderdussen, and 3 bomb ships, and proceed
with them into Gibraltar Bay; and upon advice he shoud

receive from the Prince of Hesse, to bring them before the town and reduce it by cannonading and bombarding. Then the marines of his squadron were put into the other ships of the fleet, that in case the winds shoud continue westerly they might all land together on the east side of Gibraltar Bay, and July 20. land the marines there between the windmills and the river.

* * * * *

July 21. The next morning, the wind springing up easterly, the whole fleet stood in the bay likewise, and that afternoon came there. Admirall Byng was with his squadron before the town, and Sir George Rooke, with the rest of the fleet, anchored from him in the bite of the bay towards the river. When Admirall Byng anchored, the town fired, but the shot went over them; yet the mainmast of his own ship was wounded; and having orders not to attack the town before the Prince of Hesse had sent a summons in and an answer was returned, he ordered the ships with him to warp a little further out. In about an hour after the fleet came to an anchor, the signall was made to land the marines; which was done without any more opposition than that a party of about 50 horse went out of the town, and marched down to the place where they landed, and made an effort as if they woud make some opposition; but upon the fire of the grenadiers that first landed, they retired into the town, with the loss of one trooper only. The marines then marched in good order to the mills, that are within shot of the north part of the town; and, posting themselves, the Prince of Hesse, who commanded them, sent a summons to the town to declare July 22. for King Charles 3d. But no answer returning that night nor the next by break of day, Admirall Byng made a signal in the morning for the squadron to draw into a line before the town, according to the manner he had before directed; which was to anchor near to one another as conveniently they coud; and no ship was to leave the line, tho' disabled, before he was acquainted with it. Accordingly they proceeded to their station before the town by warping. It being then calm, the town kept firing on them now and then, while the governor sent his answer to the Prince of Hesse that he woud defend the town to the last as loyall soldiers for King Philip the 5th, to whom they had sworn fealty. When Sir George Rooke was ac-

86

quainted with this answer, he sent five ships more to Admirall
Byng, whose squadron now consisted of 22, which were disposed of in a line as near as possible they coud be from the head
of the new mold, which is to the southward of the town, to
the old mould and to the northward of it; the English to the
southward of it, and the Dutch to the northward. He placed
two of the bomb ships with the Dutch, the other without his
own ship; in which form, such ships as were near kept warping
all the next night, sending their boats to sound before; and
those ships that were more out sailed with the land breeze, and
early in the morning most of them had placed themselves
pretty regularly. In the night, Sir George Rooke sent Capt.
Whitaker with some boats mann'd, arm'd and with fireworks,
within the old mould, to burn a French privateer or merchant
ship that lay there; and while he performed that service,
Admirall Byng at the same time, to amuse the ennemy,
ordered the bombs to play into the town, which had some
effect. The next morning, as soon as it was day, seeing that July 23.
some of the ships coud not get into the line as directed, he
ordered them to place themselves in the best manner they
coud where they saw an intervall, which they did as well as the
nature of the place permitted; there being deep water off the
new mould, but shoaler to the northward of the old mold and
midle of the town, where his ship the Ranelaugh went in so
near that at low water she lay in less than 3 fathom and $\frac{1}{2}$, tho'
she drew but one quarter more. About 5 in the morning the
town began to fire at the ships; upon which Admirall Byng
made the signall to begin to cannonade, and for the bomb
ships to play; which they did with so furious a fire that the
frightened inhabitants run out of the town up the hill. Yet
Admirall Byng observing the smoak was so great that the
object to fire at coud not be so true, he sent orders along the
line to forbear firing all they coud, only now and then firing
their lower tier, as being best for battery, and to forbear altogether firing their upper tier and small guns; and about noon
he directed a general cessation, that he might see what effect
their firing had. These orders he sent by Capt. Edward
Whitaker who was then on board him; and who being in the
Lenox (that lay nearest in with the mould), observed, as did

Capt. Jumper who commanded her, that severall of the cannon of castle and batteries over the new mould were dismounted, and thought the men beat from their guns, which had been silent for some time. Capt. Whitaker then returned to Admirall Byng with their observation, and opinion that with the boats manned and armed they might take possession of those fortifications. Thereupon he made imediately the signall for the boats of the line, sending Whitaker at the same time to Sir George Rooke, to desire that the remaining boats of the fleet manned and armed might be sent him. In the meantime he directed the boats that were with him to the southward of the mould head, under the comand of Capt. Hicks, the senior officer; and he was to employ them in taking possession and reducing the place if it was practicable; if not, to order the boats to their respective ships. Not long after, Capt. Whitaker returned from Sir George Rook with a letter to Admirall Byng, for his comanding the attack and the men designed to be landed; and with him to send such other captains as he thought fit. Accordingly Capt. Byng ordered Capt. Whitaker, and with him Capts. Fairfax, Roffey, Mighells, and Acton, with the men sent in the boats, to attack the new mould, castle and fortifications adjoyning; and in case he shoud become master of them, he was to endeavour to lodge himself and make good his possession of them. But before he could get to the shoar with the boats Sir George Rook had sent, Capts. Hicks and Jumper were gone with those they had got together in persuance of Admirall Byng's former orders to them; who as they were rowing to the shoar perceived a great number of priests, women and children (that to avoid danger in the town had got out of it, and were to the southward towards the chappell of Our Lady of Europa, and who now saw the boats going to land), making all haste possible into the town again; and being by the narrow passage of the rock, Sir Clodesly Shovell, then on board Admirall Byng's ship, desired our cannon to be fired that way, to frighten them back again; which as soon as was done they all ran away to the Convent of Our Lady again. The firing of this gun was likewise taken by all the rest of the ships for a signal to begin again; so they renewed their fire upon the town, under the cover of which the sailors landed on the new mould, and marched up to attack the castle and fortifications. Lieutenant Davenport went with about 30 men to the left of the covered way, and at the breach that was made got over to the eastward of the castle, while the main number that landed went up the covered way under the bastion, and finding the gates shut and the draw bridge up, mounted on the wall and pallasadoes that joined the gate, clambering over every thing in their way with great valour and much more courage than prudence. But when many were got over the paliasodes and were mounting, the castle blew up; the blast and fall of which killed and wounded, it is thought near 100 men, and Mr. Master, his own leftenant and brother in law, was much hurt in the leg. It is very uncertain if this was done by a train laid to the magazines by the Spaniards, or by some accident; for there was some Spaniards in the fort who met the same fate as the English had. This, however, so much discouraged the sailors that, apprehending more mines, made the best of their way down to the boats. By this time, as some were going off and the rest going down to do so, Capt. Whitaker met them with his boats, turned them back, and marching up without oposition, he took possession of the remaining part of the castle and bastion adjoining. He then marched further on and took the redoubt half way between the new mould and the town, planting there the union-jack; then marching to view the grounds, he found no opposition, so posted his men well to defend the ground they had possession of. As soon as Admirall Byng saw they were landed and had possession of the works, he strengthened them by sending more men and desired another supply of Sir George Rooke, and ordered Captain Whitaker to secure himself in the strongest places untill he was suported with more force; and that he should send an intelligble officer to give him an account of his proceedings; and, being in want of boats, directed him to send as many as he coud spare and what others coud be got from the line, in order to supply him with men. Then Admirall Byng went on board Sir George Rooke, when it was concluded Admirall Byng should send in a sumons to the town by a drum at the south gate, from his camp of sailors; and that the Prince of Hesse be acquainted therewith and desired to summons the town in the name of the King of Spain, from his camp of marines. Upon receiving these orders he [Byng] went imediately ashoar to the seamen's camp, and after sending a sumons to the governor in the manner agreed on, he went to view the posts, and ordered the out-guards and sentinells not to suffer any person to pass to the chapell of our Lady of Europa, wherein was many of the most considerable women of the town, priests and others, to prevent any rudeness and insult they might otherwise receive. In the evening the governor sent back the drum sent by Admirall Byng with answer, That he would deliver up the town, and the next morning send hostages and capitulate on terms that were July 24. promised him should be honourable. The next morning Admirall Byng went to the Prince of Hesse's camp to acquaint him with what had been done, the manner of their encampment, and the posts they were in to the southward of the town. While he was with the Prince, the governor of the town sent out hostages, in order to capitulate, and Admirall Byng by them was desired that the women in his possession might be kept from the rudeness of the sailors, and to release them. This seems to have been one of the greatest inducements of the citizens towards a capitulation, being very apprehensive that some injuries might be offered them. Admirall Byng assured them that none had been offered to any of them, and acquainted them with the care he had taken to protect them by the guards he had posted for their security, which was a great satisfaction he gave those gentlemen; and after talking to the Prince assured them upon his honour he woud imediately visit the women and carry them himself to the gates of the town; upon the performance of which they promised to deliver up the gate of it next to the camp of the Prince of Hesse; and then the articles of capitulation for a surender were agreed upon with the governor, and are as follows:—

1. That the garrison, both officers and souldiers, may depart with their arms and necessary baggage; and the souldiers to have what they can carry on their shouldiers. The officers and gentlemen of the town may carry their horses with them, and may have boats to carry their things if they shoud have occasion for them.

90

2. That they may take out of the garrison three peicees of brass canon of different natures, with 12 charges of powder and ball.

3. That they may take provision of bred, wine, and flesh for 6 days march.

4. That none of the officers' baggage be searched, altho' it be in chests or trunks, and that the garrison depart in three days; and such of their necessaries as they cannot carry out with them may be sent for, and that they be permitted to have some carts.

5. That such inhabitants of the citty as are willing to remain have the same priviledges they enjoyed in the time of Charles 2d, and their rights and religion to remain untouched, upon condition that they shall take an oath of fidelity to Charles 3d, their legitimate king and master.

6. That they shall discover all their magazines of powder and other amunition or provisions or arms that may be in the citty.

7. That all the subjects of the French king be excluded from any part of these capitulations, and all their effects to be seised, and their persons to be prisoners of warr.

Upon the signing of these articles the governor delivered up the north gate, bastions, and fortifications of that part of the town, which the Prince of Hesse with the marines took possession of. At the same time Admirall Byng delivered up the women at the south gate, passing by him unvailed. The same evening he embarked the seamen that were encamped, leaving only 200 men in the castle and 50 in the redoute for 2 or 3 days, till relieved by some marines; and he likewise ordered the ships that were before the town to return to their propper flags; and soon after the Spaniards, both garrison and inhabitants, marched all out of the town, except about 20 families.

Thus did the fleet very unexpectedly reduce the town of Gibraltar, very much owing to the gallantry of the sailors, with the loss only of 61 killed and 260 wounded; tho' the furious canonading, in which it is reckoned were fired 1400 shot, had done the town so little damage that it is said orders were sending to draw of the ships and reimbark the men, who might have met with greater oposition in their landing than they did; and it was looked on as a surprising negligence in the Spaniards to have no more than two Spanish regiments of 40 men each in a garrison of that importance, where there was above 100 guns mounted on the walls, all facing the sea and the two narrow passages of the land.

IV. *Defence of Gibraltar*
October 1704—April 1705

I f enterprise was all that was required to capture Gibraltar, heroism was needed to preserve it. The naval action of Malaga in August 1704 preserved it from immediate re-capture (see Corbett, England in the Mediterranean, *pp. 525–35). But in the winter and early spring of 1704–5 a very inadequate English force of marines, infantry and sailors was called on to defend the fortress against fierce attacks of large Spanish and French armies. These attacks were directed against the northern defences of Gibraltar from the low-lying isthmus. The defence was only successful because Sir John Leake three times in six months relieved the town by arriving in the nick of time with an English squadron wintering at Lisbon. It was impossible for the fleet to winter in Gibraltar Bay. After the third relief in April 1705 the French General Tessé raised the long siege (see Corbett,* England in the Mediterranean, *pp. 536–44). The following dispatch describes one of the numerous crises of a defence which deserves to be remembered along with the more famous defence of Gibraltar by Eliott in 1779–82.*

Brigadier Shrimpton to Marlborough
(Coxe Papers, B.M. Add. MSS. 9115, ff. 14–15)

GIBRALTAR, Feb. 3 (O.S.), 1705.—I should not trouble your Grace with writing so often, but that I believe the consequence of the place may justify it. The enemy attacked us this day——at break of day at the round Tower and the breach above it. They began their attack with 500 grenadiers sustained by 1000 spaniards. They carried the Round Tower and the breach and came over the hill as far as the four gun battery and were possessed of that too which is within 40 paces of the Castle breach which is very easy to enter and that is the last opposition on that side and had they attacked us at the same time on the covert way the north bastion and the curtain*, we should have found it very hard to have kept them out. Our garrison being now not above 1800 men and they so harrassed that they have not half the rest that nature requires, being always at arms or at work. The enemies have had reinforcements of four french battalions and 19 companies of grenadiers. The marshal de Tesse is with them. They threaten us heavily with a general assault which keeps us night and day under arms. My Lord Galway sent a ship here that arrived three days ago and six days in her passage from Lisbon to tell us he is hastening all he can with the rest of those companies that should have come with us, and all but 270 odd men that were taken at our coming here. The ships that bring them take up 500 Portuguese at Lagos. All together they will make about a 1000 men. We pray heartily they may come time enough which if they do we assure ourselves we shall be able to beat the enemy out once more. But if Sir John Lake who stays for Admiral Whelston does not bring out at least 2 full battalions we shall not be able to hold out till the great fleet comes. Our daily loss is 20, 30, and sometimes 40 men a day wounded and killed. The round Tower and breach and another post lying so exposed to the enemys batteries were killed of the enemy in this action as 150 men a good many officers and we hear more wounded and took 40 prisoners and 6 officers. We had a 180 men killed and wounded. I must tell your Grace that our battalion of guards diminishes a pace. We have not above 250 men fit for duty and above 200 wounded and sick They begin to be very ragged with the hard duty and working daily.

* The north bastion and the curtain were to meet at the Round Tower and The Castle, on lower ground, near the Old Mole, see map p. 84 above.

IV

BLENHEIM & RAMILLIES

BLENHEIM AND RAMILLIES

THE following first-hand accounts of the two decisive battles of the war should be studied in connection with the Marlborough Papers in Section v below, and with such modern books as Atkinson's *Marlborough* (Heroes of Nations Series) and the late Frank Taylor's *Wars of Marlborough* (1921), vol. 1, where there is an excellent map of the march to the Danube. The New or Continental style of dating is used by all the writers except Col. Blackader, pp. 142–5.

I. *The March to the Danube, 1704. Hare's Journal*

THIS *account of Marlborough's famous march is taken from the semi-official narrative written by Dr Hare, Marlborough's Chaplain on that campaign, a narrative which Marlborough had himself supervised* (Marlborough's Despatches, 1, p. 332). *This section, not I think previously printed, is taken from the MSS. in the British Museum, Add. MSS. 9114. It describes the days when Marlborough gradually made public to one ally after another his intention of carrying his army to the Danube to conquer Bavaria and save the Empire, a movement for which the march to the half-way-house of the Moselle had been in part a blind. It also illustrates the special care Marlborough took to provide for the health and feeding of his troops, and the advantages he thereby obtained on this difficult march; and his relation to the various German Princes with whom he co-operated or through whose territory he marched. It will be observed that the army passed from the Rhine to the Danube in two sections, the cavalry first, under the Duke; and the infantry and artillery, some days behind, under his brother, General Charles Churchill.*

MAY 20 (N.S.) 1704.—Count Wratislaw and Baron D'Almelo accompanied His Grace to the Elector of Treves's Castle of Erenberstien, over against Coblentz, where having dined with the Elector His Grace marcht thence to Braubach a

Town belonging to the Landgrave of Hesse d'Armstadt where he was join'd by the infantry under the command of General Churchill. And still resolving to advance as fast as possible, he went forward with the Cavalry and gave orders to General Churchill to follow as close as was consistent with the March of the Artillery and heavy baggage thro' that mountainous Country, where one Hill took up a whole days march and could hardly have been ascended in that time but for the Indefatigable care and pains of Colonel Blood and the other Officers Commanding Her Majestys Train of Artillery.

*   *   *   *   *   *

28th. The next day his Grace ma'ch'd to Swalbach whither Lieutenant General Bulow came to wait upon him and where he received Letters by express from the Prince of Hesse and Lieutenant General Hompetch, that they were at Mayence, attending his Grace Orders. He had also another express from the States General, intimating that they had given Orders for the sending His Grace a Detachment of Seven Battalions and 21 Squadrons from the Army on the Maese. . . .

29—His Grace continued his march to Cassel a village upon the Rhine over against Mayence. He immediately went (accompanied by Lieutenant General Lumley) to make a visit to the Elector and was met at the Landing place, by several of His Highnesses Coaches which attended there, to conduct His Grace and his retinue to the Palace. After having Dined with his Electoral Highness, a Councill was held with the Generals about the further motions of the Army. And as in the project that had been laid for acting upon the Moselle, The Landgrave of Hesse Cassel had agreed to furnish a certain proportion of heavy Cannon, the Duke of Marlborough now represented to his Highness the imminent danger with which the Empire was threatened and particularly the sad Condition of his Imperial Majesties affairs in Hungary; That therefore he had laid aside his thoughts of proceeding to the Moselle, since his service wou'd be more necessary elsewhere, and upon that account desir'd His Highness to send his Cannon away to Manheim under the direction of the Hereditary Prince his Son, since it might be of great advantage, in setting down before Landau, or any other enterprize that might be found most convenient for annoying the Enemy.

His Grace thus resolving to march forward did also send to the Regency of the Palatinate at Heydelbourg, to tell them, that for the advantage of the Common Cause and the preservation of the Empire, he was obliged to make all the haste he cou'd, with the Forces of Her Majesty and the States General into Germany; and that therefore that no time might be lost, he desir'd that they would cause a Bridge of Boats to be laid over the Wikar at Ladenbourg where he design'd to pass over with the Army the 3ᵈ of June.

His Grace now sent to thank the States General for ordering him such a considerable and Speedy Reinforcement and acquainted them (and Prince Lewis at the same time) that he had appointed the Prince of Hesse and the two Lieutenant Generals Bulow and Hompetch to joyn him at Armchal near Philipsbourg.—

And tho his Grace had not yet openly declar'd his Resolution of Marching to the Danube, yet he sent to the Marquis of Barieth, Director of the Circle of Franconia, to the Bishop of Constance, and the Duke Regent of Wertemberg, Directors of Circle of Suabia. To the Bishop of Wormes; Grand Master of the Teutonick Order and to the Elector Palatine, Directors of the Rhine, for a free passage for his Army thro those Countries, praying withal, that Forrage and Provisions might be made ready as was desir'd before of the Elector of Mayence.—

And tho the Troop's notwithstanding all their fatigue, and ill weather had hitherto continued to be very healthy, yet his Grace thought it convenient to order a Hospital to be appointed at this place [Mainz], as well for those few which were, as for others which might become sick and unable to march.—

31st. The next morning the Army was drawn out in order of Battle and the Elector of Mayence with the Landgrave of Hesse D'Armstat, and several other Persons of Quality of both Sexes, came over the Rhine to see it.— They first rode along the lines, and then saw the Troops

March by towards the Mayne, which River they pass'd about noon, at a Village call'd Cortheim [=Kostheim] and encamp'd that night at Great Gerau.—

June 1st.—Afterwards the Army made a long march to Zuingenberg and the next day proceeded to Weinheim where his Grace was quartered in a fine Castle, belonging to the Elector Palatine. The Roads at this time were very difficult, and almost impassible and therefore his Grace sent an Express to General Churchill to be inform'd of the condition of the Foot and Artillery, and ordered him to change the Route, and to march with them towards Heydelbourg, and to send the same Messenger immediately back to acquaint his Grace where he design'd to encamp every Night, and what day he proposed to be at Heydelbourg, that his Grace might take his measures accordingly.—

2ᵈ—That General [= Churchill] was now advanced as far as Cassel [near Mainz], where he made a halt to refresh his Troops. The Day he halted, the Elector of Mayence invited him and the commanding Officers to Dinner and had a Ball appointed that Evening at his Brother the Count Schonborns House, for the entertainment of them. The same Day the Elector and Nobility aforesaid came to see the infantry re- ceiv'd. All the Regiments were drawn out on purpose, and were so fresh, and so clean, that the Elector and all that at- tended him were greatly surprised at their handsome ap- pearance. But when his Highness came to Her Majesties Battalion of Guards, which then consisted of above 700 able men, and was drawn up by itself, on the Right of all, he seem'd to view each man from Head to Foot, and observing not only their order, but the cleanliness, and their Arms, Accoutre- ments Clothes, Shoes and Linnen he said to the General "Certainly all these Gentlemen are Dressed for the Ball."—

By this time the Duke of Marlborough had got as far as Ladenbourg where he had passed the Neckar and encamped on the side of that River over against the Tower.—Here his Grace Halted likewise, as well to recover the Cavalry, as to give an opportunity to the Infantry and Artillery to come up to him. Here he had advice from the Count Vehlen General of the Palatine Horse, who commanded the Forces in the lines of Stolhosfen, that Monsieur Tallard had repassed the Rhine the second instant at Altenheim and was marching towards Landau, in order to join Mareschall Villeroy or to oppose the Dukes passage over the Rhine. This motion of Marshall Tallard was occasioned by the Governour of Philipsbourg's offering to make a Bridge of Boats over the Rhine, which gave Monsieur Tallard a jealousie that the Duke was going to sit down before Landau.

* * * * * *

His Grace supposed the detachments from the Netherlands to be now in the Neighbourhood of Cologn, and therefore sent to the Bishop of Raab, to expedite the march of it, acquainting him at the same time with his resolution of Marching to the Danube. He also now acquainted the States General that he expected to be there within ten Days, having prepar'd everything for coming up with the Elector of Bavaria.—

* * * * * *

General Churchill was now come up to Heidelbourg where his Grace by a letter to that General expressed his concern for the infantry under his command. He was very sensible of the Hardships the Cavalry had endur'd by so many hard Marches, and therefore by more Necessary Consequences, reflected on the sufferings of the Foot, and so order'd that General to call the commanding Officers of each Regiment together, to cause them to make an early provision of shoes and other necessaries, which would not be so easily found in an Enemies Country [viz. in Bavaria whither they were going].—

And to make things yet more easy both to the Armies and the Countries it march thro, his Grace was not unmindfull to provide money and order Regular payments for everything that was brought into the Camp; a thing hitherto unknown in Germany, where in all former Wars, both the Imperial and French Generals have subsisted their Armies at the Expences of those Princes whose Countrys they march'd thro; and to prevent any failure herein he order'd the Treasurer of the Army to be always in Cash to answer Bills, and duly to have a

Months Subsistance before hand, and that the supplies should be laid from Frankfort to Nurenberg, And that he should loose no time in sending Credit to those places, since Specie was scarce in those Parts (Especially now Ausbourg the Chiefest Town for Returns was in the Elector of Bavaria's hands) and that the Bankers might have time to get any considerable sum together.

*   *   *   *   *   *

The 8th His Grace March'd to great Gardach and repassing the Neckar at Lauffen, the next day came to Mundelsheim where he had advice, that the Elector of Bavaria had come over the Danube with his Army, and encampt near Ulm. The next morning an Adjutant General came to acquaint his Grace that Prince Eugene of Savoy and Count Wratislaw were on the road intending to dine with him that day. About 5 in the afternoon that Prince came to his Graces Quarters, where he was several Hours in Conference with his Grace and the next day accompanied him on the March to Gros Heppach.—

On this Ground the Troops were drawn out in Order of Battle and his Grace accompanied the Prince to review them. his Highness Prince Eugene was very much surprized to find them in so good Condition, after so long a March, and told his Grace That he heard much of the English Cavalry and found it to be the best appointed and the finest he had ever seen, But says he Money (which you don't want in England) will buy fine Clothes and fine Horses, but it cannot buy that lively air which I see in every one of those Troopers Faces. To which his Grace reply'd that that must be attributed, to their heartiness for the Publick Cause, and the particular pleasure and Satisfaction, they had in seeing his Highness.

Here his Grace halted for the Convenience of meeting more of the Emperors Generals, to advise with them about the properest methods of putting their projects into execution. The Duke Regent of Wirtemberg General of the Imperial Cavalry, came to him, thither from Prince Lewis's army and brought him an account from thence, that upon the Instances of his Grace for the Security of the Rhine, Prince Lewis had sent 9000 Prussians and 3 Regiments of Horse (of 400 each Regiment) towards the Lines of Stolhoffen, And as Count Wratislaw inform'd his Grace, that Prince Lewis himself was coming Post to meet him. His Grace sent Colonel Cadogan to Compliment and Conduct that Prince to the Camp; The Colonel met him with Prince Lobkowitz his Nephew, at Elsinghen, and brought them to his Grace's quarters; where a Conference was held that Evening in which it was resolv'd, that all the Troops of the Allies in that Neighbourhood should join the Army on the Danube; and act in conjunction for some Days, to give time for the rest of the Troops to come up. To this end his Grace wrote to the Duke of Wertemberg and Lieutenant General Scholten to hasten the March of the Danish Forces, that were to come with them from Flanders, and Orders were sent for the other Troops which were most distant to make all possible haste to the place of Rendezvouz. And where as there are too many fatal Instances wherein a Confederate Army, the Common Cause has Suffer'd and many fair Advantages have been lost by the intestine disputes, and disagreements of the Principall Generals Commanding different Corps. There was now no likelyhood of any such thing, for Prince Lewis readily own'd what Obligations the Emperor and the House of Austria lay under to Her Majestie and sufficiently applauded the Wisdom and Conduct of the Duke her General; and therefore, tho as an Elder General and Lieutenant General of the whole Empire he might have pretended to a sole command of the Army, yet he insisted upon no such point, but that each of them shou'd have their Day of Command alternatively, one in the Name of the Emperor and the other in the name of Her Majestie, as long as they continued together. In short instead of disputing about priority of Command, they rather strove who should obey; and this good agreement between them at first, was a happy presage of future success....

II. *Marlborough's letters to Harley, describing the actions of Schellenberg and Blenheim*

TO MR SECRETARY HARLEY.

Camp at Ebermergen, 3rd July, 1704.

SIR,

I now acknowledge the favour of your letters of the 6th and 9th past, and am very glad to acquaint you at the same time with a considerable advantage we have had over the Elector of Bavaria. Upon my coming on Tuesday with the army to Onder Ringen I received advice that the Elector had sent a great body of his best troops to reinforce those on the Schellenberg near Donawert, where they had been fortifying and intrenching themselves for some time. This being a post of great consequence to the enemy, I resolved to attack it, and accordingly yesterday, about three in the morning, I marched with a detachment of six thousand foot, thirty squadrons of horse, and three regiments of Imperial grenadiers, leaving the whole army to follow; but the march being long and the roads very difficult, I could not reach the river Wernitz till about noon. We immediately used all the diligence we could in laying over the bridges, which being finished about three o'clock, the troops with the artillery marched over, and all things being ready the attack began about six. We found the enemy very strongly intrenched, and they defended themselves with great obstinacy for an hour and a half, during which there was a continued fire without any intermission; at last the enemy were forced to yield to the bravery of our troops, who made a great slaughter and possessed themselves of their camp, the Comte d'Arco, the Elector's general, with their other general officers, being obliged to save themselves by swimming over the Danube. We took fifteen pieces of cannon, with their tents, baggage, and ammunition; part of the latter, being underground and not discovered by our men, blew up in the night and did some mischief to a squadron of Dutch dragoons.

The loss on our side has been considerable, but I must refer you to my next for the particulars. Our horse were commanded by Lieut.-Gen. Lumley and the foot by the Earl of Orkney and Major-Gen. Withers. The battalion of guards, one of my Lord Orkney's regiments, and Ingoldesby's were those that suffered the most. Major-Gen. Wood, Col. Palmer of Lieut.-Gen. Lumley's regiment, and Col. Meredyth are the most of note of the English that were wounded; Lieut.-Gen. Goor and Major-Gen. Beinheim in the States service are killed, with the Prince of Wolfenbuttel, a major-general in the Emperor's service; Prince Louis and Gen. Thungen were slightly wounded; Comte Stirum is shot through the body, but it is hoped may recover. The Hereditary Prince of Hesse and Count Horne, who commands the Duke of Wirtemberg's troops, are likewise wounded. All our troops in general behaved themselves with great gallantry, and the English in particular have gained a great deal of honour in this action, which I believe was the warmest that has been known for many years, the horse and dragoons appointed to sustain the foot standing within musket-shot of the enemy's trenches most part of the time.

A little before the attack began an adjutant-general arrived from Prince Eugène to give an account that the Maréchals de Villeroi and Tallard were at Strasburg, preparing to send the Elector a great reinforcement through the Black Forest, and I have advice from other hands that they design him fifty battalions and sixty squadrons of their best troops, which made me the more earnest to push on this attack, all which you will please to lay with my humble duty before her Majesty and his Royal Highness.

I am, with great truth, Sir, &c. M.

To Mr Secretary Harley

SIR,   *Camp at Hochstet, 14th August, 1704.*

I gave you an account on Sunday of the situation we were then in, and that we expected to hear the enemy would pass the Danube at Lavingen, in order to attack Prince Eugene. At 11 that night we had an express from him, that the enemy were come over, and desiring he might be reinforced; where-

upon I ordered my brother Churchill to advance at one o'clock
in the morning with his twenty battalions, and by three the
whole army was in motion; for the greater expedition I
ordered part of the troops to pass over the Danube, and follow the march of the twenty battalions, and with most of the
horse, and the foot of the first line, I passed the Lech at Rain,
and came over the Danube at Donawert, so that we all joined
the Prince that night, intending to advance and take this camp
of Hochstet, in order whereto we went out on Tuesday early
in the morning with forty squadrons to view the ground, but
found the enemy had already possessed themselves of it,
whereupon we resolved to attack them, and accordingly we
marched between three and four yesterday morning from the
camp at Munster, leaving all our tents standing. About six
we came in view of the enemy, who we found did not expect
so early a visit. The cannon began to play at half an hour after
eight. They formed themselves in two bodies; the Elector,
with M. Marsin and their troops opposite our right, and M.
de Tallard with all his opposed to our left, which last fell to
my share. They had two little rivulets besides a morass before
them, which we were obliged to pass over in their view, and
Prince Eugene was forced to take a great compass to come to
the enemy, so that it was one o'clock before the battle began:
it lasted with great vigour till sunset, when the enemy were
obliged to retire, and, by the blessing of God, we obtained a
complete victory. We have cut off great numbers of them, as
well in the action as in the retreat, besides upwards of thirty
squadrons of the French, which we pushed into the Danube,
where we saw the greatest part of them perish, M. de Tallard
with several of his general officers being taken prisoners at the
same time; and in the village of Blenheim, which the enemy
had intrenched and fortified, and where they made the greatest
opposition, we obliged twenty-six battalions and twelve
squadrons of dragoons to surrender themselves prisoners at
discretion. We took likewise all their tents standing, with their
cannon and ammunition, as also a great number of standards,
kettle-drums, and colours in the action, so that I reckon the
greatest part of M. Tallard's army is taken or destroyed. The
bravery of all our troops on this occasion cannot be expressed;

the generals as well as the officers and soldiers behaving themselves with the greatest courage and resolution, the horse and
dragoons having been obliged to charge four or five several
times.

The Elector and M. Marsin were so advantageously posted
that Prince Eugene could make no impression on them till the
third attack at or near seven at night, when he made a great
slaughter of them, but being near a wood side, a good body of
Bavarians retired into it, and the rest of that army retreated
towards Lavingen, it being too late and the troops too much
tired to pursue them far. I cannot say too much in praise of
the Prince's good conduct and the bravery of his troops on
this occasion.

You will please to lay this before her Majesty and his Royal
Highness, to whom I send my Lord Tunbridge with the good
news.

I pray you will likewise inform yourself and let me know
her Majesty's pleasure as well relating to M. de Tallard and
the other general officers, as for the disposal of near 1200 other
officers, and between 8000 and 9000 common soldiers, who
being all made prisoners by her Majesty's troops are entirely
at her disposal; but as the charge of subsisting these officers
and men must be very great, I presume her Majesty will be
inclined that they be exchanged for any other prisoners that
offer.

I should likewise be glad to receive her Majesty's directions
for the disposal of the standards and colours, whereof I have
not yet the number, but guess there cannot be less than a
hundred, which is more than has been taken in any battle
these many years.

You will easily believe that in so long and vigorous an
action, the English, who had so great a share in it, must have
suffered, as well in officers as men, but I have not yet the
particulars.

I am, Sir, your most obedient humble servant. M.

III. *Blenheim, described by Cardonnell,*
Marlborough's Secretary

(B.M. Ellis Papers II, Add. MSS. 28918, ff. 287–288 *b*)

PRINCE LEWIS of Baden having march'd the 9th with twenty
two Battallions and thirty four Esquadrons all Imperial to
beseige Ingoldstadt, the Duke of Marlborough tooke post
with the rest of the army between the Saar and Danube for
as to either to cover the seige, or be ready to joine Pr. Eugene
in case the Elector should passe the Danube. The 11th uppon
advice that hee had done soe neer Dillingen, our army passed
itt att two several places and joined the Prince who had retired to Donewaert, and that evening our army encamped
att Munster within a league and halfe of the Electors camp,
who made a movement and beat in our advanc't guards as if
he would have attacked us, for hee did nott then know that
Prince Eugene and wee were joined.

Our Tents and Baggage being sent away wee marched on
the 13th in eight Collumns towards the enemyes camp, without their having any knowledge thereof till about seven in the
morning that wee appeared in sight of them, att which time
wee began to extend, and forme in the enemyes front, who
had a small river and a morasse from right to left before them,
the passing whereof had some difficulty in itt, for wee were
obliged to make severall bridges in the very face of their army
and some of ours attackt on the left the Electors forces. Lord
Cutts with twenty Battalions att the same time or rather a
little before attackt a village on their right [Blenheim] wherein
Marchal Tallards foote were posted. General Churchill Lord
Orkney and Lt Genll Ingoldsby were in the center.

The enemyes frame consisted of about eighty peices of
Cannon which began to play about nine a clock, and killed us
a great many men. Our first attack begun att two in the
afternoone, in a short time after which our horse and foote
passed in the Center when all the french horse and some
Battalions of foote were drawne up.

Our whole army having now passed the river & Morasse
the horse formed and charged the enemy with the greatest

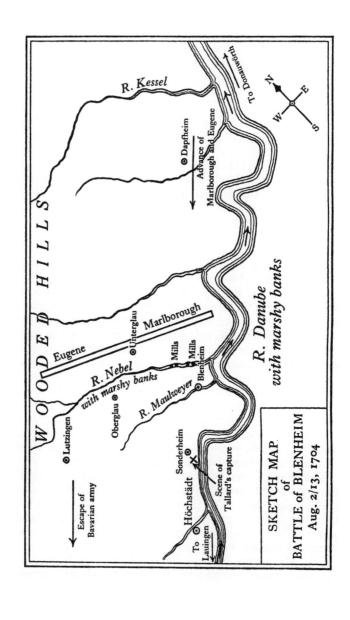

R. Kessel

To Donauwörth

N
W — E
S

Dapfheim

Advance of
Marlborough and Eugene

WOODED HILLS

Unterglau

Marlborough

Eugene

R. Nebel
with marshy banks

Mills   Mills
Blenheim

Oberglau

R. Maulweyer

R. Danube
with marshy banks

Lützingen

Escape of
Bavarian army

Sonderheim

Scene of
Tallard's capture

Höchstädt

To
Lauingen

SKETCH MAP
of
BATTLE of BLENHEIM
Aug. 2/13, 1704

bravery imaginable, though in some places they were repulsed
for want of foote to sustaine them, those who had first past
with Gen^ll Churchill being march't to sustaine Lord Cutts
whom the enemy pusht very hard: Lord Orkney marcht the
foote under his command to sustaine the horse, and having
interlined them (whoe were in some disorder for want of
foote) brought up some cannon, and then wee charged both
their foote and horse.

Our horse in a very little time routed theirs, butt their foote
stood their ground (being drawn up in Battalion quarres) till
they were all cutt to peices. Then their whole line retired a
considerable way to the ground where they had encampt.
After this Lord Orkney moved towards the right of the
enemy, and joined Lt Gen^ll Ingoldsby whoe both passed another rivulet and came into the right of the enemyes camp,
butt could not gett the cannon over, wherefore they were
planted on the other side, from whence they played on the
enemyes flanke in the village which att the beginning Ld
Cutts had attackt [Blenheim].

Itt was agreed that att the same time Orkney and Ingoldsby should attack the village the Prince of Hesse & L^t
Gen Lumley should charge the enemyes horse to prevent
their flanking our foote, which they did with great bravery
and successe.

Our foote uppon the first attack gott into the village, on
the side where Orkney & Ingoldsby were, Lt Cutts whoe
attackt att the same time being repulsed, butt were in a little
time beat of, butt they kept possession of the avenues of the
village, whilst Brig. Web with his Regiment maintained his
foot on the side of the Danube which shutt the enemy
quite up.

Lord Orkney made two other attacks, in the latter of
which hee went into the very middle of the village, but was
beaten out againe both times; by means of some houses which
covered the enemy, and out of which they fired and killed a
great many of our men. Hee then made another attack.
(Having first given orders for firing those houses as soone as
they could come att them, which was accordingly done) and
saw a Brigade advancing towards him, with intention as hee

supposed to fight their way through, his Lordship ordered the beating a parley, which Brig: Denonville (whoe commanded) accepted of In a very little time hee submitted to become prisoner att discretion, (being the onely conditions his L^ds^p would graunt) provided they might nott bee plundered; which was very punctually perform'd.

Lt Gen^ll Ingoldsby att the same time capitulated on like formes with a second [Brigadier] whoe comãnded another Brigade in the village. Brigad^r being examined touching the number of forces in the village answered above twenty Battalions and twelve Squadrons. Ld Orkney proposd his returning into the village with his Lordships aid de camp to offer Monsr Blanzac Maresshall de camp and whoe comãnded there in cheife the like conditions which Denonville had accepted; accordingly they went, and returned in a short time Blanzac coming out with them. Ld Orkney acquainted him that their Maresshal was actually our Prisoner with an infinite number of other officers, that my Ld Marlborough was by this time att least a league of, in pursuite of their horse whoe were entirely routed, that his Grace had sent him word that he should bee immediately sustained by twenty Battalions and all the cañon (which noe doubt had its weight with Blanzac for you must know that Ld Orkney had att this time butt nine Battalions & three troops of Dragoons comãnded by Brig. Rosse, whoe behaved themselves very gallantly, & were of very great use) and therefore offered him quarter which hee advised his acquiting of.

Marquesse Blanzac promised returning to Ld Orkney after having consulted his officers in the village. Ld Orkney sent his aid de camp back into the village with Blanzac with directions that in case the officers should bee of opinion to capitulate hee should then goe to Lord Cutts whoe was on the other side the village to acquaint him that the enemy were treating in order to prevent his firing or making any farther attack; Blanzac in a short time returned butt seemed very unwilling to become prisoners insisting on marching away, butt this or any other or better conditions than what hee had grauntd to Denonville his Lordship peremptorily refusing Blanzac accepted the same and marcht out prisoners twenty seven Battalions (including the two who had first capitulated) and twelve squadrons of Dragoons.

As to what passed on the right where Pr. Eugene comãnded wee must bee wholly ignorant, save that I heard him say that hee had been very sore presst, having repulsed the enemy severall times, and often repulsed by them, wherefore hee did nott thinke fitt to push the Bavarians too hard in their retreat which they made regularly and in good order.

The Duke of Marlborough exposd himselfe in every place, from one attacque to another, beyond what is thought advisable in a General, butt hee saw the good effect of his doing soe, and noe doubt knew the necessity of a battaille better then any of us, for I beleive had the opinion of a majority of us prevaild, wee should nott have been for itt under our circumstances; in short orders were never better given or better executed.

You must hereafter expect a perticular acco^{tt} of the slaine and prisoners on ye enemyes part, for of the latter there are none of us I beleive I shall bee greatly within compasse in saying wee have twelve hundred officers and as many thousand Soldiers prisoners.

IV. *The Blenheim Campaign as Captain Parker saw it.*

THESE *extracts are from the Memoirs of Captain Robert Parker, late of the Royal Regiment of Foot in Ireland, published by his son in* 1746. *They give a marching officer's experiences.*

Now the Duke of *Marlborough* upon confidering the ftate of the *Empire*, faw plainly, that unlefs fomething extraordinary was undertaken this year for its defence, the Eleɕtor of *Bavaria* would inevitably place himfelf on the *Imperial* Throne; and in that cafe he and *France* would give laws to *Europe*. Upon this he formed a bold and daring fcheme, for marching a good body of Troops from the *Netherlands* to the *Danube*. He firft communicated it to the Queen, and a few of the Privy-Council; then to fuch of the *States-General* as he

could confide in; for the fuccefs of the undertaking depended
in a great meafure on the fecrecy of it. In order to cover his
defign, he gave out that he would make this Campaign on the
Mofelle; and had ordered great Magazines of all manner of
neceffaries to be laid up at *Coblentz*, at which place the *Mofelle*
falls into the *Rhine*. This anfwered his purpofe, for the Court
of *France* made no doubt, but his defigns lay that way; in
confequence of which, they made great preparations to receive
him on that fide.

* * * * * *

And now when we expected to march up the *Mofelle*, to
our furprize we paffed that river over a ftone bridge, and the
Rhine over two bridges of boats, and proceeded on our march
through the country of *Heffe-Caffel*, where we were joined
by the hereditary Prince (now King of *Sweden*) with the
Troops of that country; which made our Army 40,000
fighting men compleat.

When we had paffed the *Rhine*, the Duke for the convenience of forage, advanced a day's march, and took his rout
with the Horfe, different from that of the Foot, which was
left under the command of General *Churchill*. We frequently
marched three, fometimes four days, fucceffively, and halted
a day. We generally began our march about three in the
morning, proceeded about four leagues, or four and half each
day, and reached our ground about nine. As we marched
through the Countries of our Allies, Commiffaries were appointed to furnifh us with all manner of neceffaries for man
and horfe; thefe were brought to the ground before we arrived,
and the foldiers had nothing to do, but to pitch their tents, boil
their kettles, and lie down to reft. Surely never was fuch a
march carried on with more order and regularity, and with
lefs fatigue both to man and horfe. From the country of *Heffe*
we marched through that of *Naffau*, into the Electorate of
Mentz, then through that of *Heffe-Darmftadt*, and through
the *Palatinate* till we came to *Heydelberg*, where we halted
three days; and now, and not before, was it publickly known
that the Duke's defign was againft the Elector of *Bavaria*. It
was fo much a fecret, that General *Churchill* (the Duke's

Brother) knew nothing of the matter till this time; and *Villeroy*'s conftant attendance on our marches, fhewed that the Court of *France* was as much in the dark as we were.

*   *   *   *   *   *

The fituation and difpofition of the enemy was as follows: They had the *Danube* on their Right, clofe to which was the village of *Blenheim:* They had on their Left a large thick wood, with the village of *Lutzingen* clofe by it, from whence runs a rivulet, which empties itfelf into the *Danube* a little below *Blenheim*. This rivulet they had in their Front, which made the ground in moft places about it fwampy and marfhy. The Electnr and *Marfin* drew up their part of the Army clofe to the Morafs, and determined not to fuffer a man to pafs, but what fhould come on the points of their Bayonets. But *Tallard* made quite another fort of a difpofition of his Troops; he pofted in the village of *Blenheim* 28 Battallions and 12 Squadrons of Dragoons. There were two mills on the rivulet a little above *Blenheim*, in which he pofted two Battalions; he had therefore but 10 Battalions in the field with him; and being joined by 20 Squadrons of *Marfin*'s, he had 70 Squadrons, on whom was his great dependence. Thefe and his 10 Battalions he drew up on the height of the plain, almoft half an *Englifh* mile from the Morafs. The village of *Auberclaw* lay partly on the Morafs toward our fide, and was near their center; in it *Marfin* had pofted 8 Battalions. Now thefe, with the troops in *Blenheim* and in the mills, were to march out as foon as they faw the Duke pafs the Morafs, and fall on his rear, by which means *Tallard* was fure of having him in a trap between two fires. Now as the main part of this Battle was fought between the Duke and this mighty Marefhal of *France*, I fhall be very particular in defcribing it.

The Duke of *Marlborough*, a man of uncommon penetration and prefence of mind, foon perceived *Tallard*'s defign; and thereupon ordered General *Churchill*, with 19 Battalions to attack the troops in *Blenheim*, and Lieutenant-General *Wood* with 8 Squadrons to fupport him. He alfo ordered the Prince of *Holftein-beck* with fix Battalions to attack the village of *Auberclaw*, and two battalions to attack the mills. The

Duke having thus fecured his rear, a little before one ordered the fignal to be made for attacking the villages and mills; at which time Brigadier *Rue* [Row] at the head of the *Britifh* Guards, and two *Britifh* Brigades, attacked thofe in *Blenheim*, but were repulfed, the Brigadier and a great many men being killed. At this time the reft of the Foot coming up, they renewed the charge; and thofe that had been repulfed, having foon rallied, returned to the charge, and drove the enemy from the fkirts of the village, into the very heart of it. Here they had thrown up an intrenchment, within which they were pent up in fo narrow a compafs, that they had not room to draw up in any manner of order, or even to make ufe of their arms. Thereupon we drew up in great order about 80 paces from them, from whence we made feveral vain attempts to break in upon them, in which many brave men were loft to no purpofe; and after all, we were obliged to remain where we firft drew up. The enemy alfo made feveral attempts to come out upon us: But as they were necefarily thrown into confufion in getting over their trenches, fo before they could form into any order for attacking us, we mowed them down with our platoons in fuch numbers, that they were always obliged to retire with great lofs; and it was not poffible for them to rufh out upon us in a diforderly manner, without running upon the very points of our Bayonets. This great body of Troops therefore was of no further ufe to *Tallard*, being obliged to keep on the defenfive, in expectation that he might come to relieve them.

Prince *Holftein-beck* was repulfed on his attack of *Auberclaw*: Yet, though he could not force the enemy from thence, he anfwered the Duke's intention however, in not fuffering them to fall on his rear. They in the mills made but little refiftance; fo fetting them on fire they made off to *Tallard*, and joined the Battalions he had with him.

It may be prefumed that the Lord *Marlborough* was not idle all this while. The very moment that the villages were attacked, he ordered Colonel *Palms* with three *Britifh* Squadrons of Horfe to enter the Morafs. Thefe having paffed it without oppofition, drew up at fome diftance from it. Upon which the Duke gave orders, that all the Troops fhould pafs with the greateft expedition, while his Grace followed clofe after *Palms*. *Tallard*, as a man infatuated, ftood looking on, without firing a fhot great or fmall; thefe formed their Lines as faft as they paffed. At length *Tallard* feeing *Palms* advanced with his Squadrons fome diftance from our Lines, ordered out five Squadrons, (fome faid feven) to march down and cut *Palm*'s Squadrons to pieces, and then retire. When the commanding Officer of thefe Squadrons had got clear of their Lines, he ordered the Squadron on his Right, and that on his Left to edge outward, and then march down till they came on a line with *Palms*; at which time they were to wheel inward, and fall upon his flanks, while he charged him in front. *Palms* perceiving this, ordered Major *Oldfield*, who commanded the Squadron on his Right, and Major *Creed*, who commanded that on his Left, to wheel outward, and charge thofe Squadrons, that were coming down on them; and he, not in the leaft doubting but they would beat them, ordered them when they had done that, to wheel in upon the flanks of the other Squadrons that were coming upon him, while he charged them in front; and every thing fucceeded accordingly. This was a great furprize to *Tallard*, who had placed fuch confidence in his Troops, that he verily thought there were not any on earth able to ftand before them. And now in no fmall hurry, he ordered his Lines to advance, and charge the Duke, who by this time had all his Troops over, and his Lines formed.

Here was a fine plain without hedge or ditch, for the Cavalry on both fides to fhew their bravery; for there were but few Foot to interpofe, thefe being moftly engaged at the villages. *Tallard* feeing his five Squadrons fo fhamefully beat by three, was confounded to that degree, that he did not recover himfelf the whole day, for after that, all his orders were given in hurry and confufion.

When the Duke faw *Tallard*'s Lines advance, he ordered his Troops alfo to advance and meet them. The Front-line of the enemy was compofed moftly of the *Gendarmery*, on whofe bravery *Tallard* had the greateft dependence. Thefe therefore were pitched upon to begin the Battle; and they indeed made fo bold and refolute a Charge, that they broke through our firft Line: but our fecond meeting them, obliged them to retire. This check allayed that fire, which the *French* have always been fo remarkable for in their firſt onfets: And it was obfervable, that they did not make fuch another puſh that day; for when once they are repulfed, their fire immediately abates. And now our Squadrons charged in their turn, and thus for fome hours they charged each other with various fuccefs, all fword in hand. At length the *French* courage began to abate, and our Squadrons gained ground upon them, until they forced them back to the Height on which they were firſt drawn up. Here their Foot which had not fired a ſhot interpofed; whereupon the Duke ordered his Squadrons to halt. At the fame time our Foot came up, and Colonel *Blood* with nine Field-pieces loaded with Cartridge-ſhot, fired on their Foot, which obliged them to quit the Horfe, and ſtand on their own defence.

The Cavalry had this breathing-time, in which both fides were very bufy in putting their Squadrons and Lines in order. And now *Tallard* finding that the Troops in *Blenheim* did not anfwer his expeſtation, fent to them to quit the Village, and come to his affiſtance: But alas! they were not able to affiſt themfelves. He then fent to Marefhal *Marfin* for help: But he fent him word, he had too much work on his own hands. The Duke now finding the enemy very backward in renewing the Battle, and, as it feemed, rather in a tottering condition, fent orders to all his Troops to advance gently, until they came pretty near them, and then to ride on a full trot up to them. This they did fo effeſtually, that it decided the fate of the day. The *French* fire was quite extinguiſhed, they made not the leaſt refiſtance, but gave way and broke at once. Our Squadrons drove through the very centre of them, which put them to an intire rout. About 30 of their Squadrons made toward a Bridge of boats they had over the *Danube:* But the Bridge (as it frequently happens in fuch cafes) broke under the crowd that ruſhed upon it, and down they went. At the fame time our Squadrons purfued clofe at their heels, cutting down all before them; for in all fuch clofe purfuits, 'tis very rare that any Quarter is given. In ſhort, they were almoſt all of them killed or drowned; and the few that reached the far fide of the River, were killed by the Boors of the Villages they had burnt. *Tallard* fled that way, but finding the Bridge broken, he turned up the River toward *Hochftet*, and was taken. The reft of his Troops fled toward *Lawingen*, but were not purfued, becaufe the Elector and *Marfin* ftill made good their ground. The Duke obferving this, ordered Lieutenant General *Hompefch* to draw together what Troops he could, and fall on their Flank: But by this time they found that *Tallard* was routed, and feeing our Squadrons drawing toward them, they inftantly, and with great dexterity and expedition, formed their Troops into three Columns, and marched off with the greateft difpatch and order imaginable. Prince *Eugene* by this time had got a good part of his Troops over the Morafs, and was juft ready to fall on their Rear: But perceiving the Squadrons under *Hompefch* coming down that way, he took them to be fome of *Tallard*'s Squadrons drawing down to join the Elector; whereupon he halted, left they fhould fall on his Flank. The Duke alfo feeing Prince *Eugene*'s Troops fo near the Rear of the Elector's, took them to be a Body of *Bavarians*, making good the Elector's retreat; and thereupon ordered *Hompefch* to halt. Here they both remained until they were informed of their miftakes by their Aids de Camp; and it was by this means that the Elector and *Marfin* had time to get over the Pafs of *Nordlingen* which was juft before them. Our Troops alfo were much fatigued, and night drew on, all which favoured their retreat. Or perhaps it may rather be faid, that Providence interpofed, which feeing the flaughter of the day, thought it fufficient: Otherwife few, if any of them, could have efcaped. As to the Battalions which *Tallard* had with him in the Field, they were cut in pieces to a man, fuch only excepted, as threw themfelves down among the dead. I rode through them next morning as they lay dead, in Rank and File. As foon as the Troops in *Blenheim*, faw the fate of their Army in the Field, they threw down their arms, and furrendered at difcretion; but the Troops in *Auberclaw* made off with *Marfin*.

V. *Blenheim through French eyes*

(*Mémoires militaires sous Louis XIV*, extraits par le général de Vault, revus etc. par le général Pelet, 1841, tome IV, pp. 562–73, 584–8.)

IN the first two of these four documents, Marshal Tallard gives his apology for the great defeat that has made his name immortal. The third and fourth documents (pp. 128–133) are narratives of other French officers present at the battle.*

Lettre de M. le maréchal de Tallard à M. de Chamillart.

Hanau, 4 septembre 1704.

Je viens de recevoir, monsieur, la lettre que vous m'avez fait l'honneur de m'écrire le 25 de l'autre mois; je compte que M. de Silly sera arrivé le même soir auprès de vous, qui aura satisfait à tout ce que vous désiriez de moi. Je l'ai prié et chargé de dire la vérité de tout au roi et à vous; c'est mon unique instruction, et je suis persuadé qu'il se sera acquitté fidèlement de la commission dont il avait bien voulu se charger. Si, outre cela, monsieur, vous voulez encore un mot de moi, je vais vous obéir.

J'ai prévu le malheur qui est arrivé, en partant d'Alsace; le malheureux projet de M. de Legall, spécieux en apparence, était en effet une source d'abîmes. Si j'étais resté à la tête du pays de Wurtemberg, mes forces étant connues et les ennemis en état de venir à moi avec toutes celles qu'ils jugeraient nécessaires pour m'accabler, il fallait que je le fusse ou que je me retirasse en Alsace avec honte et précipitation; ma perte ou ma retrait faisait faire la paix de M. de Bavière, et l'armée du Danube était également perdue; les ennemis, par parenthèse, ne la voulaient laisser retirer par le projet de paix que brigade par brigade. C'est M. de Bavière qui leur a fait parler le premier, et il n'est pas vrai qu'il y ait jamais offert Ulm, Memmingen ni Augsbourg. Comptez, s'il vous plaît, monsieur, sur ce que j'ai l'honneur de vous mander, et excusez cette petite digression.

Je n'étais pas en moindre risque en allant en Bavière, les choses y étant dans l'état qu'elles étaient, sans aucun magasin, pas pour six jours de vivres en nul endroit, tous les postes occupés par les ennemis, et l'armée que je menais affaiblie par la désertion de tous les étrangers, et la mortalité dans les dragons surtout, et dans plusieurs régiments de cavalerie, telle que vous aurez appris par M. le duc de Quintin qu'elle était

dans son régiment. Au surplus, monsieur, une ignorance
totale de la force des ennemis, et M. de Bavière ayant toutes
ses troupes, à cinq bataillons et vingt-trois escadrons près, dans
son pays, pour couvrir ses salines, le château d'un gentilhomme,
enfin tout, hors ce qu'il fallait couvrir, qui était la frontière.

Je lui parlai dans la première audience que j'eus avec lui
là-dessus avec tant de force, qu'il me promit de faire venir
jusqu'à quarante escadrons et dix-huit bataillons.

Cependant, les ennemis étant partis de Friedberg et mar-
chant au Danube, il eut de faux avis qu'ils avaient passé cette
rivière; il fut question d'aller à Lauingen pour empêcher
qu'ils ne s'en saisissent. Je demandai si, quand on y serait, il
y avait quelque poste qu'on pût occuper avec sûreté pour
attendre le renfort de Bavarois qui devait venir. Tout le
monde m'assura que oui: on prit la résolution de passer le
Danube; le poste de Lauingen, qui était le seul qui nous
restât, était si important, que cette démarche était nécessaire.
Je consentis donc à la faire, sans même donner qu'un séjour
à l'armée que j'amenais: nous marchâmes trois jours, au bout
desquels nous passâmes le Danube. Je trouvai des pays
ouverts et point de poste. M. l'électeur, se moquant de mes
craintes, me força de lui dire que, si je connaissais moins sa
droiture, je croirais qu'il voudrait hasarder les forces du roi
sans les siennes, pour voir sans risque ce qui en arriverait.
Il voulut marcher dès le soir à M. le prince Eugène, ignorant
ses forces et ne sachant pas qu'il avait ramené trente escadrons
des lignes et dix-huit bataillons, qui, avec le détachement que
les alliés lui avaient envoyé et un nouveau corps de leur armée
dont il avait été joint, le faisaient d'une force considérable.
Je ne m'y opposai point, disant que c'était à lui et à M. le
maréchal de Marcin, qui connaissaient le pays et qui savaient
le fond qu'il y avait à faire sur ceux qui leur donnaient des
nouvelles, à juger de ce qui se devait entreprendre; qu'en gros
je savais qu'il ne fallait pas manquer une occasion, si on la
croyait sûre, mais qu'il fallait prendre garde aussi à trouver
toute l'armée. Après une longue délibération, on conclut de
ne point marcher ce soir-là.

Le lendemain je pris la liberté de représenter à M. le
maréchal de Marcin qu'il me semblait que, dans la situation

des choses, il ne fallait rien risquer; que les affaires du roi allaient bien partout; que nous avions les principales forces de l'état entre les mains, et qu'à mon sens nous ne devions rien tenter qu'au mois d'octobre, pour les quartiers d'hiver, et nous contenter jusqu'à ce temps-là de ne point laisser mettre les ennemis entre le pays de Wurtemberg et nous.

Dès le lendemain M. l'électeur nous repressa de marcher en avant; comme il n'y avait point de fourrage où nous étions, et que j'avais envie, au lieu d'avoir le cul au Danube, comme nous avions, que nous y missions notre droite et notre gauche vers la montagne, afin de traverser le pays, je consentis à aller chercher un camp, étant convenus que nous laisserions la rivière d'Höchstett devant nous, ou qu'au plus nous n'irions que jusqu'à Höchstett, laissant le marais à la tête du camp.

Quand nous y fûmes le lendemain, M. l'électeur proposa de passer outre et d'aller jusqu'à Lutzingen, où le combat s'est donné. Poussé, tourné en ridicule sur mes représentations, je consentis qu'on fût reconnaître le nouveau camp proposé. Je revenais toujours à dire qu'il fallait rester derrière Höchstett. M. de Legall dit que les ennemis se viendraient mettre à Lutzingen: s'ils y fussent venus et que nous fussions restés à Höchstett, vous eussiez eu cent lettres contre moi par la première occasion; et en effet c'était leur dessein. M. le maréchal de Marcin me tira à part là-dessus, et me dit qu'il ne voyait pas d'inconvénient à y venir; las de refuser, j'y consentis, et nous y marchâmes le lendemain sans l'avoir trop reconnu par nous-mêmes, mais sur la foi de ceux qui y étaient l'année dernière avec M. le maréchal de Villars. Cette diversité d'avis, monsieur, qui rend ce qu'on veut faire public, fait bien voir et est une belle leçon pour jamais de n'avoir qu'un homme pour commander une armée, et que c'est un grand malheur que d'avoir à ménager un prince de l'humeur de M. l'électeur de Bavière, surtout quand des lieutenants généraux s'adressent à lui directement pour l'échauffer et lui inspirer leurs sentiments, comme faisaient certains de l'armée de M. le maréchal de Marcin.

Quand nous fûmes arrivés, nous vîmes l'armée des ennemis campée à une lieue et demie de nous. M. l'électeur de Bavière dit qu'il venait de recevoir des lettres de Donawert, par où

on lui mandait qu'il n'y avait que le duc de Marlborough qui
eût joint le prince Eugène, et sur ce principe il voulait qu'on
marchât aux ennemis pour les attaquer. Il criait qu'on perdait
une occasion qu'on ne trouverait jamais. Enfin M. le maréchal
de Marcin et moi lui dîmes que, puisqu'il voulait marcher à
eux, il fallait au moins démêler si M. de Bade y était ou non,
parce que d'aller attaquer des gens beaucoup plus forts que
soi, dans un beau poste, comme ils le seraient s'ils étaient tous
réunis, n'était pas chose faisable. Cependant, pour ne pas
perdre cette prétendue occasion, on détacha M. de Silly avec
huit troupes soutenues de huit autres, puis de seize, enfin de
quatre régiments de dragons et de mille chevaux, pour en-
gager une escarmouche à la tête du camp des ennemis, afin de
faire des prisonniers à quelque prix que ce fût. Il nous en
envoya quatre en fort peu de temps, qui nous assurèrent que
toutes les forces des ennemis y étaient. M. l'électeur convint
donc de faire entrer les troupes dans le camp, disant à tout le
monde qu'on perdait une occasion qu'on ne retrouverait jamais.

Je le priai de vouloir bien passer à ma droite, parce que je
n'en étais pas content; on trouva même que je faisais diguer le
ruisseau, afin de le faire regonfler. M. de Zurlauben m'avertit
que M. d'Arco riait de ce qu'on croyait que les ennemis
pussent venir à nous; et M. l'électeur, sachant que j'avais
envie de faire faire une redoute sur un grand chemin qui
traversait le ruisseau, me dit, "J'espère que vous ne ferez pas
lever terre;" ce sont ses propres mots. Tout cela changea fort
le lendemain à cinq heures du matin, quand on vit que l'armée
des ennemis marchait à nous; et ceux qui étaient ennemis des
précautions la veille cherchaient à en prendre quand il n'était
plus temps. On se mit en bataille: je mis seize bataillons dans
le village de Blindheim et quatre régiments de dragons à pied,
leur étant mort tant de chevaux qu'ils rendaient un double
service de cette manière-là. Ce village était trop éloigné du
ruisseau pour en défendre le passage, et trop près pour qu'on
pût faire passer les lignes devant et le laisser derrière. J'ap-
puyai la gendarmerie au village. Je mis trois brigades d'infanterie le long du canal d'un moulin qui était derrière; la
brigade de Broglie et celle du mestre de camp général joignaient
la gendarmerie, puis commençait la droite de l'armée de M. le

maréchal de Marcin. J'avais neuf bataillons dans ma seconde ligne, et n'en avais point dans ces trois brigades de cavalerie de la première, parce que ce corps était destiné à se porter promptement sur le ruisseau et charger les ennemis avant qu'ils fussent formés. Je ne m'étendrai pas davantage sur un détail que M. le marquis de Silly vous aura expliqué bien plus nettement que je ne pourrais faire dans cette lettre; j'aurai simplement l'honneur de vous dire que, voyant que les ennemis assemblaient un gros corps de troupes dans le centre de leur ligne, j'envoyai un de mes aides de camp en avertir M. le maréchal de Marcin, pour le supplier d'envoyer la réserve derrière ce centre: il crut en avoir besoin à la gauche.

Il faut considérer, s'il vous plaît, monsieur, que je n'avais que trente-six bataillons et quarante-quatre escadrons, ayant été obligé de doubler mes escadrons à cause de la mortalité des chevaux. Je fus attaqué par quarante-huit bataillons et quatre-vingt-neuf escadrons anglais ou à la solde de Hollande et d'Angleterre, les moindres escadrons à cent soixante maîtres, les moindres bataillons passant cinq cents hommes. M. le maréchal de Marcin fut attaqué par dix-huit bataillons et quatre-vingt-douze escadrons. Il avait quatre-vingt-trois escadrons et quarante-deux bataillons, parce que les troupes de l'électeur étaient à la gauche.

Je renvoyai encore lui demander du secours dans le cours de l'action: il ne crut pas être en état de m'en donner. Enfin j'envoyai le maréchal des logis de la cavalerie lui dire que je le priais de me mander de ses nouvelles; que je ne pouvais plus soutenir l'effort des ennemis, d'autant plus qu'une colonne de cavalerie de la droite de leur armée repliait encore sur moi d'augmentation; M. du Plessis ne put me rejoindre, et je ne l'ai pas vu depuis.

M. de la Vallière et son régiment, M. de Broglie et le régiment du Roi, cavalerie, et le régiment de Forsat, ont fait des merveilles; les officiers de la gendarmerie sont de très-braves gens; mais les gendarmes n'ont rien fait qui vaille. Le gros de la cavalerie a mal fait, je dis très-mal; car on n'a jamais rompu un escadron des ennemis. J'ai pourtant vu un instant où la bataille était gagnée par la brigade de Robecq et celle d'Albaret, si la cavalerie, qui s'était avancée plus près des ennemis, à la faveur de l'infanterie, qu'elle n'avait fait auparavant, n'avait tourné tout d'un coup et abandonné cette pauvre infanterie.

M. de Zurlauben a fait des merveilles et en officier et en brave homme; M. de Valsemé a très-bien fait aussi. J'ai lieu de me fort louer de M. de Silly et de M. de Lignier, brigadier d'infanterie. La tête qui tourna à M. de Clérambault, qui préféra de se noyer à rester à son poste, est cause que, sa mort étant arrivée à l'insu de M. de Blanzac et des autres, l'on n'a point pris, dans le village où était l'infanterie [Blenheim], les partis qu'il y a eu à prendre. M. de Clérambault y avait rappelé à mon insu les trois brigades qui soutenaient mon aile droite, à la faveur desquelles on eût toujours été le maître de retirer l'infanterie du village. J'en étais sorti, il y avait trois quarts d'heure, pour retourner à la cavalerie, quand ce qui en restait s'enfuit sans que les ennemis marchassent à eux; je voulus la rallier, mais inutilement.

Je voulus me rejeter dans le village pour faire un dernier effort, afin de me retirer avec l'infanterie; je fus suivi par un régiment de dragons des troupes de Hesse, qui m'enveloppa, l'officier m'ayant reconnu à l'ordre du Saint-Esprit. Le village se défendit encore une heure et demie et puis capitula, abandonné par toute la cavalerie, par celui qui y commandait et par la moitié de ceux qui étaient dedans. M. de Silly vous aura informé, monsieur, d'un détail que je ne puis répéter ici. Ce fut la fin d'une journée malheureuse; cependant ce que le village tint de trop a donné lieu à M. le maréchal de Marcin de se retirer; et comme je sais qu'il est arrivé en Alsace avec son armée, la cavalerie de la mienne, qui n'a perdu que cinq ou six cents hommes, et l'armée de l'électeur, je puis vous assurer, monsieur, en homme d'honneur, que je crois les affaires du roi plus solidement bonnes que si les forces du roi étaient en Bavière. Ratisbonne étant pris et Ingolstadt assiégé, comme il l'était sans que l'électeur en sût rien quand le combat s'est donné, car il eût fait sa paix, ses troupes eussent servi l'empereur, et l'armée du roi aurait eu beaucoup de peine à se retirer. Il ramène un corps de cavalerie considérable dont nous manquions, et je vois présentement plus de deux cents escadrons et plus de cent dix bataillons en Alsace.

Permettez-moi, je vous supplie, monsieur, de n'en pas dire davantage sur une matière qui me perce encore le cœur. Le plus grand mal est sauvé quand les ennemis n'ont point suivi l'armée. Sans le miracle de l'année dernière à Höchstett, M. de Bavière était perdu dès la campagne passée; sans celui de Spire, il l'était l'hiver; il en fallait un double cette campagne pour le sauver, et c'est un bonheur que l'armée de M. le maréchal de Marcin et la sienne soient arrivées à bon port.

J'en suis la victime; mais, pourvu que les affaires du roi n'en souffrent point, je suis content de mon sort. Vous savez, monsieur, que, hors l'attachement que j'avais pour le roi et un certain point d'honneur, je souhaitais peu de chose pour moi; et si ces deux raisons ne m'avaient retenu, j'aurais désiré d'être en repos et hors de but aux cabales qui me persécutaient, et qui cherchaient toujours à empoisonner ce que je faisais de mieux. J'avoue que j'aurais bien voulu sortir du service par une autre porte que celle-ci; mais je n'ai rien a me reprocher. J'ai prévu, j'ai voulu empêcher, ma disposition était bonne; j'ai soutenu jusqu'au dernier moment, et je voudrais quasi que c'eût été aussi le dernier de ma vie.

Au reste, monsieur, je suis aussi sensible que je le dois à toutes les bontés que vous me témoignez dans la lettre que vous me faites l'honneur de m'écrire. Soyez persuadé, je vous supplie, que j'en conserverai le souvenir tant que je vivrai, et que vous aurez toute ma vie en moi un serviteur que sa méchante fortune vous rend bien inutile.

P. S. J'ajoute un mot à cette lettre pour avoir l'honneur de vous dire, monsieur, qu'il peut y avoir des gens qui ont bien fait, que je ne nomme pas; mais je ne parle que de ce que j'ai vu.

Au reste, monsieur, vous voyez bien par la franchise avec laquelle j'ai l'honneur de vous écrire, que cette lettre n'est que pour vous, et pour le roi, si vous jugez à propos de la lui montrer.

Je ne rendrais pas justice à M. de Montperoux, si je ne disais pas qu'il a fait en galant homme et en homme de courage.

M. le maréchal de Tallard et M. le maréchal de Marcin, étant à la tête des gardes le 13 du mois d'août dernier, virent les ennemis qui marchaient à nous sur huit colonnes. On fit prendre les armes aux deux armées, qui n'étaient point encore mêlées, pour ne pas communiquer à celle de Bavière, en faisant le service conjointement, la fatale maladie que nos chevaux avaient apportée d'Alsace.

La situation de notre droite était assez embarrassante; il y avait un village [Blenheim] qui joignait le Danube, trop éloigné du ruisseau qui nous couvrait [Nebel] pour en défendre le passage, et qui en était aussi trop proche pour pouvoir faire passer les lignes entre ledit village et ledit ruisseau, d'autant plus que le terrain qui était entre deux était absolument soumis à une hauteur qui était du côté qu'occupaient les ennemis.

Cela réduisit M. le maréchal de Tallard à la nécessité de garder ce village. Il y mit d'abord neuf bataillons et quatre régiments de dragons à pied, parce que les chevaux de ces derniers étant presque tous morts de la contagion, ils étaient plus en état de rendre service de cette façon qu'ils n'auraient pu faire à cheval.

Il appuya la droite de la gendarmerie à Blindheim: elle était composée de huit escadrons; la brigade de Broglie, composée de cinq, la joignait; ensuite la brigade de Grignan, réduite à pareil nombre, la maladie ayant si fort diminué les escadrons qu'il les avait fallu doubler.

Ce corps composait toute la première ligne de cavalerie de l'armée de M. de Tallard; l'aile droite de M. le maréchal de Marcin commençait après sans intervalle.

Comme l'ordre qu'avaient ces troupes était de charger les ennemis, sans les laisser former, quand ils passeraient le ruisseau, on n'y avait point mêlé d'infanterie, afin qu'elles pussent se porter plus diligemment où elles seraient nécessaires, et parce que le terrain était absolument ouvert devant elles; mais on avait placé les trois brigades de Royal, de Languedoc et de Zurlauben derrière, qui tenaient presque la même étendue que la cavalerie, tant pour la soutenir si elle était poussée, y ayant des sources propres à poster de l'infanterie où elles étaient, que pour être à portée de rattaquer le village s'il venait à être forcé, parce que de ce poste dépendait

Relation de la bataille d'Höchstett par M. le maréchal de Tallard. Aix-la-Chapelle, 3 décembre 1704.

tout, et que les ennemis avaient jeté les deux tiers de leur infanterie sur leur gauche, qui y étaient directement opposés.

Notre seconde ligne était composée de dix escadrons de la brigade de Silly, de neuf bataillons et deux brigades de la Baume, de Stref; celle de la Vallière était en une espèce de réserve auprès du village.

Voilà la première disposition, très-forte, puisque ledit village était bien garni, puisqu'il y avait une ligne de cavalerie qui le joignait prête à se porter sur le ruisseau, que cette ligne était soutenue d'une ligne d'infanterie, celle-là, d'une autre mêlée de cavalerie et d'infanterie, et enfin qu'il y avait, outre cela, un petit corps de réserve.

C'était là la situation des troupes quand la bataille commença.

Voici ce qui arriva: les ennemis firent passer vingt bataillons pour venir attaquer notre village. Ceux qui le défendaient soutinrent cet effort avec vigueur; et comme ces premiers se retiraient, M. de Zurlauben les chargea en flanc avec trois escadrons de la gendarmerie qui firent assez bien leur devoir.

Les ennemis, voulant soutenir leur infanterie, firent passer le ruisseau à de leur cavalerie; cinq escadrons se formèrent en deçà et vis-à-vis de la gendarmerie. D'abord on la fit marcher pour les charger. M. de Zurlauben était à la tête; mais quoiqu'il y eût huit escadrons de notre côté, ainsi que je viens de le dire, les cinq des ennemis soutinrent leur choc et les firent plier.

La seconde ligne de l'aile droite de cavalerie marcha pour les attaquer; mais elle ne les enfonça pas non plus. Pendant ce temps-là ces premiers défilaient toujours; et, avant que nos gens fussent ralliés, il se trouva un corps assez considérable de formé.

Les ennemis ne passaient pas le ruisseau avec moins de diligence vis-à-vis l'aile droite de M. le maréchal de Marcin. La cavalerie qui la composait et l'aile gauche de l'armée de M. de Tallard marchèrent conjointement pour les charger; mais, quoique supérieure en nombre, la charge des nôtres fut inutile: les ennemis ne furent point rompus.

La seconde ligne, qui vint pour soutenir la première qui avait été repoussée, ne fut pas plus heureuse; en sorte que le

temps qu'il fallut pour rallier tout cela ayant donné aux
ennemis celui d'achever de se former en deçà, ils firent passer
tant de cavalerie, qu'ils se trouvèrent en état de se servir contre
nous de la supériorité que leur donnait le nombre; car les deux
tiers de leurs forces et de leurs troupes d'élite étaient employés
contre notre droite, qui ne faisait pas le tiers des nôtres, le
corps d'armée de l'électeur étant encore sur la gauche de
l'armée de M. de Marcin.

Je ne dirai point que les ennemis, ayant rattaqué le village
pendant ce temps-là, en furent encore repoussés, ni que M. de
Clérambault, qui y commandait, croyant être trop faible,
avait dégarni sans ordre cette ligne d'infanterie qui était
derrière la cavalerie, pour en faire rentrer une partie dans le
village et en rapprocher l'autre.

Je ne parlerai point non plus d'une charge qui se fit avec ce
qui s'était rallié de cavalerie et de neuf bataillons de la seconde
ligne d'infanterie, laquelle pourtant ébranla la première ligne
des ennemis, et qui aurait eu plus de succès si la gendarmerie
et la cavalerie n'avaient pas plié et n'avaient pas abandonné
cette pauvre infanterie, parce qu'il faudrait étendre cette relation à l'infini, et je me contenterai de faire voir que la
bataille a été perdue, premièrement, parce que la gendarmerie
n'a pu enfoncer les cinq escadrons anglais dont j'ai parlé ci-
dessus; parce que la droite de M. de Marcin et la gauche de
M. de Tallard n'ont pu non plus accabler ce qui était devant
elles, avant qu'ils fussent fortifiés en continuant de passer le
ruisseau; parce que les deux secondes lignes de droite et de
gauche de la cavalerie n'ont pas mieux réussi, et enfin parce
que la seconde ligne d'infanterie a été abandonnée.

Il y a eu tant de relations sur ce qui s'est passé dans le village,
qu'il serait inutile d'en reparler; et je crois que, quand celle-ci
aura été lue, on verra bien clairement que le malheur qui nous
est arrivé est venu de ce qu'on n'a pas fait plier les ennemis aux
premières charges, et de ce que toute leur force, ayant tourné
vers la droite, la gauche, qui n'était attaquée que par un corps
inférieur, s'est contentée de soutenir avec succès sans s'être
crue en état de nous secourir.

*   *   *   *   *   *

Lettre de
M. de...
Du camp
de Tuttlin-
gen, 21 août
1704.

Je vous envoie, monsieur, la copie de la lettre que j'écris à M. de Chamillart, pour lui demander la charge de commissaire général de la cavalerie. Je lui fais un petit détail de ce qui s'est passé de mon côté, M. le maréchal de Tallard, qui est pris prisonnier, ayant assez de choses à mander sur son compte sans parler des particuliers. Il m'a vu charger trois fois avec ma brigade, et me fit l'honneur de me dire qu'il était content, et qu'il aurait souhaité que la gendarmerie qui était sur ma droite eût fait de même; je n'ai pas vu d'officier général pendant toute l'action à ma tête. Toute l'armée crie fort contre la disposition de M. de Tallard, et effectivement je crois qu'il aurait mieux fait de ne pas mettre toute son infanterie dans le village où sa droite était appuyée, et de mettre plus de troupes à son corps de bataille, qui est l'endroit par où les ennemis ont gagné la bataille. On peut dire aussi sans médisance que MM. les officiers généraux n'ont été d'aucun secours à M. le maréchal; ils ont laissé passer aux ennemis un marais et petit ruisseau que nous avions devant notre camp sans le défendre, et les ennemis étaient en deçà sur trois lignes avant que personne eût chargé. M. de Marcin de son côté n'a pas voulu aider de ses troupes l'armée de M. de Tallard, quoiqu'il lui en ait envoyé demander pendant l'action. Je ne vous ferais pas tous ces détails si je ne vous envoyais ma lettre par M. le marquis de Rieux, qui est de mes amis, et qui a bien voulu s'en charger. Je vous prie de ne la montrer à personne. Ce qu'il y a de plus malheureux dans cette action, c'est que M. de Clérambault, lieutenant général, qui commandait les vingt-sept bataillons qui étaient dans le village de la droite et douze escadrons de dragons, n'ait pas songé à se retirer avec ce corps; il s'est noyé dans le Danube à quatre heures du soir, deux heures avant la fin de l'affaire, la tête lui ayant tourné. On condamne fort M. de Blanzac, qui commandait sous lui, de ne s'être pas retiré, et d'avoir fait une capitulation aussi honteuse. Si ce corps s'était retiré, comme il n'y avait rien de plus possible, les ennemis perdaient autant que nous, et nous n'aurions pas été obligés de quitter le pays. L'armée de M. de Tallard perd vingt mille hommes dans cette occasion, tués ou pris, et les ennemis avouent dix mille hommes tués ou blessés. Les ennemis avaient plus de vingt-cinq mille

hommes plus que nous, de leur aveu. Le canon a commencé
à tirer de part et d'autre entre huit et neuf heures du matin; il
y en avait plus de quatre-vingts pièces de chaque côté. On a
commencé à charger à onze heures du matin, et cela a duré
jusqu'à six heures du soir. Voilà en gros le détail de cette
affaire. Comme je ne sais pas si mon père est en Auvergne, je
vous prie de lui envoyer ma lettre avec l'état des officiers du
régiment tués ou blessés. Son pauvre régiment d'infanterie a
été tout tué; il n'en reste que le sieur Sauge, major, qui a deux
coups de mousquet, qui serait mort si je ne l'avais retiré chez
moi et n'avais pris soin de le faire panser. Je vous serai très-
obligé de vouloir bien écrire à M. de Chamillart en ma faveur.
Quoique je sois persuadé que le roi ne me donnera pas cette
charge, je ne veux pas avoir à me reprocher de ne l'avoir pas
demandée. Je viens de faire une campagne bien fatigante et
bien périlleuse, et qui, je vous assure, fera prendre à bien des
gens le parti de la retraite; et si le roi ne donne pas quelque
gratification aux officiers du régiment, il leur sera impossible
de le remettre.

    Voici, monsieur, le seul moment que j'ai pu avoir depuis   Lettre de
notre malheureuse bataille d'Höchstett; et comme mes   M. le baron
blessures me donnent un peu de relâche, j'essayerai de vous   de Montigny-
informer de ce que j'ai vu dans cette affaire, que j'avais crue Languet.
être le comble de notre bonheur, et qui a été tout le contraire, 25 août 1704.
par l'envie que M. le maréchal de Tallard a eue de combattre.
    Les ennemis, ayant été avertis que nous avions passé le
Danube à Lauingen, quittèrent la Bavière, et, ayant assemblé
à Donawert toutes leurs forces, passèrent en même temps,
supérieurs à nous de quarante à cinquante escadrons et de
quelques bataillons. Nous marchâmes les uns aux autres, et
nous nous portâmes en bataille sur deux lignes à une petite
lieue d'Höchstett, la droite au Danube et la gauche à la montagne et à un bois, une réserve derrière un village à notre droite
dans un coude du Danube [Blenheim], ce qui a été la perte de
M. le maréchal de Tallard, faute d'un pont pour retraite en cas
de besoin; un autre village [Oberglau] au centre à la tête de
nos deux lignes, où nos forces d'infanterie étaient sous les ordres
de M. de Blainville, et qui ont toujours battu les ennemis. A

notre gauche, nous avions un village devant nous que nous brûlâmes [Lutzingen]; cette gauche était appuyée sur un bois qui valait mieux que tous les villages, puisqu'il n'était pas d'une si grande garde.

Le long de ces villages régnait seulement un ruisseau de deux pieds de large, qui formait un petit marais très-desséché à cause des grandes chaleurs, ce qui a trompé beaucoup de nos généraux, qui le croyaient plus mauvais. Ce ruisseau était la seule séparation qu'il y eût entre les deux armées. Celle des ennemis vint se mettre devant nous en bataille à six heures du matin, de manière que cette grande plaine se trouva toute noire et couverte de troupes; et à sept heures trois quarts commença une canonnade des plus rudes de part et d'autre, et où la droite de M. de Tallard avait toujours la supériorité sur les ennemis, leur ayant fait replier deux fois leur gauche qui venait se former devant nous.

Sur les dix heures, les Anglais qui composaient cette gauche voulurent tenter le passage de ce ruisseau devant M. de Tallard; mais ils furent repoussés avec perte considérable. Son altesse électorale, qui se portait par tous les lieux les plus exposés, partit à toutes jambes de la gauche pour venir à la droite de M. le maréchal de Tallard, où l'affaire commença fort vigoureusement au moment qu'elle arriva, qui était sur les onze heures. Notre aile droite de cavalerie, composée de la gendarmerie du roi qui était près du village [Blenheim], fut attaquée par la cavalerie anglaise, laquelle fut d'abord repoussée jusque sur l'infanterie qui se disposait à attaquer ledit village de M. le maréchal de Tallard, ce qui fut cause que son altesse électorale s'y porta en même temps; mais y ayant trouvé une fière disposition, notre infanterie retranchée à vingt pas des ennemis, retourna sur l'heure à la cavalerie; mais, en sortant du village entre les deux feux, nous aperçûmes quelques escadrons de notre gendarmerie en fuite qui ne se ralliaient pas, ce qui obligea l'électeur à dire à ses adjudants généraux, auxquels il avait ordonné de ne le pas quitter: "Voilà la gendarmerie qui se sauve; est-il possible? Allez, messieurs; dites-leur que je suis ici présent; ralliez-les, et qu'ils retournent à la charge."

Ce fut dans ce moment que, partant de la main, je courus aux gendarmes, et leur ayant dit plus que l'électeur ne nous avait ordonné, quelques-uns se rallièrent et revinrent à la charge; ce fut dans cette occasion qu'ayant enfoncé un escadron anglais, quelques gendarmes qui étaient avec moi ayant été tués, je reçus deux coups de sabre sur la tête, un coup d'épée qui me perce le bras, une contusion d'une balle à la jambe, et mon cheval blessé; alors étant environné de toutes parts sans espérance de salut, je fus pris par un officier, lequel, m'ôtant un de mes pistolets qui me restait, me dit, "Il y a bon quartier, suivez-moi; je vous ferai bien panser, et donnez-moi votre croix," qui est celle de l'ordre de Wurtemberg que je portais. Il la détacha lui-même et la prit avec la chaîne d'or; et pour en être mieux traité et éviter tout autre malheur, j'eus la faiblesse de lui donner cent trente-quatre louis d'or que j'avais en une bourse; mais tout autre en pareil cas en aurait peut-être fait autant pour les attendrir et éviter d'être massacré.

Il y eut, dans le même temps encore, une autre charge de la gendarmerie, qui fut également repoussée; mais quelques escadrons ayant fait plier la cavalerie anglaise, ceux qui m'emmenaient furent obligés de se retirer au galop et d'essuyer toute la bordée de la mousqueterie de M. de Tallard qui était dans le village, ce qui les rompit, et par un grand bonheur je ne fus blessé d'aucune des balles qui pleuvaient de tous côtés; mais celui qui m'emmenait en main, ayant reçu un coup qui le fit tomber sur son cheval et l'obligea de lâcher la bride du mien qu'il tenait, je la repris au plus vite, aussi bien que mes éperons, pour retourner à nos gens; mais quel chagrin pour moi quand je vis que les grenadiers à cheval anglais, qui avaient déjà été repoussés, retournaient à la charge avec la cavalerie anglaise, et culbutaient derechef toute notre gendarmerie et la cavalerie qui la soutenait, et qu'à la faveur d'un si vilain mouvement, toute la cavalerie de leur gauche débouchait le ruisseau et occupait déjà notre terrain, de manière qu'en passant au travers de leurs lignes je regagnai notre centre, qui était mêlé avec la cavalerie ennemie, mais cependant qui soutenait encore mieux son terrain, qu'il perdit pourtant à la fin.

Pendant cette mauvaise manœuvre de notre droite, la gauche, qui était composée de la cavalerie et infanterie bavaroise, et de toute l'armée de M. le maréchal de Marcin, comme aussi ce que commandait au centre M. de Blainville, enfonçaient les ennemis, et par cinq différentes charges avaient entièrement battu toute leur droite, de sorte que M. l'électeur, qui s'était porté partout dans le centre et à la gauche pour encourager tout le monde par sa présence, qui croyait alors la première fuite de la gendarmerie rétablie, et qui se trouvait maître non-seulement de l'artillerie de la droite des ennemis, mais de quantité de drapeaux et étendards, croyait la bataille entièrement gagnée. Mais il sut que la droite de notre armée était vigoureusement repoussée, à quoi il ajouta foi d'autant plus aisément, que les fuyards étaient déjà à plus de demi-lieue sur leurs derrières, et que tout leur terrain était occupé par quantité de troupes des ennemis; et comme on se battait depuis le matin, et qu'il était huit heures du soir, il craignit que la gauche ne fût coupée, et fit battre la retraite.

C'est là où l'habileté de M. de Marcin parut, puisqu'il ne se retira aucun bataillon ni escadron en désordre, mais toujours redoublant des salves sur ceux qui les voulaient suivre; et près de Dillingen et Lauingen il rejoignit les étendards de la gendarmerie et la cavalerie, qui s'y étaient retirées. Alors il apprit avec beaucoup de chagrin que M. le maréchal de Tallard avait voulu périr dans le village, et ne s'était pas voulu retirer, comme on le lui avait mandé, avec vingt-sept bataillons et quatre régiments de dragons, et fit par là la perte de la plus grande bataille qui ait été donnée. Si ce maréchal se fût retiré avec ses troupes, il est certain que l'avantage était de notre côté, les ennemis ayant perdu beaucoup plus de monde que nous dans le choc; nous avions quantité de drapeaux, et les ennemis ne nous auraient pu rien faire de toute la campagne, au lieu que, par la perte que nous avons faite, nous avons été obligés de nous retirer, abandonnant tous nos magasins, et nos vivres nous étant coupés aussi bien que toute la meilleure infanterie de l'électeur et vingt-trois escadrons, tant de ses dragons que de sa cavalerie qui étaient vers le Tyrol, lesquels, suivant toute apparence, ne nous pourront plus rejoindre. Nous sortons avec peu de pain, après avoir brûlé une bonne partie de nos équipages. Nous sommes enfin venus joindre M. de Villeroy avec les débris de trois armées.

Je ne puis vous dire de la faute de qui vient une perte si

considérable; mais il est certain que la gendarmerie et la cavalerie de M. de Tallard sont la cause de la perte de cette grande bataille; que nous avions trop de bataillons à cette droite, et que dans le centre il nous en manquait. D'ailleurs rien n'a été si bien conduit que la marche des ennemis, qui nous étaient supérieurs, et qui, outre leurs lignes égales aux nôtres par leurs trois attaques, étaient en colonnes de cinq à six lignes qui se soutenaient. Si nous avons tort, c'est d'avoir risqué cette bataille dans le temps où les armes de France étaient glorieuses de tous côtés; il valait bien mieux faire tenir ensemble toutes les forces de l'empire réunies, nous retrancher et ne rien hasarder. Les ennemis se seraient consumés et ruinés, et auraient été obligés de s'en retourner. Vous savez, monsieur, mieux que moi à qui en est la faute. Son altesse électorale et M. de Marcin ne voulaient pas hasarder; et s'il l'avait fallu, au moins fallait-il rassembler toutes les forces de Bavière qui étaient dispersées de part et d'autre, pour la garde des places et passages, qui présentement n'en sont pas moins perdues.

VI, VII. *Ramillies*

THE following are two accounts of the battle of Ramillies; the first (VI) by Capt. Parker, whose account of Blenheim will be found on pp. 111–117, above; the second (VII) by Lord Orkney, who commanded the bulk of the English infantry, and made the successful feint against the enemy's left that fatally weakened his centre at Ramillies. It is clear from Orkney's account that the feint had been carried further and with more vigour before it was stopped than many narratives of the battle have allowed. On this see also *Hist. MSS. Com. Portland*, IV, p. 310, where Lieut.-Colonel Cranstoun writes: "The Earl of Orkney who commanded the British infantry upon the right had marched them over the ruisseau and bog and was himself on the head of the English guards and first battalion marching into the village of Offuz, and was already come under the enemy's fire, when Brigadier Cadogan came with orders, as he pretended from the Duke, and obliged him to retire." Lord Orkney's letter is in *E.H.R.*, April 1904.

VI. *Ramillies* (Capt. Parker)

Upon our taking the field, the Duke of *Marlborough* ordered fix hand-mills for grinding corn, to be delivered to every *Britifh* Regiment, as well Horfe as Foot. This occafioned a report, that he defigned to march us to *Italy*, to the relief of the Duke of *Savoy*, which had been a fine jaunt indeed: But whatever his Grace's defign was, it is ftill a myftery, for any thing I have been able to learn; for we never had occafion of hand-mills in *Flanders*.

In the beginning of *May* our Army took the field, and affembled at *Burklome* near the demolifhed Lines. Here the Duke had an account, that the Eleftor and *Villeroy* were affembling the *French* Army on the plains of *Mont St. Andrea*; whereupon he advanced to *Hanoy*. At this place he had intelligence, that the enemy had the fame day taken up the ftrong camp of *Ramillies*, which was within three leagues of us. Thereupon he fent an exprefs to the Duke of *Wirtenberg*, who commanded the *Danifh* Horfe, to let him know that he defigned to engage the enemy next day, and therefore that he would join him as foon as poffible.

Our Army at this time confifted of 117 Squadrons (including the *Danifh* Horfe, which were fourteen of them), and 80 Battalions; and the next day, being *Whitfunday* the 12th of *May*, O.S. by three in the morning, we marched up to the enemy in four Columns.

The enemy had 132 Squadrons, and 90 Battalions, befide the advantage of the ground. It was a fpot they had made choice of two months before; for in the month of *March*, the Eleftor and *Villeroy* had taken two Engineers with them, and rode out, as it were to divert themfelves with hunting and hawking. At this time they examined all the ground from *Louvain* to the *Mehaign*, and finding the ground about *Ramillies* the fitteft place to draw the Duke of *Marlborough* to a Battle; they ordered the Engineers to draw a Plan of it, and of the Order of battle, and fent it to Court for their approbation. The Plan was highly approved of, and fuch a number of Troops fent them as they required; and among them were as many of the Houfhold Troops, as could be fpared.

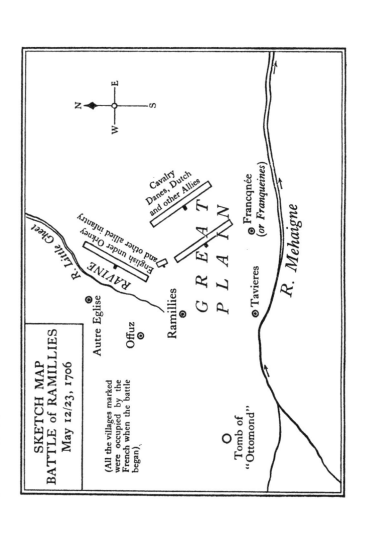

SKETCH MAP
BATTLE of RAMILLIES
May 12/23, 1706

(All the villages marked
were occupied by the
French when the battle
began).

N
W — E
S

R. Little Gheet

RAVINE

Autre Eglise

Offuz

Ramillies

English under Orkney
and other allied infantry

Cavalry
Danes, Dutch
and other Allies

G R E A T
P L A I N

Tavieres

Francqnée
(or Franqueines)

Tomb of
"Ottomond"

R. Mehaigne

The nature of the ground, and difpofition of their Army was as follows. They had the *Mehaign* on their Right, with the Village of *Franqueines* on the bank of it; in this Village they had placed a good body of Foot and Dragoons, and had alfo thrown up fuch an Intrenchment, as the time would admit of. From hence to the Village of *Ramillies*, (which was a little to the Left of their Center) was a fine plain of near half a League in length, where they knew the main ftrefs of the Battle muft fall. On this Plain therefore, they drew up the choiceft, and the greateft number of their Cavalry, interlined with their beft Infantry. In the Village of *Ramillies*, (before which they had alfo thrown up a trench) they placed twenty Battalions with ten pieces of Cannon. From *Ramillies* runs the River *Gheete*, which makes the ground on both fides marfhy, and not paffable, efpecially for Horfe. Along this River to the Villages of *Offufe* and *Autereglife*, which covered their left flank, was pofted a thin Line of the worft of their Infantry, with Squadrons after a fcattering manner pofted in their Rear. This was the difpofition of the enemy, when our Army came up to them.

We drew up in two Lines oppofite them, having a rifing ground on our Right, whereon a great part of our *Britifh* Troops were drawn up. From hence the Duke had a fair view of the enemy, and faw evidently, that the ftrefs of the Battle muft be on the Plain, where they were drawn up in a formidable manner: He faw alfo, that things muft go hard with him, unlefs he could oblige them to break the difpofition they had made on the plain. On this occafion his Grace fhewed a genius vaftly fuperior to the *French* Generals; for though he knew the ground along the *Gheete* was not paffable, yet he ordered our right wing to march down in great order, with Pontoons to lay bridges, as if he defigned to attack them in their weak part. The Elector and *Villeroy* perceiving this, immediately ordered off from the Plain, an intire Line both of Horfe and Foot, to reinforce thofe on the *Gheete*. When the Duke obferved that thefe had arrived there, he fent orders to our right wing to retire eafily up the hill, without altering their afpect. This we did, until our Rear line had got on the back of the rifing ground, out of fight of the enemy: But the

Front line halted on the fummit of the hill in full view of them, and there ftood, ready to march down, and attack them. As foon as our Rear line had retired out of fight of the enemy, they immediately faced to the Left, and both Horfe and Foot, with a good many Squadrons, that flunk out of the Front line, marched down to the Plain, as faft as they could; by this time the greater part of our Horfe of the Left wing had arrived there alfo, and we were now fuperior in numbers to them in that quarter. The Duke foon put them in order for attacking the enemy on the Plain; and about one o'clock fent orders to the Veldt Marefhal, to begin the battle on the Left. At the fame time he ordered four Brigades of Foot, to attack the Village of *Ramillies*, and then ordered the Troops on the plain to advance and charge their main body.

In this engagement there was great variety of action; fome-times their Squadrons and fometimes our's giving way in different places; and as the fate of the day depended intirely on the behaviour of the Troops on the plain; fo both fides exerted themfelves, with the utmoft vigour for a long time. The Duke was in all places where his prefence was requifite; and in the hurry of the action happened to be unhorfed, and in great danger of his life; but was remounted by Captain *Molefworth*, one of his Aid de Camps, the only perfon of his Retinue then near him; who feeing him in manifeft danger of falling into the hands of the purfuing enemy, fuddenly threw himfelf from his horfe, and helped the Duke to mount him. His Grace, by this means, got off between our Lines; the Captain being im-mediately after furrounded by the enemy; from which danger (as well as that of our fire) he was, at laft, providentially de-livered. His Grace, about an hour after, had another narrow efcape; when in fhifting back from Captain *Molefworth*'s horfe to his own, Colonel *Bringfield* (his firft Efcuyer) holding the Stirrup, was killed by a cannon-fhot from the Village of *Ramillies*. Notwithftanding which, the Duke immediately rode up to the head of his Troops; and his prefence animated them to that degree, that they preffed home upon the enemy, and made them fhrink and give back. At this very inftant the Duke of *Wirtenberg* came up with the *Danifh* Horfe, and perceiving an open between the Village of *Franqueines* and their main body, fell in on the Right flank of their Horfe, with fuch courage and refolution, that he drove them in upon their Center. This put them into great diforder; and our Troops taking this advantage, preffed fo clofe upon them, that they could never recover their order. The Elector and *Villeroy* did all that was poffible to keep them from breaking: But our Troops ftuck fo clofe to them, that they were put to the rout. The Houfhold-Troops, who had behaved to admiration during the whole action, rallied and made a ftand for fome time: But as all the reft had fled, they were obliged to follow them, leaving the Foot that had been drawn up with them in the field (who were of no manner of ufe to them), to be cut to pieces.

The Veldt Marefhal had alfo routed thofe where he attacked, who fled in a fcattering manner toward *Charleroy*. The Troops in *Ramillies* defended themfelves to the laft, till they faw their Troops drove out of the Field; upon which they drew off, and made toward their Left Wing: But were moft of them cut to pieces before they could reach it. Their Left Wing, which was pofted along the *Gheete*, and the Front Line of our Right Wing, (in which was our Regiment) ftood looking on without firing a fhot; and as we were pofted on an eminence, and were difengaged, we had a fair view of the whole Battle on the Plain.

When the Elector and *Villeroy* faw all was loft, they, with fuch Troops as they could bring together, made the beft of their way for *Louvain*, and fent to their Left Wing to join them there, in order to make a ftand at the *Dyle*, as they had done the laft year: But the Lord *Marlborough* (perhaps fenfible of his miftake at that time) purfued fo clofe with the Horfe, that he cut between their Left Wing and *Louvain*, which obliged them to difperfe and fly the other way, every man fhifting for himfelf. The Elector and *Villeroy* finding that the Duke was clofe at their heels, turned off from *Louvain*, and made toward *Vilvorde*, hoping to make the Canal which runs from *Bruffels* thither: But the Duke ftill purfuing them clofe, they quitted *Vilvorde*, and never ftopped, until they fled to *Lifle*, with about 2000 Horfe only. The Duke having paffed the Canal of *Vilvorde*, halted at *Grimn-*

berg, where he waited for the coming up of the Foot. Thefe continued marching after him with all the expedition they could, without obferving any other order than this, that every Regiment kept their men as clofe together as they poffibly could; and none of them halted above an hour at a time, till they joined him.

Thus ended the famous Battle of *Ramillies.* The enemy had at leaft 7000 killed, and a great many more taken prifoners; and as they were difperfed about the Country, their lofs by defertion was very confiderable. Upon the whole, their lofs was computed to be upwards of 30,000, befide 60 pieces of Cannon, 8 Mortars, a great number of Colours, Standards and Kettle-drums, taken. Their Tents and Baggage efcaped us, having been fent off before the Battle. The lofs on our fide was computed to be more than 5000 killed and wounded.

VII. *Ramillies* (Lord Orkney)

Camp at Braunchein, 24th May 1706, 7 o'clock.

You will be extremely glad to hear we have fought a very great battle yesterday and beat the French, and I in very good health, but am hardly able to hold up my head, I am so weary and faint; for it is 48 hours I have not eat nor drank, but once or twice a glass of wine and bit of bread. I really cannot tell you any particulars yet of this battle, nor well what loss we have, nor what they have.

We could hardly fail of meeting, since we marched with a firm resolution to attack them; and I find they did the same out of their line to attack us. However, they seeing us coming up to them, they took up a very good post at the head of the Geet, and possessed themselves of several villages on their front, and a marshy ground with a little ruisseau before them; so that, when we came to attack, it was impossible for us to extend our line, so were drawn up in several lines, one behind another, and indeed even in confusion enough, which I own gave me at first a very ill prospect of things. But, since it was so, we made our effort at a village in the centre, which they call Ramillies; and that post was attacked very furiously by chiefly stranger troops, except Churchil's and Mordaunt's regiments, who have suffered greatly. This post was at last forced and taken, and our army pierced into others by that village, where our horse and theirs had some sharp activity. My Lord Malbro' was rid over, but got other squadrons, which he led up again. Major B[r]ingfield, holding his stirrop to give him another horse, was shot with a canon bullet which went thro' my Lord's leggs; in truth there was no scarcity of 'em.

Where I was with most of the English foot, there was a morass and ruisseau before us, which they said was impossible to pass over. But however we tryd, and, after some difficulty, got over with ten or twelve battalions; and Mr Lumley brought over some squadrons of horse with very great difficulty; and I endeavoured to possess myself of a village, which the French brought down a good part of their line to take possession of, and they were on one side of ye village, and I on the other; but they always retired as we advanced. As I was going to take possession, I had ten aid-de-camps to me to come off, for the horse could not sustain me. We had a great deal of fire at this, both musquetry and canon; and indeed I think I never had more shot about my ears; and I confess it vexed me to retire. However we did it very well and in good order, and, whenever the French pressed upon us, with the battalion of guards and my own, I was always able to make them stand and retire. Cadogan came and told me it was impossible I could be sustained by the horse if we went on then, and, since my Lord could not attack everywhere, he would make the grand attack in the centre and try to pierce there, which, I bless God, succeeded.

I don't know myself what prisoners we have; I am told several major-generalls and others of less note. Lord John Hay's dragoons and others got in upon the Regiment de Roy, which they beat intirely. There is at least 7 or 800 of 'em prisoners, and everywhere you see colours and standards, and I hear there is at least 40 pieces of canon and a great deal of their baggage. For, whenever they saw that village forced, they immediately retired with such expedition that one could hardly think it possible. We pursued them till dark night, but their horse it was impossible to get at. Their foot Mr Lumley with severall English squadrons came nigh, but without foot it was impossible to attack them. He sent to me that, if I could come up with the foot, he did not doubt but we would take eight or nine batallions of 'em that were in a body together. I marched I am sure as fast as it was possible for men to march, and ordered them to lose no time, and that I would ride up to Mr Lumley myself. I own it vexed me to see a great body of 'em going off, and not many horse with them; but, for my heart, I could not get up our foot in time; and they dispersed and got into strong ground where it was impossible to follow them.

We are just now met with the left of the army, for all night we knew nothing of one another, and Mr Lumley and I had resolved to march streight to the Dyle to their lines. But here we are endeavouring to make a camp and form in some order, for we look like a beaten army. I really fancy we shall march to morrow to the Dyle to see if it be possible to force their lines now in the consternation they are in. That is the place certainly they will make head again, for their lines are strong. I am sure, whenever we can get at 'em with any kind of reason, these troops will never stand us. They were 74 batallions, 128 squadrons, of the best troops in France with orders to attack us; we 73 battalions, 123 squadrons, so there was a pretty near equality if there had been any in ye ground. We had two young gentlemen prisoners with us all night, both men of great quality—a nephew of Marishal Luxembourg and Marishall Tallard's only son.

I am afraid the express will be gone; so, being extremely fatigued, God bless you and send us a happy meeting. I doubt these lines will be a troublesome piece of work; yet pray don't fail to send a copy to brother Hamilton and Selkirk. I have several of your letters, but cannot answer them till I have some rest. The battle begun yesterday at 12 and ended chiefly about 5 at night, when we pierced and got the better. Tho' this be of great consequence, it is nothing like Hochstet because of the numbers taken in ye village. Maybe they have lost 5 or 6 thousand men, but truely it is hard to guess.

VIII. *A Scottish Cameronian Colonel in the Blenheim and Ramillies Campaigns*

A DOUR *covenanting Scots Colonel goes through the campaigns of 1704–6 with little love for the English or his other allies, particularly the Popish ones, but with a firm conviction that it is God's will the French should be beaten. The following extracts are from his Diary (ed. 1824). His dates are Old Style, eleven days behind the dates as given by authorities quoted above.*

1704. *April* 30. *Sabbath.* Marching all day, but alas, involved in sin by company and idle discourse. A sad place to be in an army on Sabbath, where nothing is to be heard but oaths and profane language....

May 17. . . . Lord, I tremble to think on the profanity and wickedness of this army that I am in, and what judgments we are like to pull down upon our own heads; for the English army are sinners exceedingly before the Lord, and I have no hopes of success, or that this expedition shall prove to our honour....

May 19—22. Marching every day. Arrived at Mentz after a long journey.

May 27. Army resting this day. I went into Heydelberg in company and hurry, and have no time for retirement.

May 28. *Sabbath.* Army marching. By being in town I had retirement, for I shook off all company, and retired alone upon the banks of the Neckar the whole forenoon. I hope I had communion with God; my covenant with Christ ratified; my Ebenezer here set up; his presence implored: And this I beg, dear Lord, if this be an unlawful expedition, that thou wouldst yet turn me back; if thou go not with me, carry me no farther. When I consider this, that we are here assisting those oppressors that have wasted the church and people of God, persecuted and oppressed them, it makes me afraid the quarrel is not right, and that we shall not prosper; though I be satisfied that our quarrel against France is a very just one....

June 21. Easy and serene all day; cheerfully committing myself and all that concerns me into the hands of God; fetching all my supplies of courage, and strength, and furniture, for going through the duties of my function, from him alone; for indeed I pretend to no stock of my own either of courage or conduct. In the evening I witnessed one of the hottest actions I have seen. It continued from six to eight o'clock. We gained our point, and beat the enemy from their post, and yet we have no reason to boast or think highly of ourselves. The British value themselves too much, and think nothing can stand before them. We have suffered considerably on this occasion, and have no cause to be proud. During the action I was straitened in praying for success and victory to our people, and had not enlargement to seek any thing but that God would get the praise to himself, and work so as the arm of flesh might not rob him of his glory. O that God might reform this army, that good men might have some pleasure in it. When we see what an uncertain thing our life is—now in health, and the next moment in eternity, it is wonderful we are not more affected by it. I see also that the smallest accidents give a turn to the greatest actions, either to prosper or defeat them: that human wisdom, courage, or any thing else we value ourselves upon, is but weak and fallible. There was only a detachment of 130 of our regiment engaged in this battle [Storming of the Schellenberg, p. 103, above].

June 22. In the evening I went alone into the field of battle, and there got a preaching from the dead. The carcases were very thick strewed upon the ground, naked and corrupting; yet all this works no impression or reformation upon us, seeing the bodies of our comrades and friends lying as dung upon the face of the earth. Lord, make me humble and thankful! I trusted in thee that I should set up many Ebenezers through Germany, and here in the field of the slain do I set up my memorial, *Hitherto thou hast helped me.*

*   *   *   *   *   *

August 2. Many deliverances I have met with, but this day I have had the greatest ever I experienced. We fought a bloody battle [Blenheim], and, by the mercy of God, have obtained one of the greatest and completest victories the age can boast of. In the morning, while marching towards the enemy, I was enabled to exercise a lively faith, relying and encouraging myself in God, whereupon I was easy, sedate, and cheerful. I believed firmly that his angels had me in charge, and that not a bone should be broken. During all the little intervals of action, I kept looking to God for strength and courage, and had a plentiful through-bearing, both to keep up my own heart, and help to discharge my duty well in my station. My faith was so lively during the action, that I sometimes said within myself, Lord, it were easy for thee to cause thy angels to lay all these men dead on the place where they stand, or bring them in all prisoners to us. And for encouraging our regiment, I spoke it aloud, That we should either chase them from their post, or take them prisoners; and I cannot but observe the event at seven o'clock at night, when they laid down their arms to us. Twenty-six regiments (some say thirty) surrendered themselves prisoners at discretion, to the Duke of Marlborough, and our regiment was one of those that guarded them.

This victory has indeed cost a great deal of blood, especially to the English. I was always of opinion that the English would pay for it in this country; and when I consider, how, on all occasions, we conquer, yet with much blood spilt, I am at a loss to know what the reason may be. Perhaps it is that our cause is good, and therefore God gives us success in our enterprises, but our persons very wicked, and therefore our carcases are strewed like dung upon the earth in Germany. Among the rest I have also got a small touch of a wound in the throat.

*   *   *   *   *   *

1706. *May* 12. *Sabbath.* Day of the battle; and here I have one of the most remarkable Ebenezers of my life to set up. This day we fought with the French, and by the great mercy of God did beat them. The battle was not general, but it was hot to those that were engaged. Our regiment was no farther engaged, but that we were cannonaded for some hours, and had several men killed and wounded. I was not near the Duke; but upon our wing we had great want of Generals and distinct orders; and some of those we had, seemed somewhat confused: So it was not our conduct, but kind Providence. I observe also that the English had but small part in this victory. They are the boldest sinners in our army, therefore God will choose other instruments. Also the English have got a great vogue and reputation for courage, and are perhaps puffed up upon it; and so God humbles their pride, as it were, by throwing them by. I was easy, and helped to discharge my duty well. We were very much fatigued with the pursuit, and lay all the night in the open fields without cover. Give me grace, O Lord, never to forget this great and glorious day at Ramillies.

*   *   *   *   *   *

May 19. A fatiguing march this Sabbath. All day I met with what I fear and hate in this trade, viz. cursing, swearing, filthy language, &c. yet though it was a hell around me, I bless the Lord there was a heaven within. We are still pursuing our victory, and they are still fleeing before us. There is certainly something in this affair beyond human working.

V

MARLBOROUGH PAPERS

MARLBOROUGH PAPERS

THIS SECTION is drawn from two well-known sources, firstly the Marlborough papers printed in Coxe's *Memoirs of Marlborough*, and secondly two short extracts from the famous *Conduct of the Duchess of Marlborough*, written by herself.

These letters, especially the Duke's own, show the connection between home and foreign affairs, the course of political faction at home and the course of the war abroad. They should be studied in the lights afforded by such modern authorities as Leadam, *Political History of England, 1702–60* (Longman), chapters I–V, pp. 1–107; Atkinson, *Marlborough* (Heroes of Nations Series); and chapters XIII–XIV of Keith Feiling's *History of the Tory Party*.

These letters of Marlborough, particularly those to his wife, are the best key we have to that very difficult problem of the character and motives of the great man whose action dominates the history of the time.

TABLE OF THE DUKE OF MARLBOROUGH'S RELATIONS

Sir Winston Churchill
a west country cavalier, *ob.* 1688

Arabella Churchill, 1648–1730
Mistress of James Duke of York
(*James II*). She bore him the
famous *Duke of Berwick* and
other children

Sarah Jennings, 1660–1744 = *John Churchill*, 1650–1722
Duchess of Marlborough   Baron Churchill, 1682
married 1678   Earl of Marlborough, 1689
    Duke of Marlborough, 1702

Henrietta Churchill = Francis Godolphin
(married 1698)   son of *Sidney,*
afterwards Duchess   *Lord Godolphin,*
of Marlborough   *Treasurer*
in her own right
from 1722–1733

Charles Spencer. = Anne Churchill
3rd *Earl of Sunderland*   "the little Whig,"
on his father's death   married 1701,
in 1702; one of the   died 1716
Whig "Junto"

Duke of Marlborough
after his aunt Henrietta's
death in 1733

Charles, Marquis of
Blandford,
died Feb. 1703,
at King's College
Cambridge

I. *Coxe. Memoirs of Marlborough*

Marlborough to *Godolphin* (July 22, 1701*)

A GREAT deal of time was spent in the emperor's ministers complaining of the Treaty of Partition, and when we came to the business for which we met, they would have the foundation of the treaty to be for lessening the power of France, and assisting the emperor in his just rights to the monarchy of Spain. But the pensionary would not consent to any thing further, than that the emperor ought to be satisfied with having Flanders, which would be a security to the Dutch, and Milan, as a fief of the empire. After four hours' wrangling, the two envoys went away; and then I endeavoured to let the pensionary see that no treaty of this kind would be acceptable in England, if there were not care taken of the Mediterranean and the West Indies. When I gave the king [William III] an account, he was of my mind, so that the pensionary has promised to use his endeavours with the town of Amsterdam; for they are unwilling to consent to any thing more than Flanders and Milan.

Lady Marlborough to *Godolphin*
(Anne's reign begun)

MARGATE, Tuesday, the 29th of May, 1702.—Since you have been so kind as to write so long a letter for my satisfaction, I hope it will hold out to read my answer, though I know my opinion is very insignificant upon most occasions. In the first place, I will begin without any compliment, and say that if any thing could give me a worse thought of the meetings of those gentlemen (the Tories) than I had before, it would be their desire to turn any man out of an employment to put in my lord Sandwich. This looks to me as if every thing were to be governed by faction and nonsense; and 'tis no matter what look things have in the world, or what men are made use of,

* This letter refers to the negociations conducted at the Hague in the last year of William's reign, which resulted in the Grand Alliance against France; see the Treaty, Section I, pp. 5–9, above. Marlborough represented England at these negociations.

if they are but such creatures as will, right or wrong, be at the disposal of two or three arbitrary men that are at the head of them. How long they will be able to support that way of government I can't tell; but if they are strong enough to go on with it, I am apt to think it will not end in hardships only to the lords lieutenants of England.

Marlborough to Lady Marlborough

MAY 15/26, 1702.—It is impossible to express with what a heavy heart I parted with you when I was by the water's side. I could have given my life to have come back, though I knew my own weakness so much that I durst not, for I knew I should have exposed myself to the company. I did for a great while, with a perspective glass, look upon the cliffs, in hopes I might have had one sight of you. We are now out of sight of Margate, and I have neither soul nor spirits, but I do at this minute suffer so much that nothing but being with you can recompense it. If you will be sensible of what I now feel, you will endeavour ever to be easy to me, and then I shall be most happy; for it is you only that can give me true content. I pray God to make you and yours happy; and if I could contribute any thing to it with the utmost hazard of my life, I should be glad to do it.

Marlborough to Godolphin (July 13, 1702)

I AM ashamed to write from this camp, for we ought to have marched from hence three or four days ago; but the fears the Dutch have for Nimeguen and the Rhine created such difficulties when we were to take a resolution, that we were forced to send to the Hague, and the States would not come to any resolution, but have made it more difficult, by leaving it to the general officers, at the same time recommending, in the first place, the safety of the Rhine and Nimeguen. However, we came last night to a resolution of marching to-morrow, and passing the Meuse a little below Grave. Accordingly we have this day made three bridges over the said river. The intention is, that we should keep ourselves masters of those bridges, and that as soon as the battering pieces can be got to Nimeguen, which we hope may be in eight days, then to pass the Meuse, and march to the siege of Rheinberg. The reason of our passing the Meuse to-morrow is, in hopes it may in some degree alarm the French, and hinder us from eating up that part of the country, which must be our subsistence during the siege. It is hoped this might be a secret, but I am afraid they have too good intelligence, and then they may act so as that we may be obliged to take new measures. If the fear of Nimeguen and the Rhine had not hindered us from marching into Brabant, they must then have had the disadvantage of governing themselves by our motions, whereas we are now obliged to mind them.

I am obliged to you for the compliment you make me for the station I am now in. It would have been a great deal more agreeable to me, if it could have been without disputes, and a little less trouble; but patience will overcome all things.

Marlborough to *Lady Marlborough* (July 17)

WE have now very hot weather, which I hope will ripen the fruit at St. Alban's. When you are there, pray think how happy I should be walking alone with you. No ambition can make me amends for being from you. If it were not impertinent, I should desire you in every letter to give my humble duty to the queen, for I do serve her with all my heart and soul. I am on horseback or answering letters all day long; for besides the business of the army, I have letters from the Hague, and all places where her majesty has any ministers. So that if it were not for my zeal for her service, I should certainly desert, for you know of all things I do not love writing.

Marlborough to *Godolphin* (July 20)

I AM afraid of giving you any trouble, knowing you have but little time to yourself. However, I cannot forbear sending you a copy of a letter I received last night from Gueldermassen, who went to the Hague to hasten every thing for the siege of Rheinberg, which by his letter I am afraid will not be made.

And should we follow what he thinks to be best, I think the French may have it in their power to beat us. But to comply as far as I can, I have this night proposed to them the leaving twenty squadrons of horse, and eighteen battalions of foot, to entrench themselves before Nimeguen, and to pass the Meuse with the rest of the army, or to march with the whole towards Cleves, in order to get between Venloo and the French, if possible, so as to be able to attack them. The fear the States have of Nimeguen and the passage of the Rhine hinders the advantage of having the superiority.

Marlborough to *Godolphin*

HELCHTEREN, Aug. 16/27, 1702.—The inclosed letter to the States will let you see the account I have given of the two days being in presence of the enemy. I have but too much reason to complain, that the ten thousand men upon our right did not march as soon as I sent the orders, which if they had, I believe we should have had a very easy victory, for their whole left was in disorder. However, I have thought it much for her majesty's service to take no notice of it, as you see by my letter to the States. But my Lord Rivers, and almost all the general officers of the right were with me when I sent the orders, so that notwithstanding the care I take to hinder it, they do talk. I could not believe the French were so strong as we now know they are; for my lord Carr, one of my aides-de-camp, was taken, so that he marched with them the day they retreated, and the duke of Berwick showed him the whole army. He counted 72 battalions and 109 squadrons, but he says that our battalions are much stronger than theirs.

Venloo will be invested to-morrow, and I have pressed the pensioner that if we have good success there, the States might give such timely order for the stores, that we might have it in our power to attack Ruremond, if the season be favourable.

I am in so ill humour that I will not trouble you, nor dare I trust myself to write more; but believe this truth, that I honour and love you, my lady Marlborough, and my children, and would die for the queen.

Marlborough's letters from the campaign of 1703
(A year of disappointment)

To *Godolphin.* July 19/30, 1703

ON Friday, I went with 4000 horse to see the lines. They let us come so near, that we beat their out-guard home to their barrier, which gave us an opportunity of seeing the lines; which had a fosse of twenty-seven feet broad before them, and the water in it nine feet deep; so that it is resolved that the army return to the Meuse, and in the first place take Huy. Upon the whole matter, if we cannot bring the French to a battle we shall not do any thing worth being commended. My letter of the 8th, which began with Sir, and was directed by Cardonnel, was intended for you, but was writ by candle light, as this is; and my eyes are so bad that I do not see what I do, so that I hope you will excuse me, that I do not answer all in your two letters of the 9th and 13th. We shall begin to march from hence on Thursday.

To *Godolphin* (July 26)

I AM but too much of your mind, that the going back to the Meuse is, as the French expression is, a *pis aller.* But as Cohorn has managed his business for these last six weeks, we had nothing else to do. I know that Huy will make very little noise in the world: however, if we will make the war in this country, it is very convenient for us to have that place....

Anne to *the Duchess of Marlborough* (1703)

WINDSOR, Saturday.—The thoughts that both my dear Mrs. Freeman and Mr. Freeman seem to have of retiring give me no small uneasiness, and therefore I must say something on that subject. It is no wonder at all that people in your posts should be weary of the world, who are so continually troubled with all the hurry and impertinences of it; but give me leave to say you should a little consider your faithful friends and poor country, which must be ruined if ever you put your melancholy thoughts in execution. As for your poor unfortunate faithful Morley, she could not bear it; for if ever you should forsake me, I would have nothing more to do with the world, but make another abdication; for what is a crown when the support of it is gone? I never will forsake your dear self, Mr. Freeman, nor Mr. Montgomery*, but always be your constant and faithful friend; and we four must never part till death mows us down with his impartial hand.

Marlborough to *Duchess*

CAMP AT HANEF, June 3/14.—By my last I had not time to give any answer to your two letters of the 23d and 25th of this last month. There is nothing more certain than what you say, that either of the parties would be tyrants if they were let alone; and I am afraid it is as true that it will be very hard for the queen to prevent it. I think nothing should be omitted to do justice, and then God's will be done. What you say of Lord Nottingham concerning the park is very scandalous, but very natural to that person. I wish with all my heart the queen were rid of him, so that she had a good man in his place, which I am afraid is pretty difficult.

We are bound not to wish for any body's death, but if 14 [Sir Edward Seymour] should die, I am convinced it would be no great loss to the queen nor the nation; and you may be sure the visit intended by 19 [Lord Rochester] and his friend could be for no other end than to flatter 14 [Sir Edward Seymour] to do such mischief as they dare not openly own.

JUNE 10, 1703.—I did yesterday receive yours of the 3d, and do agree with you that the seven persons you mention in that letter do not do the queen that service they ought to do; but I can't but be of the opinion, that if they were out of their places, they would be more capable of doing her hurt. Some of them might, in my opinion, be removed, as 15 [Lord Jersey] and 42 [Lord Nottingham]; but who is there fit for their places? I do protest before God I know of none. I am of your mind, that if the queen spoke to Lord Rochester in the manner you mention in your letter, I believe it would make him very cautious; not that I think it would make him honest, but he would be afraid. The conversation that was between Lord Rochester and the speaker is no doubt the language that

* Godolphin: Freeman=Marlborough: Morley=Anne.

he entertains the whole party with; and if they can once be strong enough to declare which way the war shall be managed, they may ruin England and Holland at their pleasure, and I am afraid may do it in such a manner as may not at first be unpopular; so that the people may be undone before they can see it. I can't say a word for the excusing the Dutch for the backwardness of their sea preparations this year; but if that, or any thing else, should produce a coldness between England and Holland, France would then gain their point, which I hope in God I shall never live to see; for our poor country would then be the miserablest part of all Christendom; for we should not only lose our liberty, but our religion also must be forced, and those gentlemen that would be helping to this, would then be as miserable as others; for the French, when they are the masters, make no distinctions. I could say a great deal upon this subject, but I dare not, for fear of accidents. In short, I think the two parties are so angry, that, to ruin each other, they will make no scruple of venturing the whole.

Marlborough to *Duchess*

ALDERBEESTEN, Sept. 30, 1703.—I see by this last letter, that you have mistaken my meaning in some of my letters; for though I may have complained of some you call your friends, yet it never entered into my thoughts that they should be spoke to in order to have a better thought of me; for I know they would be as unreasonable as the others in their expectations, if I should seek their friendship: *for all parties are alike.* And as I have taken my resolution of never doing any hardship to any man whatsoever, I shall by it have a quiet in my own mind; not valuing nor desiring to be a favourite to either of them. For, in the humour I am now in, and that I hope in God I shall ever be of, I think both parties unreasonable and unjust. I am very sensible of several errors I have committed; but I must not endeavour to mend them by running into greater: so that I shall make complaints to neither, but endeavour to recommend myself to the world by my sincere intentions of governing all my actions by what I shall think is for the interest of my queen and country. I hope in God this will agree with what you desire, and then I can have no uneasiness.

Marlborough to *Duchess* (Winter 1703–4)

I do own a great deal of what you say is right; but I can by no means allow that all the Tory party are for King James, and consequently against the queen, but the contrary; I think it is in her power to make use of almost all, but some of the heads, to the true interests of England, which I take to be the Protestant succession, to the supporting of which, by the help of Almighty God, I will venture my last drop of blood. As you are the only body that could have given me happiness, I am the more concerned we should differ so much in opinion. But as I am firmly resolved never to assist any Jacobite whatsoever, or any Tory that is for persecution, I must be careful not to do the thing in the world which my Lord Rochester would most desire to have me do, which is to give my vote against this bill: but I do most solemnly promise that I will speak to nobody living to be for it; and to show you that I would do any thing that were not a ruin to the queen, and an absolute destruction to myself to make you easy, at this time by what has been told me, the bill [The Occasional Conformity Bill] will certainly be thrown out, unless my lord treasurer and I will both speak to people and speak in the House, which I do assure you for myself I will not do.

HAGUE, April 24/May 5, 1704.—Your dear letter of the 15th came to me but this minute. My lord treasurer's letter in which it was inclosed, by some mistake was sent to Amsterdam. I would not for any thing in my power it had been lost; for it is so very kind, that I would in return lose a thousand lives if I had them to make you happy. Before I sat down to write this letter, I took yours that you wrote at Harwich out of my strong box and have burnt it; and if you will give me leave it will be a great pleasure to me to have it in my power to read this dear dear letter often, and that it may be found in my strong box when I am dead. I do this minute love you better than ever I did before. This letter of yours has made me so happy, that I do from my soul wish we could retire and not be blamed. What you propose as to coming over, I should be extremely pleased with; for your letter has so transported me, that I think you would be happier in being here than where you are; although I should not be able to see you often. But you will see by my last letter, as well as this, that what you desire is impossible; for I am going up into Germany, where it would be impossible for you to follow me; but love me as you now do, and no hurt can come to me. You have by this kindness preserved my quiet, and I believe my life; for till I had this letter, I have been very indifferent of what should become of myself. I have pressed this business of carrying an army into Germany, in order to leave a good name behind me, wishing for nothing else but good success. I shall now add, that of having a long life, that I may be happy with you.

Marlborough to *Duchess*

WEINHEIM, May 22/June 2, 1704.—I take it extreme kindly that you persist in desiring to come to me; but I am sure when you consider that three days hence will be a month that the troops have been in a continual march to get hither; and we shall be a fortnight longer before we shall be able to get to the Danube, so that you could hardly get to me and back again to Holland, before it would be time to return into England. Besides, my dear soul, how could I be at any ease? for if we should not have good success, I could not put you into any place where you would be safe.

I am now in a house of the elector palatine, that has a prospect over the finest country that is possible to be seen. I see out of my chamber window the Rhine and the Neckar, and his two principal towns of Manheim and Heidelberg; but would be much better pleased with the prospect of St. Alban's, which is not very famous for seeing far.

Marlborough to *Godolphin*

JUNE 4.—The cannon and infantry being six days' march behind me, and the troops of Luneburg, Holland, and Hesse being in several quarters, I shall halt here to-morrow, to give the necessary orders, and then shall advance towards the Danube, with what troops I have here, leaving the English and cannon to be brought up by my brother, and the Danes by the duke of Wirtemberg. I hope in eight days to meet with Prince Louis and Prince Eugene. I am afraid the first will

not go to the Rhine, he being, as I am told, desirous to stay
on the Danube. When I see them, you shall be sure to know
what we have concerted.

Marlborough to *Godolphin*

MAY 28/JUNE 8, 1704.—Having received intelligence yesterday that in three or four days the duke of Villeroy, with his
army, would join that of the marshal de Tallard about Landau,
in order to force the passage of the Rhine, I prevailed with Count
Wratislaw to make all the haste he could to Prince Louis of
Baden's army, where he will be this night, that he might make
him sensible of the great consequence it is to hinder the French
from passing that river, while we are acting against the elector
of Bavaria. I have also desired him to press, and not to be
refused, that either Prince Louis or Prince Eugene go immediately to the Rhine. I am in hopes to know to-morrow
what resolution they have taken. If I could decide it by my
wishes, Prince Eugene should stay on the Danube although
Prince Louis has assured me, by the count de Frise, that he
will not make the least motion with his army but as we shall
concert. At this time it is agreed that Prince Louis shall act
on the Iller, and I on the Danube. If the marshal de Villeroy
can be kept on the other side of the Rhine, we must be contented to suffer him to do what he pleases there, whilst we are
acting in Bavaria. If we can hinder the junction of more
troops to the elector, I hope six weeks after we begin may be
sufficient for the reducing of him, or the entire ruining of his
country. It will be the 10th of June our style, before the
English foot and cannon can join me on the Danube; and if
the cannon, which Prince Louis has promised, can be ready,
which I much doubt, I shall in two days after the junction
march directly to Donawerth. If I can take that place I shall
there settle a magazine for the army, at the same time that the
other army is to force their passage over the Iller, which
Prince Louis thinks himself sure of, that river having several
fords.

Marlborough to *Duchess*

JUNE 4/15, 1704.—Since my last, I have had Prince Louis with me, so that we have taken the necessary measures for our first motions. Prince Eugene was with me from Monday till Friday, and has in his conversation a great deal of my Lord Shrewsbury, with the advantage of seeming franker. He has been very free with me, in giving me the character of the prince of Baden, by which I find I must be much more on my guard than if I was to act with Prince Eugene....

When I had writ thus far, Count Wratislaw came to me, having just received an express from his master. After very great expressions it ended in saying that his master was desirous to write to the queen, that he might have her consent to make me a prince of the empire, which he would do by creating some land he has in the empire into a principality, which would give me the privilege of being in the college, or diet, with the sovereign princes of the empire. You know I am not good at compliments; however, I did assure him that I was very sensible of the honour his master intended me, but in my opinion nothing of this ought to be thought on till we saw what would be the fate of the war. He replied, that what already had been done, had laid obligations on his master above what he could express, and that if the queen would not allow him to do this, he must appear ungrateful to the world, for he had nothing else in his power worth giving, or my taking. What is offered will in history for ever remain an honour to my family. But I wish myself so well that I hope I shall never want the income of the land, which no doubt will be but little, nor enjoy the privilege of German assemblies. However, this is the utmost expression that they can make, and therefore ought to be taken as it is meant.

I know you wish the queen and me so well, that you would be glad that nothing should be done that might do either of us hurt. Therefore my opinion of this matter is, that there can be no inconvenience in allowing Count Wratislaw's master to write to the queen to ask her consent for the doing this, and then to bring the letter to the cabinet council. In the mean time I shall take care with Count Wratislaw, that no further step be made till I know the queen's pleasure, and the opinion of lord treasurer.

Marlborough to Duchess

GIENGEN, June 18/29, 1704.—Since my last, I have had the happiness of receiving yours of the 30th of the last month, and the 1st and 2d of this. It is not only by yours, but by others, that I find that there are several people, who would be glad of my not having success in this undertaking. I am very confident, without flattering myself, that it is the only thing that was capable of saving us from ruin, so that whatever the success may be, I shall have the inward satisfaction to know that I have done all that was in my power, and that none can be angry with me for the undertaking, but such as wish ill to their country and their religion, and with such I am not desirous of their friendship.

The English foot and cannon joined me two days ago, but I do not expect the Danish horse till six or seven days hence, till which time we shall not be able to act against the elector of Bavaria, as I could wish. You will easily believe that I act with all my heart and soul, since good success will in all likelihood give me the happiness of ending my days with you. The queen's allowing you to say something from her is very obliging. I shall endeavour to deserve it; for I serve her with all my heart, and I am very confident she will always have the prayers and good wishes of this country.

You have forgot to order Hodges to send me a draught of a stable, as I directed him, for the lodge; for it ought not to be made use of till the year after it is built; and as I see you set your heart on that place I should be glad all conveniences were about it.

Marlborough to Duchess (the burning of Bavaria)

JULY 30.—The succours which the elector expects on Sunday, have given him so much resolution, that he has no thoughts of peace. However, we are in his country, and he will find it difficult to persuade us to quit it. We sent this morning 3000 horse to his chief city of Munich, with orders to burn and destroy all the country about it. This is so contrary to my nature, that nothing but absolute necessity could have obliged me to consent to it, for these poor people suffer for their master's ambition. There having been no war in this country for above sixty years, these towns and villages are so clean, that you would be pleased with them.

(In another letter to *the Duchess* he says)

You will, I hope, believe me, that my nature suffers when I see so many fine places burnt, and that must be burnt, if the elector will not hinder it. I shall never be easy and happy till I am quiet with you.

Marlborough to *Duchess* (the famous note)

AUGUST 13, 1704.—I have not time to say more, but to beg you will give my duty to the queen, and let her know her army has had a glorious victory. M. Tallard and two other generals are in my coach, and I am following the rest. The bearer, my aide-de-camp, Colonel Parke, will give her an account of what has passed. I shall do it in a day or two, by another more at large.—MARLBOROUGH.*

Celebrating the Victory

'Twas then great Marlborough's mighty soul was prov'd,
That in the shock of charging hosts unmov'd,
Amidst confusion, horror, and despair,
Examin'd all the dreadful scenes of war:
In peaceful thought the field of death survey'd,
To fainting squadrons sent the timely aid;
Inspir'd repuls'd battalions to engage,
And taught the doubtful battle where to rage.
So when an angel by divine command,
With rising tempests shakes a guilty land,

* This note is preserved in the family archives at Blenheim, as one of the most curious memorials which perhaps exists. It was written on a slip of paper, which was evidently torn from a memorandum book, and contains on the back a bill of tavern expenses. The book may probably have belonged to some commissary, as there is an entry relative to bread furnished to the troops. (Note by Coxe.)

Such as of late o'er pale Britannia past,
Calm and serene he drives the furious blast;
And, pleas'd the Almighty's orders to perform,
Rides in the whirlwind, and directs the storm.

ADDISON'S *Campaign*.

From *Hare's Journal* (after Blenheim)

AFTERWARDS the two commanders, accompanied by counts Wratislaw and Maffei, and several general officers, visited Marshal Tallard, at the quarters of the prince of Hesse. In their way, they ordered all the standards, colours, cannon, &c. taken from the enemy to be committed to the care of Colonel Blood. Reaching the marshal's quarters, they found him very much dejected, and wounded in one of his hands. His grace humanely inquired how far it was in his power to make him easy under his misfortune, offering him the convenience of his quarters, and the use of his coach. The marshal thankfully declined the offer, saying, he did not desire to move, till he could have his own equipage. His grace accordingly despatched one of his own trumpets to the electoral army, with a passport for bringing it to the marshal. During the interview the marshal directed the conversation to the events of the preceding day, which Marlborough would fain have avoided from motives of delicacy. He told the duke, that if his grace had deferred his visit, meaning his attack, a day longer, the elector and he would have waited on him first.

The duke asking why they did it not on the 12th, when they were expected, the marshal answered, they would have done it before, had they not been informed that Prince Louis of Baden had joined his grace, with his army from Ingoldstadt; and that four prisoners, whom their squadrons had taken that day from our army, had given the information, and had agreed in their intelligence, though questioned separately* [see p. 121, above].

At this interview many of the French generals crowded about his grace, admiring his person, as well as his tender and generous behaviour. Each had something to say for himself,

---

* It has been supposed that these four prisoners had instructions to suffer themselves to be taken, in order to make this report. (Coxe.)

which his grace and Prince Eugene heard with the greatest modesty and compassion. Prince Eugene much commended the conduct of the elector of Bavaria, as well as the behaviour of his troops, and frankly told how often and how bravely he had been repulsed by them. When he spoke of his own troops, he said, "I have not a squadron or battalion, which did not charge four times at least."

Marlborough to *Duchess*

AUGUST 14.—Before the battle was quite done yesterday, I writ to my dearest soul to let her know that I was well, and that God had blessed her majesty's arms with as great a victory as has ever been known; for prisoners I have the Marshal de Tallard, and the greatest part of his general officers, above 8000 men, and near 1500 officers. In short, the army of M. de Tallard, which was that which I fought with, is quite ruined; that of the elector of Bavaria and the Marshal de Marsin, which Prince Eugene fought against, I am afraid, has not had much loss, for I cannot find that he has many prisoners. As soon as the elector knew that Monsieur de Tallard was like to be beaten, he marched off, so that I came only time enough to see him retire. As all these prisoners are taken by the troops I command, it is in my power to send as many of them to England as her majesty shall think for her honour and service. My own opinion in this matter is, that the Marshal de Tallard, and the general officers, should be sent or brought to her majesty when I come to England; but should all the officers be brought, it would be a very great expense, and I think the honour is in having the marshal and such other officers as her majesty pleases. But I shall do in this, as in all things, that which shall be most agreeable to her. I am so very much out of order with having been seventeen hours on horseback yesterday, and not having been able to sleep above three hours last night, that I can write to none of my friends. However I am so pleased with this action, that I can't end my letter without being so vain as to tell my dearest soul, that within the memory of man there has been no victory so great as this; and as I am sure you love me entirely well, you will be infinitely pleased with what has been done, upon my account as well as the great benefit the public will have. For had the success of Prince Eugene been equal to his merit, we should in that day's action have made an end of the war.

STEINHEIM, August 18.—I have been so very much out of order for these four or five days, that I have been obliged this morning to be let blood, which I hope will set me right; for I should be very much troubled not to be able to follow the blow we have given, which appears greater every day than another, for we have now above 11,000 prisoners. I have also this day a deputation from the town of Augsburg, to let me know that the French were marched out of it yesterday morning, by which they have abandoned the country of Bavaria, so that the orders are already given for the putting a garrison into it. If we can be so lucky as to force them from Ulm, where they are now altogether, we shall certainly then drive them to the other side of the Rhine. After which we flatter ourselves that the world will think we have done all that could have been expected from us. This day the whole army has returned their thanks to Almighty God for the late success, and I have done it with all my heart; for never victory was so complete, notwithstanding that they were stronger than we, and very advantageously posted. But believe me, my dear soul, there was an absolute necessity for the good of the common cause to make this venture, which God has so blessed. I am told the elector has sent for his wife and children to come to Ulm. If it be true, he will not then quit the French interest, which I had much rather he should do, if it might be upon reasonable terms; but the Imperialists are for his entire ruin. My dearest life, if we could have another such a day as Wednesday last, I should then hope we might have such a peace as that I might enjoy the remaining part of my life with you. The elector has this minute sent a gentleman to me, I think only to amuse us; we shall see the truth in a day or two, for we march to-morrow. The blood they have taken from me has done me a great deal of good, which is very necessary, for I have not time to be sick.

Marlborough to *Godolphin*

SEFELINGEN, Aug. 28.—The troops under my command are advanced three days on their march towards the Rhine, but I have been obliged to stay here to finish, if possible, the treaty with the electress, who has assured me by letter that one of her ministers shall be here this day with full powers. If he comes before I am obliged to seal this letter, you shall have an account of it. By the letters we have intercepted of the enemy's, going to Paris from their camp at Dutlingen, they all own to have lost above 40,000 men. If we have not Ulm by treaty, we shall leave Monsieur Thungen with the troops that should have had the siege of Ingoldstadt. We are endeavouring all we can to get sixty pieces of cannon for the siege of Landau, which place would be of great advantage to our winter quarters. Although we have had a very great loss of officers and soldiers, our army is in so good heart, and so entirely united, that if the enemy gives us an occasion, I do not doubt but God will bless us with a farther success.

Marlborough to *Duchess*

SEFELINGEN, August 21.—The poor electress has taken five of her children with her, and is following her husband, who seems to be abandoned to the French interest. Prince Eugene and I have offered him by a gentleman that is not yet returned, that if he will join in the common cause against France, he shall be put in possession of his whole country, and receive from the queen and Holland 400,000 crowns yearly, for which he should only furnish the allies with 8000 men; but I take it for granted he is determined to go for France and abandon his own country to the rage of the Germans.

AUGUST 25.—The elector of Bavaria has sent his wife and children back to Munich, and this morning by a trumpet has writ to me, and in it a letter to the electress open. It has made my heart ache, being very sensible how cruel it is to be separated from what one loves. I have sent it to her by a trumpet of my own, with assurances that her answer shall be carefully delivered to the elector, for I take pleasure in being easy when the service does not suffer by it.

AUGUST 28.—Although the troops be marched I shall stay here a day or two longer, to finish a treaty with the electress of Bavaria, which I own would be a great satisfaction to me; for when the public are served I should be glad the family were not quite ruined.

CELEBRATING THE VICTORY

The *Queen* to *Duchess*

WINDSOR, August 10/21.—Since I sent my letter away by the messenger, I have had the happiness of receiving my dear Mrs. Freeman's, by Colonel Parke, with the good news of this glorious victory, which, next to God Almighty, is wholly owing to dear Mr. Freeman, on whose safety I congratulate you with all my soul. May the same Providence that has hitherto preserved, still watch over, and send him well home to you. We can never thank God Almighty enough for these great blessings, but must make it our endeavour to deserve them; and I hope he will continue his goodness to us, in delivering us from the attempts of all our other enemies. I have nothing to add at present, but my being sincerely, &c.

Mrs Burnet to *Duchess*

AUGUST 12 (O.S.).—Though your grace's moments are so valuable that I should fear to trouble you with my most humble thanks, till you had more leisure to receive such worthless tributes, yet I cannot defer letting your grace know the joy I see in every one I meet. The common people, who I feared were grown stupid, have and do now show greater signs of satisfaction and triumph, than I think I ever saw before on any good success whatever; and after the first tribute of praise to God, the first cause of all that is good, every one studies who shall most exalt the Duke of Marlborough's fame, by admiring the great secrecy, excellent conduct in the design, and wonderful resolution and courage in the execution. The emperor can give no title* half so glorious as such an action. How much blood and treasure has been spent to reduce the

---

* Alluding to the title of Prince.

exorbitant power of France, and to give a balance to Europe; and when, after so long a struggle, the event remained under great uncertainty, to have the glory to break the chain, give the greatest blow to that tyranny that it ever had, have an emperor to owe his empire to the queen's armies, as conducted by his grace, are splendours that outshine any reward they can receive.

I do not wonder you are all joy. You have just cause for it, and to recount every day with the utmost thankfulness the amazing blessings God has heaped upon you. The bishop heartily prays for the continuance of the duke's success, so that the queen may have the greatest glory that is possible, that is, the restoring peace and liberty, to Europe, and, what is greater, the free profession of the Protestant religion, wherever it has been persecuted or oppressed; and that after her, her ministers, who are the instruments, may share in the lasting blessings and glory due to such benefactors to mankind. Sure no honest man can refuse to unite in such noble designs. I am really giddy with joy, and, if I rave, you must forgive me. I can lament for no private loss, since God has given such a general mercy. In death it would be a matter of joy to me to have lived so long as to hear it.

The bishop said he could not sleep, his heart was so charged with joy. He desires your grace would carefully lay up that little letter*, as a relic that cannot be valued enough. Some wiser people than myself think the nation is in so good a humour with this great success, and the plentiful harvest, that better circumstances can hardly meet for a new parliament; and, with a little care, it may be as good a one as the depraved manners of this nation is capable of. I pray God direct and prosper all her majesty's counsels and resolutions in this, and every thing else, and make her the universal protectress of truth and charity. And may your grace be ever a happy favourite, happy in all your advices and services, and happy in her majesty's kind approbation and esteem; and may every honest heart love you as well, and endeavour to serve you as faithfully, as does your grace's most obedient, &c.

* Private letter from the duke, ante, p. 162.

Marlborough to *Duchess*

SEFELINGEN, August 25 (N.S.).—Since my last I have received four letters of my dearest soul's, of the 16th, 21st, and 28th, for which I return her a thousand thanks. I find by some of your's that I am very much obliged to 22 [Rochester?], and some of his friends, that take the action of Donawerth [Schellenberg] not to be a victory. I wish that and our last battle could have been obtained without the hazard of any but myself; his lordship then would not have complained; for this last action I will be answerable his friend, the king of France, will own the victory. It is not to be imagined with what precipitation they have quitted this country.

CAMP AT GROSS-GARTACH, Sept. 2, 1704.—I must beg, my dearest soul, to make my acknowledgments to the queen for her very obliging letter, believing it much easier than to trouble her with a letter of mine. I hope the elector of Bavaria and the remainder of the French army (who, notwithstanding they were joined by the duke of Villeroy and his army, did not think themselves strong enough to stay for us, but are glad to put the Rhine between us), will be able to convince 17 [Nottingham?] that the French think themselves beaten. I am sure we can never bless God enough for the success he has given us, it being much above our own expectations. But if those sort of gentlemen think there has not been enough done, I hope he will bless us with a farther success, which at last must bring us to happiness in spite of them, which shall be the prayers and endeavours of him that loves you dearly.

. . . OCTOBER 20, 1704.—I have just now received your's of the 23d from the Lodge, and am a good deal concerned to find by it that 37* is still of the opinion that 16 and 86 play a game that must be fatal, if the designs of 92 do not prove successful. I was in hopes that 86 had done so much towards

---

* The ciphers in this and the following letters to the duchess are difficult to explain; and the difficulty is increased by several mistakes in the originals, which were evidently written in haste. It is certain, however, that 17 means the earl of Nottingham. (Coxe's note.)

the hindering 92 succeeding, that his greatest enemies would not deem him so weak and foolish as to think they could ever forgive him. I do assure you as for myself, my pretending to be of no party, is not designed to get favour, or to deceive any body, for I am very little concerned what any party thinks of me; I know them both so well, that if my quiet depended upon either of them I should be most miserable, as I find happiness is not to be had in this world, which I did flatter myself might have been enjoyed in a retired life. *I will endeavour to leave a good name behind me in countries that have hardly any blessing but that of not knowing the detested names of Whig and Tory.*

Marlborough to *Godolphin* (about the Nottingham Tory partisans)

CAMP NEAR TRAERBACH, Nov. 3, 1704.—If I do not succeed at Berlin, it will not be necessary for me to stay at either of these courts above two or three days. However, it will make my coming into England very late this year, so that I can't forbear writing to you about 19, for I have it from other letters as well as your's, that he is in measures with 17 [probably Nottingham] and 18, to give all the obstruction that is in their power to the carrying on of the public business with vigour this sessions, on which I think not only the queen's honour, but her safety depends; for France is now in that condition, that if her majesty's arms have good success this next year, she will have it in her power to make such a peace as may make Christendom quiet as long as it may please God to bless us with her life. I do not think that 19 has any personal interest; but should he be left in the employment he is now in, it would be a great encouragement to others to do like him, which might be very prejudicial. . . .

Marlborough to *Duchess* (Oct. 3, 1704)

AFTER I have disposed of every thing for the taking such winter quarters as I wish to have, I shall not stay a day longer with the troops than what is absolutely necessary; for if the service should require my going to Berlin, that will cost me at least a fortnight. I am very much afraid that my going may do no good; but if I should not go, the emperor and the States may think the eight thousand men might have been had, if I could have taken the pains of going: so that you see if they insist upon it, I must undertake that trouble.

Marlborough to *Duchess* (1704)

HANOVER, Dec. 2.—On my arrival here I found two of your dear letters; and could you know the true satisfaction I have when they are kind, you will ever make me happy. I shall go from hence on Thursday, so that on this day se'nnight I hope to write from the Hague, where I will make as little stay as the business will allow of. I have so much respect shown me here that I have hardly time to write. The king of Prussia did me all the honour he could; and indeed I have met with more kindness and respect everywhere than I could have imagined. But by my letters from England I find that zeal and success is only capable of protecting me from the malice of villanous faction; so that if it were not for the great obligation I owe to the queen, nothing should persuade me evermore to stir out of England. We have the news here that Landau and Traerbach are taken, so that thanks be to God this campaign is ended, to the greatest advantage for the allies that has been for a great while. I long extremely to be with you and the children, so that you may be sure I shall lose no time when the wind is fair.

Marlborough to *Duchess* (1705)

MELDERT, August 3.—I received yours of the 17th yesterday, in which you complain of my having writ a cold letter, which you think may be occasioned by one I had then received from you. It is most certain that upon many occasions I have the spleen, and am weary of my life; for my friends give me much more uneasiness than my enemies, as you may guess by a copy of a letter I have sent to my lord treasurer. But for you, my dearest life, I love you so well, and have placed all my happiness in ending my days with you, that I would venture ten thousand lives to preserve your good opinion. You sometimes use the expression of my Tory friends. As I never will enter into party and faction, I beg you will be so kind and just to me, as to believe that I will have no friends but such as will support the queen and government. Yours of the 13th, which had the draught of the house and gardens, I received but this day, the French having taken the postilion, but they sent the letters back unopened. I hope some time this summer you will go down to Woodstock for three or four days, and that you will let me know if Mr. Wise be still of the opinion that he shall be able to make all the plantations this next season, which would be a great pleasure to me at my return, if I could see the walks in the park planted.

Marlborough to *Duchess*
(The forcing of the lines of Brabant)

TIRLEMONT, July 7/18, 1705.—My dearest soul, this bearer, Durel, will acquaint you with the blessing God has been pleased to give me; for I have this morning forced the enemy's lines, and beaten a good part of their army, taken their cannon, two lieutenant-generals, and two major-generals, and a great many of their officers, besides standards and colours, of all which I shall have a perfect account to-morrow. It is impossible to say too much good of the troops that were with me, for never men fought better. Having marched all night, and taken a good deal of pains this day, my blood is so hot that I can hardly hold my pen; so that you will, my dearest life, excuse me if I say no more, but that I would not let you know my design of attacking the lines by the last post, fearing it might give you uneasiness; and now, my dearest soul, my heart is so full of joy for this good success, that should I write more I should say a great many follies.

Marlborough to *Godolphin*

TIRLEMONT, July 7/18, 1705.—As I had in this action no troops with me but such as I brought from the Moselle, I believe the French will not care to fight with them again. This bearer will tell you that Monsieur Overkirk's army was not in the lines till the whole action was over, and that I was forced to cheat them into this action; for they did not believe I would attack the lines, they being positive that the enemy were stronger than they were. But this is what must not be spoke of, for it would anger the Dutch, with whom, I think, at this time, I am very well, for their deputies made me the compliment this afternoon, that if I had not been here the lines would not have been forced. I intend to march to-morrow towards Louvain, by which march I shall see what Monsieur de Villeroy will do. This day has given me a great deal of pleasure; however, I think 500 pounds is enough for the bearer.

I beg you will make my compliments to the queen, and assure her that I have infinite pleasure in thinking this action may do good to her service.

Marlborough to *Duchess* (1705)

AUGUST 19 (N.S.).—When I had writ this far I took the resolution of not letting the post go, believing I should have engaged the enemy as yesterday, which I certainly had done if it had been in my power. But all the Dutch generals, except M. Overkirk, were against it, so that the deputies would not consent to our engaging, notwithstanding we were in battle, within cannon shot of the enemy; and I do assure you that our army were at least one third stronger than theirs. We are now returning, for we cannot stay longer than the bread we have brought with us will give us leave. It is impossible to make the war with advantage at this rate. I have sent a copy of my letter to the States to lord treasurer. I should have writ in a very angry style, but I was afraid it might have given the French an advantage.

Marlborough to *Duchess* (inter-allied difficulties)

TIRLEMONT, Aug. 31, 1705.—I have so many things that vex me, that I am afraid the waters, which I think to begin to-morrow, will not do me much good. That I may be the more quiet during the siege of Leuwe, I have taken my quarters in this town, and will trouble myself with business as little as possible. My letters from the Hague tell me that the factious there are divided concerning the last disappointment I had. Those that are for a peace think their generals acted prudently; but the others are angry with them and their deputies, so that it is with them as with us in England, they judge by parties. I wish the French may make no advantage of these unhappy divisions; for it is most certain that the French are so desirous of a peace, that the Dutch may have whatever they will ask; but should we be so unfortunate as to have a peace concluded as things now are, it is most certain it could not last long, and I fear that at last it would be their ruin. But, if it be possible, they have more faction than we have, by which we may fear every thing.

Marlborough to *Godolphin*

AUGUST 31, 1705.—You do in yours complain of some things at home; but if you could know all I suffer here abroad, you would agree with me in begging of the queen that I might never more go out of England; for in Holland they have not only taken care that my letter should not be printed, but there is another printed, and my name put to it, of which there is not one word of it mine. I have complained to the pensioner of this, and should have done it to the States, but then it must have been public, which might have caused some disorders among the people there, for they are of my side against their generals. By this you may see how difficult a part I have to act, being obliged to take care that neither the French nor Dutch common people know how I am used; for it is most certain I have not the tenth part of the authority I had last year; and it is as certain that if I had the power of fighting, with the blessing of God, the French must have been beaten. By all this, you will easily believe me that I shall make it my endeavour to be in England early. But if any misfortune should happen to the army after I were gone, I should never forgive myself; for though I am used ill, the public must not suffer; and should I think of putting this army into winter quarters before the end of October, it would give an opportunity to the French of sending troops to Germany; but be assured my heart is with you. My vexing has put me so much out of order, that I am obliged to take a vomit this night, and to-morrow I shall begin the Spa waters, and shall drink them during the time we shall stay in this camp.

Marlborough to *Duchess*

TIRLEMONT, Sept. 2, 1705.—I received last night yours of the 17th and 18th, o.s., of the last month. It is impossible for me to express the trouble the last disappointment has given. However, I must be careful not to speak all the truth, for fear of offending the Dutch, which would give a great advantage to the common enemy.

It is a pleasure to me when I find by yours that you are easier with 79 [the queen]. I think, for the good of every thing, you should make it your business to have it so; for I am very confident by 72 [Lord Godolphin's] letters, it would be of great use to him. I wish 79 [the queen] and 72 [Lord Godolphin] all the happiness imaginable. But really my spirit is so broke, that whenever I can get from this employment I must live quietly or die.

Marlborough to *Godolphin* (1705)
(The Dutch make amends)

TIRLEMONT, Sept. 14.—. . . I will send you a copy of the States' letter by the next post. They have writ one to their deputies and generals, in which they have expressed themselves so that their generals are not pleased, for they would now have their army fight. I am afraid there will not be an opportunity for it; but should an occasion offer, I do verily believe every body would consent to it, now that we have the happiness of not having Slangenberg, he being gone to Maestricht; and I do, with all my heart, pray to God that I may never be in an army with him. The waters have made my head ache so, that I can write no more, and after to-morrow I intend to leave them off, though I had resolved to have drunk them all this week.
TIRLEMONT, Sept. 17.—I send you a copy of the letter I have received from the States, by which you will see they are desirous we should venture; and I do verily believe, if an occasion should offer, all their generals would readily consent, now that M. Slangenberg is gone. It would have been happy for the common cause had he been sick two months ago.

Marlborough to *Godolphin*

AERCHOT, Sept. 24, 1705.—...Pensioner Buys has confirmed me in my opinion, that the constitution of the States is such that they cannot take away the power the deputies have had at all times in the army; for in the king's time they had the same authority, but he took care to choose such men as always agreed to whatever he had a mind to. Now this may, if they please, be put in practice. I have also underhand assurances that they will never employ Slangenberg in the army where I may be. By the whole I find they would be very glad to content me, but I am afraid would be glad also to have it in their power to hinder a battle, for they do seem to apprehend very much the consequences of such a venture.

Lord Peterborough to his *Lady*
(Taking of Barcelona)

OCTOBER 6, 1705.—I can now give you joy upon taking Barcelona, which is effected. I can modestly say such an attempt was never made by such a handful of men. We have taken, in three days, the castle of Montjuich, sword in hand, that resisted 30,000 men three months. There were five hundred men in it. We marched with a thousand men thirteen hours, and with scaling ladders took a place upon a rock, much stronger than Portsmouth, and had but eight hundred men, two [hundred] having lost us in the night. This enterprise, which some people would reckon impossible or rash, will save many thousand lives. I was forced to lead them on with the Prince of Hesse, who was killed; I escaped without hurt, though both my aide-de-camps were much wounded. I would rather you should hear of this earlier from others than myself.

Lord Peterborough to the *Duchess of Marlborough*

OCTOBER 29, 1705.—If some few I esteem and respect are as much pleased as our enemies are surprised and made uneasy, I would desire no more. I know the good nature of England, especially towards the month of November; but I hope at least they will find no fault.

The ceremony is now over, and we have two kings acknowledged in Spain. Give me leave to say, if I had now two hundred thousand pounds I would be answerable for our being, madam, possessed, in a month's time, of the better part of all Catalonia, Valencia, and Aragon; but our coarse English proverb is too true—"there is no making brick without straw."

Had it not been for the impatience I am under to justify to the world the countenance and good opinion you were pleased to honour me with, I never durst have entered into those measures which brought the king hither. But knowing the ill state of things in Portugal, and the prospect not answering elsewhere, I thought a retrieve was necessary for resolutions out of the common road. I have met with great difficulties, but expect greater. This letter goes by Italy, only to assure your grace of my eternal gratitude and respect, and to recommend the whole to your care and protection. I lay this enterprise at your door, my lady duchess: if we are sustained in time, and as we ought, I hope you will not be ashamed to own it. But, madam, we are far off (though I hope not forgotten). I can now assure your grace I am of the side of the church: no doubt Sir Edward Seymour will make haste to help me, and I think we have met with miracles in our favour. But we are poorer than church rats; and miracles cannot save us long, without money, and a quick and vigorous assistance.

Marlborough to *Duchess* (Ramillies)

1706, May 24th, 11 o'clock.—I did not tell my dearest soul in my last the design I had of engaging the enemy if possible to a battle, fearing the concern she has for me, might make her uneasy; but I can now give her the satisfaction of letting her know, that on Sunday last we fought, and that God Almighty has been pleased to give us a victory. I must leave the particulars to this bearer, Colonel Richards, for having been on horseback all Sunday, and after the battle marching all night, my head aches to that degree, that it is very uneasy to me to write. Poor B[r]ingfield, holding my stirrup for me, and helping me on horseback, was killed*. I am told that he leaves his wife and mother in a poor condition. I can't write to any of my children, so that you will let them know I am

* There is a monument to Col. Bringfield in Westminster Abbey, north aisle.

well, and that I desire they will thank God for preserving me. And pray give my duty to the queen, and let her know the truth of my heart, that the greatest pleasure I have in this success is, that it may be a great service to her affairs; for I am sincerely sensible of all her goodness to me and mine. Pray believe me when I assure you that I love you more than I can express.

Marlborough to *Godolphin*

MONDAY, May 24 (N.S.).—I believe my last might give you expectation of an action. We have been in perpetual motion ever since; and on Sunday last we came in presence with the enemy, who came with the same intentions I had, of fighting. We began to make our lines of battle about eleven o'clock, but we had not all our troops till two in the afternoon, at which time I gave orders for attacking them. The first half hour was very doubtful, but I thank God after that we had success in our attacks, which were on a village in the centre; and on the left we pursued them three leagues, and the night obliged us to give it over. Having been all Sunday, as well as last night, on horseback, my head aches to that degree that I must refer you to the bearer. I shall only add, that we beat them into so great a consternation, that they abandoned all their cannon; their baggage they had sent away in the morning, being re-solved to fight. They had 128 squadrons, and 74 battalions. We had 123 squadrons, and 73 battalions; so that you see the armies were near of a strength; but the general officers which are taken, tell us that they thought themselves sure of victory, by having all the king of France's household, and with them the best troops of France. You will easily believe this victory has lost us a good many men and officers; but I thank God we have but three English regiments that have much suffered; the Dutch horse and foot have suffered more than we. I am going to get a little rest, for if our bread comes by six this evening, I will then march to Louvain this night, in hopes to find them in such disorder, as that we may be encouraged to attack them behind their lines, for they can have no cannon but what they can take out of Louvain. I beg you will assure the queen, that I act with all my heart, and you know how necessary it is for her affairs that we should have good success.

Poor B[r]ingfield is killed, and I am told he leaves his wife and mother in a bad condition.

From *Mr. St. John* to *Marlborough*

MAY 17/28, 1706.—My lord, every man that wishes well to the common good of Europe must be transported with the glorious action of Sunday last; but those who are particularly devoted to the service may pretend to a greater degree of joy. The vast addition of renown which your grace has acquired, and the wonderful preservation of your life, are subjects upon which I can never express the thousandth part of what I feel. France and faction are the only enemies England has reason to fear, and your grace will conquer both; at least while you beat the French, you give a strength to the government which the other dares not contend with.

Marlborough to *Godolphin* (1706)
(Following up Ramillies)

BRUSSELS, May 16/27.—Since my last we have not only passed the Dyle, but are masters of Louvain, Mallines, and Brussels; you will see, by what I send to Mr. Secretary Harley, what has passed between me and the states of Brabant, which I found assembled at Brussels. As there could not be time for orders from England, I hope her majesty will approve of what I have done. It is not to be expressed the great success it has pleased God to give us, by putting a consternation in the enemy's army; for they had not only a greater number than we, but all the best troops of France. The consequence of this battle is likely to be of greater advantage than that of Blenheim; for we have now the whole summer before us, and with the *blessing of God*, I will make the best use of it. For as we had no council of war before this battle, so I hope to have none this whole campaign; and I think we may make such a campaign as may give the queen the glory of making an honourable and safe peace; for the *blessing of God* is certainly with us.

Marlborough to *Duchess*

BRUSSELS, May 16/27.—I have been in so continued a hurry ever since the battle of Ramilies, by which my blood is so heated, that when I go to bed I sleep so unquietly that I cannot get rid of my head-ache, so that I have not as yet all the pleasure I shall enjoy, of the blessing God has been pleased to give us by this great victory. My lord treasurer will let you see what I send by this express to Mr. Secretary Harley, by which you will see that we have done in four days, what we should have thought ourselves happy if we could have been sure of it in four years. I bless God that he has been pleased to make me the instrument of doing so much service to the queen, England, and all Europe, for it is most certain that we have destroyed the greatest part of the best troops of France. My dearest soul, I have now that great pleasure of thinking that I may have the happiness of ending my days in quiet with you.

I have appointed next Sunday for the army to return thanks to God, for the protection he has been pleased to give us. For on this occasion it has been very visible, for the French had not only greater numbers than we, but also all their best troops. I hope the queen will appoint a speedy thanksgiving day at St. Paul's, for the goodness of God is so very great, that if he had suffered us to have been beaten, the liberties of all the allies had been lost. The consequences of this battle are likely to be greater than that of Blenheim, for I have now the whole summer before me. Pray make my excuse to Lord Sunderland that I am not able to write, but he may, if he pleases, see what I write to lord treasurer. My dearest life, I am ever yours.

Brussels has submitted to King Charles the Third, and I am promised that in eight days the states of Brabant will also proclaim him.

Marlborough to *Godolphin*

MERLEBECK, NEAR GHENT, May 20/31.—We did this day design the passing the Scheldt at Gavre, by which we should have cut the French army from their old lines; but they rather chose to abandon Ghent, which they did this morning at break of day, so that I have camped the left of the army at Gavre, and the right at this place. I shall send to-morrow a detachment to Bruges, they having also abandoned that town. As soon as we can have the cannon, and what is necessary, we shall attack Antwerp; after which I should be glad the next place might be Ostend; for unless they draw the greatest part of their army from Germany, they will not be able to hinder us from doing what we please on this side their lines. I tell you my thoughts, but if you think there is any thing better for the queen's interest, I shall endeavour to do it, having that more at heart than my own life.

Marlborough to *Duchess*

MERLEBECK, NEAR GHENT, May 20/31.—We are now masters of Ghent, and to-morrow I shall send some troops to Bruges. So many towns have submitted since the battle, that it really looks more like a dream than truth. My thoughts are now turning to the getting every thing ready for the siege of Antwerp, which place alone, in former years, would have been thought good success for a whole campaign; but we have the blessing of God with us, and I hope we shall do more in this campaign than was done in the last ten years' war in this country, which is a great pleasure, since it is the likeliest way to bring me to my happiness of ending my days quietly.

MERLEBECK, June 3.—Every day gives us fresh marks of the great victory; for since my last, which was but two days ago, we have taken possession of Bruges and Damme, as also Oudenard, which was besieged the last war by the king with sixty thousand men, and he was at last forced to raise the siege. In short, there is so great a panic in the French army as is not to be expressed. Every place we take declares for King Charles. To-morrow the Marshal de Marsin joins their army with 18 battalions of foot and 14 squadrons, which will be very little assistance to them; so that if they will oppose us they must draw more troops from their other armies.

You are very kind in desiring I would not expose myself. Be assured I love you so well, and am so desirous of ending my days quietly with you, that I shall not venture myself but when it is absolutely necessary; and I am sure you are so kind to me, and wish so well to the common cause, that you had rather see me dead than not to do my duty. I am so persuaded that this campaign will bring us a good peace, that I beg of you to do all you can that the house at Woodstock may be carried up as much as possible, that I may have a prospect of living in it.

I do not trouble the queen with thanking her for her obliging letter, but beg you will, with the most dutiful expressions, do it, as also for the letter she writ to lord treasurer before the battle, which I will endeavour to deserve by venturing at all times my life with pleasure for her service.

Make my excuse to Lord Sunderland, and that I desire he would do it to the rest of our friends that I have not time by this post to thank them for their obliging letters.

Marlborough to *Godolphin* (1706)*

ROUSSELAER, July 1.—M. Hope is come this day from Brussels, and I have communicated to him the emperor's letter, and the powers from the king of Spain. He made me great compliments, but I find by him that he thinks this may give uneasiness in Holland by thinking that the court of Vienna has a mind to put the power of this country into the queen's hands, in order that they may have nothing to do with it. If I should find the same thing by the pensioner, and that nothing can cure this jealousy but my desiring to be excused from accepting this commission, I hope the queen will allow of it; for the advantage and honour I might have by this commission is very insignificant, in comparison of the fatal consequences that might be, if it should cause a jealousy between the two nations.

Marlborough to *Heinsius*
(Grand Pensionary of Holland)

ROUSSELAER, July 3.—Sir, by yours of the 30th of the last month, which I received last night, I find you had not received mine, in which I sent you the copies of what I had received from Vienna, but that the Count de Goes had acquainted you with his despatch. I write this to beg of you to do me the justice to be firmly persuaded that I shall take no step in this matter, but what shall be by the advice of the

---

* The following letters refer to important transactions between the allies. The Emperor and the King of Spain (Charles III) pressed Marlborough to take the governorship of the Netherlands which he had just reconquered for them at Ramillies. But Marlborough refused the glittering offer because of the grave jealousy it would have given to the Dutch.

States; for I prefer infinitely their friendship before any particular interest to myself; for I thank God and the queen I have no need nor desire of being richer, but have a very great ambition of doing every thing that can be for the public good; and as for the frontier, which is absolutely necessary for your security, you know my opinion of it. In short, I beg you to assure yourself, and every body else, that I shall with pleasure behave myself in this matter, and all things else, that you may think for the good of the republic, as you would have me; for next to serving the queen and my country, I have nothing more at heart, than to have your good opinions. And let me, on this occasion, assure the States, that I serve them with the same affection and zeal that I do my own country, so that they need be under no difficulty; for if they think it for their service, I shall with pleasure excuse myself from accepting this commission.

Marlborough to *Godolphin*

HARLEBECK, July 6.—...The enclosed letter of the same date confirms me, that if I should accept of the honour the emperor and the king of Spain do me, it would create a great jealousy, which might prejudice the common cause, so that I hope her majesty will approve of what I have done. And I beg you to be so just and kind to me as to assure the queen, that though the appointments of this government are three-score thousand pounds a year, I shall with pleasure excuse myself, since I am convinced it is for her service, unless the States should make it their request, which they are very far from doing; for they have told me that they think it not reasonable that the king of Spain should have possession of the Low Countries till they had assurances of what barrier they should have for their security. I hope this compliance of mine will give me so much credit as to be able to hinder them from hurting themselves; for it is certain, if they follow their own inclinations, they will make such demands upon this country, as will very much dissatisfy the house of Austria, and be thought unreasonable by all the allies, of which the French would be sure to make their advantage.

183

Marlborough to *Heinsius*

CAMP OF HARLEBECK, July 10, 1706.—Sir, I have learnt by the honour of your letter of the 3d instant, that M. Hope was to come to me on the part of the States-general, as in fact he came, Thursday night; and he has probably written to their high mightinesses, that, with the permission of the queen, I was firmly resolved not to charge myself in any manner with the commission with which his Catholic majesty has been pleased to honour me. This you will have the goodness to confirm to them on my part. This new instance ought to convince their high mightinesses how much I have their interest and particular satisfaction at heart, as well as that of the common cause.

On this occasion I take the liberty of reminding their high mightinesses that when the army came to Louvain, and in the farther progress which we have made with the advice of the army deputies, we jointly gave assurances, in writing, to all the towns and people of the country, in the name of the queen, of their high mightinesses, and of his Catholic majesty, that those who should submit to their legitimate sovereign should regain the same rights, privileges, and advantages which they enjoyed in the time of King Charles II.; and to these assurances, with the help of God, I am persuaded we must partly attribute the facility with which we entered into possession of so many strong places, where every one testified universal joy.

However, by the resolution of the States of the 19th of last month, which M. Hope sent me, translated into French, it seems as if their high mightinesses are of opinion that their deputies should sign alone the authorisation for the council of state, the chambers of finance, and other judicatures, who ought not to conclude any thing without having previously consulted, and with the approbation of the said deputies to the exclusion even of the queen.

However, according to what I have learnt, or have been able to comprehend hitherto, it has always appeared that the States had nothing else in view but a good barrier and a reasonable security for their country. I beg, then, you will, with all submission to their high mightinesses, entreat them to reflect maturely on such a step, which is perhaps the true means of attaining those objects. I am persuaded that when the States shall come to deliberate thereon with their usual prudence and wisdom, their high mightinesses will find many reasons beyond what I can suggest to them to bring them to take those measures in this government which may be most useful to the country.

I am more than gratified personally with the friendship and kindness their high mightinesses have at all times shown me, and this obliges me to give them my thoughts without disguise in every thing which I think concerns their interests. I persuade myself also, that they do me the justice to believe that I wish them as much happiness and prosperity as they can themselves desire; and I shall continue always to entertain the same sentiments of respect towards them.

Marlborough to *Godolphin*

HARLEBECK, July 14.—You will see by three or four letters that I have lately writ to you the care I have taken not to give any occasion of jealousy in Holland, and that I was in hopes that my declining the honour the king of Spain had done me would give me so much power with the States as that I might be able to hinder them from doing themselves and the common cause hurt. But such is their temper, that when they have misfortunes they are desirous of peace upon any terms, and when we are blessed by God with success, they are for turning it to their own advantage, without any consideration how it may be liked by their friends and allies. You will see, by the enclosed copy of a letter I have this day writ to the pensioner [Heinsius], that if they cannot be brought to change their resolution of the 19th of the last month, they will create so great a jealousy in this country, that they shall be under the absolute government of the Dutch, that it would turn very much to the advantage of the French. Besides that, the king of Spain will have just reason to complain. M. Hope tells me the States have directed M. Vryberg to acquaint her majesty, and her ministers, with their reasons and proceedings. In my poor opinion, her majesty cannot give too kind an answer;

but she must be careful that the king of Spain and the house of Austria have no reason given them to be angry.

Now the States have applied to her majesty, I cannot act with safety, but by her majesty's directions by one of the secretaries of state. I must beg of her majesty, for her own service and the public good, that she will be pleased to allow of my declining the honour of the king of Spain's commission; otherwise the party in Holland that are for peace, rather upon ill terms than good, would make a very ill use of it, though, in my opinion, the States might have avoided many inconveniences and irregularities, that must now happen, if they had approved of my acting; for I should have done nothing but what must have turned to their safety. And at the same time they might have treated with the king of Spain concerning their barrier; but by this step of theirs, they will very quickly be obliged to declare not only to the queen, but to every body else, that till they have their *surety*, as they call it, by having such a barrier as they shall think reasonable*. I dread the consequences of this matter, for I cannot write so freely to the States as I should otherwise if I were not personally concerned. You may be sure the French have too many partisans in Holland not to be informed of this proceeding, so that they will be sure to make their advantage of it.

Prince Eugene to *Marlborough*
(Battle of Turin, 1706)

YOUR highness will not, I am sure, be displeased to hear by the Baron de Hondorff of the signal advantage which the arms of his imperial majesty and his allies have gained over the enemy. You have had so great a share in it by the succours you have procured, that you must permit me to thank you again. Marshal Marsin is taken prisoner and mortally wounded. The troops have greatly signalised themselves. In a few days I will send you a correct account; and in the mean time refer you to that which you will hear from the bearer of this letter, who is well-informed, has seen every thing, and is competent to

* Some words omitted in the original.

give an accurate relation. Your highness will excuse the short-
ness of this letter, as I have not a moment of time*.

Marlborough to *Duchess*

SEPTEMBER 26.—I have now received the confirmation of the
success in Italy from the duke of Savoy and Prince Eugene;
and it is impossible for me to express the joy it has given me,
for I do not only esteem, but I really love that prince. This
glorious action must bring France so low, that if our friends
can be persuaded to carry on the war one year longer with
vigour, we could not fail, with the blessing of God, to have
such a peace as would give us quiet in our days; but the Dutch
are at this time unaccountable.

From *Godolphin* to *Marlborough*
(Allied quarrels in Spain 1706)

JUNE 11/22.—I have had other notices agreeing with Count
Wratislaw's letter, which you sent me concerning Lord
Peterborough; but I reckon they come all from the complaints of the prince of Lichtenstein. And though I can easily
believe occasion enough may have been given for them, yet
I certainly know, by several letters from Mr. Crowe and
others, that the conduct of him who complains has been worthless and contemptible to the last degree. Count Noyelle's
letter is very modest, and does not pretend to decide between
the two noblemen.

WINDSOR, July 18.—...The same packet brought me a
letter from my Lord Peterborough of a very old date, from
Barcelona. It is full of extraordinary flights and artificial
turns. But one may see by it that there is room for every thing
that has been thought or said of his conduct there; and, at the
same time, by that and other letters of more credit, nothing
ever was so weak, so shameful, and so unaccountable, in every
point, as the conduct of the prince de Lichtenstein, and the
rest of the king of Spain's German followers....

---

* Eugene modestly omits to allege, in excuse for the abruptness of this
letter, the pain of a dangerous wound in the head, which he received
during the attack of the lines. (Coxe.)

Marlborough to *Godolphin*

HELCHIN, Aug. 16.—I agree with you that the Germans that are with King Charles are good for nothing; but I believe the anger and aversion he has for Lord Peterborough is the greatest cause of taking the resolution of going to Saragosa, which I am afraid will prove fatal; for Mr. Crowe told me, that he once said to him, that he would never have any thing to do with Lord Peterborough—that he would not accept of health from him: I suppose this expression is better in Spanish than English. . . .

From *Godolphin* to *Marlborough*

ST. JAMES'S, Aug. 13/24.—Lord Peterborough has written a volume to Mr. Secretary Hedges. It is a sort of remonstrance against the king of Spain and his ministers, in the first place; and, secondly, a complaint against all the orders and directions sent from hence, and as if he had not authority enough given him, either at sea or land. In a word, he is both useless and grievous there, and is preparing to be as troublesome here, whenever he is called home.

WINDSOR, Aug. 15/26.—Mr. Secretary Hedges tells me he is causing Lord Peterborough's long letter to be copied, that he might send it to you. It is a sort of two-edged sword; first, a remonstrance against King Charles, in terms as unmanly as unjust; and, secondly, it is prepared to fall on any body here that shall be in his displeasure.

WINDSOR, Sept. 2/13.—I trouble you with a long letter from the king of Spain. In my answer to it I have not been able to forbear complaining of his inexcusable delays, in not advancing sooner towards Madrid; though I can agree with you that Lord Peterborough's humour may have given a handle to his ministers to prevail with him against his own interest, from a hope they had of squeezing the people of Aragon, as they had before done those of Catalonia. But they have missed their aim in it, as I find by Colonel Stanhope's letter, which I send you; and in a word, Lord Peterborough's extravagances could not have hurt us, if those Germans had not outdone him, both in folly and every thing that is worse.

Peterborough to *Duchess of Marlborough* (Sept. 4, 1706)

...You were pleased, madam, to allow me to be fortunate, till I had nothing to wish. Remember, my lady duchess, one of my first wishes is, that I may never lose your good opinion and favour, and yet I am content to suffer the punishment, whenever I deserve it, by failing in my duty to my queen or country, or my private respects due to my lord duke or yourself, for your public merits, and particular favours to me and my family.

The most disagreeable country in the world is Spain; the most pleasing England; our German ministry and Spanish statesmen much alike; their officers the greatest robbers, and their soldiers the greatest cowards; the only tolerable thing your sex, and that attended with the greatest dangers. Judge, then, madam, of my joy and disappointment, when I soon expected the honour of seeing your grace, after a war ended in a year, and a treaty finished in two months....

Marlborough to *Godolphin* (July, 1706)

...I DON'T think the Dutch are very reasonable, to be so much in pain about their barrier, as things stand; but it is a plain argument to me, they think of joining their interest to that of France, whenever a peace comes; and for that very reason the longer we can keep it off the better.

HELCHIN, Aug. 23.—I send you inclosed a letter from the pensionary and my answer. I do not doubt Mr. Secretary Harley or yourself will hear from M. Buys, as the French are making applications, I believe, at Vienna, as well as at the Hague. You must be careful what answer you make, for be assured they will not continue the war much longer; and I am afraid, in a very little time, we shall find that the court of Vienna and the Dutch are more desirous of quarrelling with each other than with France.

Marlborough to the *Pensionary* (Heinsius)

HELCHIN, Aug. 21.—I have had the favour of yours of the 13th, and shall obey your commands as far as I dare; for, as a good Englishman, I must be of the opinion of my country, *that both by treaty and interest we are obliged to preserve the monarchy of Spain entire.* At the same time, as a friend, I must acknowledge that I believe France can hardly be brought to a peace, unless something be given to the duke of Anjou, so that he may preserve the title of king. I think that of Milan is unreasonable, since it would make France master of the duke of Savoy and all Italy. As to what they pretend on the Rhine, I can't think they would insist on that. The explication of the queen's title is certainly very impertinent; for the last peace, in which they take no notice of the successor, was contrary to custom and the laws of the land. You see that in few words I let you know my thoughts. But I durst not advise what answer you should give; but I should think it were very natural for M. Buys to give an account of this proposal to Mr. Secretary Harley and lord treasurer, who will acquaint her majesty; by which means you will have the opinion of the queen.

The *Queen* to *Godolphin* (1706)*

AUGUST 30/SEPT. 10.—I think one should always speak one's mind freely to one's friends on every occasion, but sometimes one is apt to hope things may not come to that extremity, as to make it necessary to trouble them, and therefore it is very natural to defer doing so as long as one possibly can. The difficulties I labour under at this time are so great, and so uneasy to me, that they will not suffer me any longer to keep my thoughts to myself; and I choose this way of explaining them to you, rather than endeavour to begin to speak, and not be able to go on. I have been considering the business we have so often spoke about, ever since I saw you, and cannot but continue of the same mind, that it is a great hardship to per-

---

* This group of letters refers to the great move of the Whig junto to compel Godolphin and Marlborough to force the unwilling Queen to accept the services of Sunderland and so give the Ministry a distinctively Whig complexion. Sunderland was Marlborough's son-in-law.

suade any body to part with a place they are in possession of, in hopes of another that is not yet vacant. Besides, I must own freely to you, I am of the opinion, that making a party man secretary of state, when there are so many of their friends in employment of all kinds already, is throwing myself into the hands of a party, which is a thing I have been desirous to avoid. May be some may think I would be willing to be in the hands of the Tories; but whatever people may say of me, I do assure you I am not inclined, nor ever will be, to employ any of those violent persons, that have behaved themselves so ill towards me. All I desire is, my liberty in encouraging and employing all those that concur faithfully in my service, whether they are called Whigs or Tories, not to be tied to one, nor the other; for if I should be so unfortunate as to fall into the hands of either, I shall not imagine myself, though I have the name of queen, to be in reality but their slave, which as it will be my personal ruin, so it will be the destroying all government; for instead of putting an end to faction, it will lay a lasting foundation for it. You press the bringing Lord Sunderland into business, that there may be one of that party in a place of trust, to help carry on the business this winter; and you think if this is not complied with, they will not be hearty in pursuing my service in the parliament. But is it not very hard that men of sense and honour will not promote the good of their country, because every thing in the world is not done that they desire! when they may be assured Lord Sunderland shall come into employment as soon as it is possible. Why, for God's sake, must I, who have no interest, no end, no thought, but for the good of my country, be made so miserable, as to be brought into the power of one set of men? and why may not I be trusted, since I mean nothing but what is equally for the good of all my subjects? There is another apprehension I have of Lord Sunderland being secretary, which I think is a natural one, which proceeds from what I have heard of his temper. I am afraid he and I should not agree long together, finding by experience my humour and those that are of a warmer will often have misunderstandings between one another. I could say a great deal more on this subject, but fear I have been too tedious already. Therefore

I shall conclude, begging you to consider how to bring me out of my difficulties, and never leave my service, for Jesus Christ's sake; for besides the reasons I give you in another letter, this is a blow I cannot bear.

Godolphin to the *Queen*

SATURDAY MORNING, AT NINE.—I come this moment from opening and reading the letter which your majesty gave yourself the trouble to write to me last night. It gives me all the grief and despair imaginable, to find that your majesty shows inclination to have me continue in your service, and yet will make it impossible for me to do so. I shall not therefore trouble your majesty with fruitless repetitions of reasons and arguments. I cannot struggle against the difficulties of your majesty's business, and yourself at the same time; but I can keep my word to your majesty.

I have no house in the world to go to but my house at Newmarket, which I must own is not at this time like to be a place of much retirement; but I have no other. I have worn out my health, and almost my life, in the service of the crown. I have served your majesty faithfully to the best of my understanding, without any advantage to myself, except the honour of doing so, or without expecting any other favour than to end the small remainder of my days in liberty and quiet.

Sunderland to *the Duchess of Marlborough* (1706)

LONDON, Sept. 17/28.—Lord Halifax and I reckoned to have set out to-morrow for Woodstock, and it is with a great deal of regret that we are obliged to put off our journey thither; but when you know the reason of it, I dare say you won't think us in the wrong. When I writ to you last, I gave you some account of a conversation Lord Halifax and the lord treasurer had together; but since that, Lord Halifax has told Lord Somers and me several particulars of that conversation, and among other things, of the great offers of any place, or any other advantage whatever that the lord treasurer was pleased to make to me, in lieu of the thing in question. I can't but think, and we are all of the same mind, that for me to hearken to any such offer, would be in effect to be both fool and knave.

Lord Somers, Lord Halifax, and I, have talked very fully over all this matter, and we are come to our last resolution in it, that this and what other things have been promised must be done, or we and the lord treasurer must have nothing more to do together about business; and that we must let all our friends know just how the matter stands between us and the lord treasurer, whatever is the consequence of it. If the lord treasurer comes to town, either to-night or to-morrow, both Lord Somers and Lord Halifax will let him know this resolution in the plainest words, and in the fullest manner they can. If he does not come, Lord Halifax will go to Windsor to him, and let him know it in Lord Somers's name, as well as his own, so that a few days will determine whether it is to be a breach or not. But whether it is or not, you must be assured that every honest Englishman will acknowledge, that whatever good has been done is entirely owing to you; and that whatever is not done is for want of your power to do it.

There is another reason which makes Lord Halifax not think it so proper for us to go to Woodstock whilst this matter is in suspense, and Lord Somers is of the same mind; that is, that since it is plain that you are very ill with the queen, purely for acting and speaking honestly and sincerely your mind, nobody knows how far some people might make the queen believe that we were gone only to influence and engage you to be more and more uneasy to her. I beg you would let us know whether we are right in this thought or no; for nothing can be a greater mortification than to be prevented of the pleasure of waiting upon you.

Marlborough to *Duchess*

What you write me concerning the queen and the lord treasurer gives me a great deal of trouble; for should the consequence be what you say, that there is no relying upon the Tories, and that the Whigs will be out of humour, it must end in confusion, which will have the consequence of the Dutch making peace with France. I am afraid this is what will gratify many of the Tory party; but I can see no advantage that can come to the Whigs by the ruin of the lord treasurer; so that I hope they are too wise a people to expose themselves and the liberties of Europe, because some things are not done with a good grace. I would not have you mistake me; for as far as it is in my power, for the sake of my country and the queen, for whom, had I a thousand lives, I would venture them all, I would have every thing that is reasonable done to satisfy the Whigs, of which I think the lord treasurer is the best judge. If it were not for my duty to the queen and friendship to lord treasurer, I should beg that somebody else might execute my office. Not that I take any thing ill, but that the weight is too great for me, and I find a decay in my memory. Whatever may be told to you of my looks, the greatest part of my hair is grey, but I think I am not quite so lean as I was.

The *Duchess* to the *Queen* (1706)

I CONCLUDE your majesty will believe my arguments upon this subject proceed chiefly from the partiality which I have for my lord Sunderland, though I solemnly protest that I never had any for any person to the prejudice of what I believed your interest. And I had rather he had any other place, or none at all, if the party that most assist you would be satisfied without it; for, besides the very great trouble of that office*, executed as it should be, he is not of a humour to get any thing by such an employment; and I wish from my soul that any other man had been proposed to you, that you could not have suspected I had any concern for. But 'tis certain that your government can't be carried on with a part of the Tories, and the *Whigs disobliged, who, when that happens, will join with any people to torment you and those that are your true servants.* I am sure it is my interest, as well as inclination, to have you succeed by any sort of men in what is just, and that will prevent what has been done from being thrown away. Your security and the nation's is my chief wish, and I beg of God Almighty, as sincerely as I shall do for His pardon at my last hour, that Mr. and Mrs. Morley may see their errors as to this *notion* before it is too late; but considering how little im-

---

* Secretary of State, Southern Department, the office claimed for Sunderland by the Whig Junto (p. 250, below).

pression any thing makes that comes from your faithful Freeman, I have troubled you too much, and I beg your pardon for it.

The *Duchess* to the *Queen* (1706)

AUGUST 30.—Your majesty's great indifference and contempt in taking no notice of my last letter, did not so much surprise me, as to hear my lord treasurer say you had complained much of it, which makes me presume to give you this trouble to repeat what I can be very positive was the whole aim of the letter, and I believe very near the words. It was in the first place, to show the reason why I had not waited upon your majesty, believing you were uneasy, and fearing you might think I had some private concern for Lord Sunderland. I therefore thought it necessary to assure your majesty that I had none so great as for your service, and to see my lord treasurer so mortified at the necessity of quitting it, or being the ruin of that and himself together. Then I took the liberty to show, as well as I could, that it was really no hardship nor unkindness to Sir Charles Hedges; and I think I might have added, tho' I believe I did not, that your majesty, to carry on your government, must have men that neither herd with your enemies, nor that are in themselves insignificant. At last, I concluded, if I am not more mistaken than ever I was in my life, with these following words, that I did pray to God Almighty with as much earnestness as I should at my last day for the saving of my soul, that Mrs. and Mr. Morley might see their errors. This is the whole sense of the letter; and having had the honour to know your majesty when you had other thoughts of me than you are pleased to have now, and when you did think fit to take advice and information, I could not reasonably imagine that you should be offended at my earnest endeavours to serve you, and pray that you nor the prince might not be deceived. But finding that no proofs nor demonstrations of my faithfulness to your interest can make any thing agreeable to your majesty that comes from me, I will not enlarge upon this subject. I will only beg one piece of justice, and that I fancy you would not refuse to any body, if you believed it one, that you will show my lord treasurer the letter of which your majesty has complained; and I wish from the bottom of my heart, that he, or any body that is faithful to you and the prince, could see every word that ever I writ to your majesty in my life.

Godolphin to *Duchess of Marlborough* (1706)

WINDSOR, SUNDAY.—According to your commands, I gave your letter to Mrs. Morley. As she was going to put it in her pocket, I told her that you had made me promise to beg of her to read it before I went out of the room. She did so, and then said she believed she had mistaken some words at the latter end of the former letter, which she seemed to think had a different sense from that which I had given her from you; but because you desired I might see it, she would look for it, and give it me, which she did, and desired me to return it to her to-day. I come now from giving it back into her hands, and I think I have convinced her that her complaint was grounded upon her having misapprehended the sense of your letter, by not reading it right, that is to say, by reading the word *notion* for *nation*. To explain this the more clearly to you, I send you a copy of the conclusion of your first letter to her, taken as far back as I thought was enough to show the plain sense and meaning of your letter. At the same time I must own that in your original letter, that word *notion* was not so distinctly written, but that one might naturally read it *nation*, if the sense of two or three lines together before did not fully explain your meaning. As to the main point, she has only told me that she had written a letter to me, as she said she would, to explain her difficulty, but she must write it out before she could give it me.

The *Queen* to *Duchess of Marlborough*

FRIDAY MORNING.—Since my dear Mrs. Freeman could imagine my not taking notice of her letter that was writ before she went to St. Alban's, proceeded from indifference or contempt, what will she think of my not answering her other in another week's time? But I do assure you it was neither of the reasons you mention that hindered me from writing, *nor no* *other*, but the concern I have been in since the change of the secretary was proposed to me. I have obeyed your commands in showing your letter to my lord treasurer, and find my complaint was not without some ground, a mistake any body might make upon the first reading; for you had made an *a* instead of an *o*, which quite altered the word. I am very sensible all you say proceeds from the concern you have for my service, and it is impossible to be more mortified than I am, to see my lord treasurer in such uneasiness; and his leaving my service is a thought I cannot bear, and I hope in God he will put all such out of his own mind. Now that you are come hither again, I hope you will not go to Woodstock without giving me one look, for whatever hard thoughts you may have of me, I am sure I do not deserve them, and I will not be uneasy if you come to me; for though you are never so unkind, I will ever preserve a most sincere and tender passion for my dear Mrs. Freeman*.

Marlborough to *Godolphin* (1706)

HELCHIN, August 9.—What you say of both parties is so true, that I do, with all my soul, pity you. Care must be taken against the malice of the angry party; and notwithstanding their malicious affection of crying the church may be ruined by the Union, the Union must be supported; and I hope the reasonable men of the other party will not oppose the enlarging of the bottom, so that it may be able to support itself. . . . I had last night the honour of yours of the 13th, and am very glad to find that the commission has so unanimously agreed. I do with all my heart wish the parliament of both nations may do the same, so that her majesty may have the glory of finishing this great work, for which she will not only deserve to be blessed in this, but also in future ages.

* The Queen gave in and appointed Sunderland, see p. 250, below.

II. *Conduct of the Duchess of Marlborough* (by herself)

THE KING died, and the PRINCESS of Denmark took his place. This elevation of my miſtreſs to the throne brought me into a new ſcene of life, and into a new ſort of conſideration with all thoſe, whoſe attention, either by curioſity or ambition, was turned to politicks and the court. Hitherto my favour with her ROYAL HIGHNESS, though it had ſometimes furniſhed matter of converſation to the publick, had been of no moment to the affairs of the nation, ſhe herſelf having no ſhare in the councils, by which they were managed. But from this time, I began to be look'd upon as a perſon of conſequence, without whoſe approbation, at leaſt, neither places, nor penſions, nor honours were beſtowed by the crown. The intimate friend-ſhip, with which the QUEEN was known to honour me, afforded a plauſible foundation for this opinion: And I believe therefore, it will be a ſurprize to many, to be told, that the firſt important ſtep, which her MAJESTY took, after her acceſ-ſion to the government, was againſt my wiſhes and inclination: I mean, *her throwing herſelf and her affairs almoſt entirely into the hands of the tories.*

I ſhall dwell the longer, and be the more particular upon the ſubjeɛt of my diſagreement with her MAJESTY about parties, that I may expoſe the injuſtice of thoſe whigs, who, after the great change in 1710, accuſed me of being the ruin of their cauſe; a cauſe, that, in her reign, would have been always too low, to be capable of a fall, but for the zeal and diligence, with which I ſeiz'd every opportunity to raiſe and eſtabliſh it; which, in the end, proved the ruin of my favour with her MAJESTY.

The QUEEN had from her infancy imbibed the moſt un-conquerable prejudices againſt the whigs. She had been taught to look upon them all, not only as republicans, who hated the very ſhadow of regal authority, but as implacable enemies to the church of England. This averſion to the whole party had been confirmed by the ill uſage ſhe had met with from her ſiſter and king WILLIAM, which, though perhaps more owing to lord ROCHESTER than to any man then living, was now

to be all charged to the account of the whigs. And prince
GEORGE, her hufband, who had alfo been ill treated, in that
reign, threw into the fcale his refentments.

On the other hand, the tories had the advantage, not only
of the QUEEN's early prepoffeffion in their favour, but of their
having affifted her in the late reign, in the affair of her *fettlement*. It was indeed evident, that they had done this, more in
oppofition to king WILLIAM, than from any real refpect for
the PRINCESS of Denmark. But ftill they had ferved her. And
the winter before fhe came to the crown, they had in the fame
fpirit of oppofition to the KING, and in profpect of his death,
paid her more than ufual civilities and attendance.

It is no great wonder therefore, all thefe things confidered,
that as foon as fhe was feated in the throne, the tories (whom
fhe ufually called by the agreeable name of the church-party)
became the diftinguifhed objects of the royal favour.

Dr. SHARP, archbifhop of York, was pitched upon by herfelf to preach her coronation fermon, and to be her chief
counfellor in church-matters; and her privy-council was filled
with tories. My lord NORMANBY (foon after duke of BUCKING-
HAM) the earls of JERSEY and NOTTINGHAM, Sir EDWARD
SEYMOUR, with many others of the high-fliers, were brought
into place; Sir NATHAN WRIGHT was continued in poffeffion
of the great feal of England, and the earl of ROCHESTER in the
lieutenancy of Ireland. Thefe were men, who had all a
wonderful zeal for the church; a fort of public merit that
eclipfed all other in the eyes of the QUEEN. And I am firmly
perfuaded, that notwithftanding her extraordinary affection
for me, and the entire devotion which my lord MARLBOROUGH
and my lord GODOLPHIN had for many years fhown to her
fervice, they would not have had fo great a fhare of her favour
and confidence, if they had not been reckoned in the number
of the tories.

The truth is, though both thefe lords had always the real
intereft of the nation at heart, and had given proof of this, by
their conduct in their feveral employments, in the late reign,
they had been educated in the perfuafion, that the high-church
party were the beft friends to the conftitution, both of church
and ftate; nor were they perfectly undeceived but by experience.

For my own part, I had not the fame prepoffeffions. The *word CHURCH* had never any charm for *me*, in the mouths of thofe, who made the moft noife with it; for I could not perceive that they gave any other diftinguifhing proof of their regard for the *thing*, than a frequent ufe of the *word*, like a fpell to enchant weak minds; and a perfecuting zeal againft diffenters, and againft thofe real friends of the church, who would not admit that *perfecution* was agreeable to its doctrine. And as to ftate-affairs, many of thefe churchmen feemed to me, to have no fixed principles at all, having endeavoured, during the laft reign, to undermine that very government, which they had contributed to eftablifh.

I was heartily forry therefore, that, for the fake of fuch churchmen, others fhould be removed from their employments, who had been firm to the principles of the Revolution, and whom I thought much more likely to fupport the QUEEN, and promote the welfare of our country, than the wrongheaded politicians that fucceeded them.

I refolved therefore, from the very beginning of the QUEEN's reign, to try whether I could not by degrees make impreffions in her mind more favourable to the whigs; and though my inftances with her had not at firft any confiderable effect, I believe, I may venture to fay, it was, in fome meafure, owing to them, that her MAJESTY did, againft her own inclinations, continue feveral of this party in office. And it is well known, that when the QUEEN, in the firft year of her reign, had determined to create four new peers, the lords GRANVILLE, GUERNSEY, GOWER and CONWAY, I prevailed that Mr. HERVEY (the prefent earl of Briftol) might be a *fifth*, in fpite of the oppofition of the tories, and efpecially of the *four* above-named; who for a while refufed to accept of the peerage, if Mr. HERVEY, a whig, were admitted to the fame honour.

But how difficult a tafk I prefcribed to myfelf, when I undertook to moderate her MAJESTY's partiality to the tories, and to engage her to a better opinion of their oppofites, will abundantly appear from the following letter, which I had the honour to receive from her, about half a year after her acceffion to the throne.

St. James's, faturday the 24 *Oc͜tr.*

'I am very glad to find by my dear Mrs. FREEMAN'S, that
'I was bleft with yefterday, that fhe liked *my fpeech*, but I can-
'not help being extremely concern'd, you are fo partial to the
'whigs, becaufe I would not have you, and your poor, un-
'fortunate, faithful MORLEY differ in opinion in the leaft
'thing. What I faid, when I writ laft upon this fubjeƈt, does
'not proceed from any infinuations of the other party; but I
'know the principles of the church of England, and I know
'thofe of the whigs, and it is that, and no other reafon, which
'makes me think as I do, of the laft. And upon my word, my
'dear Mrs. FREEMAN, you are mightily miftaken in your
'notion of a true whig: For the charaƈter, you give of them,
'does not in the leaft belong to them, but to the church. But
'I will fay no more on this fubjeƈt, only beg, for my poor fake,
'that you would not fhow more countenance to thofe, you
'feem to have fo much inclination for, than to the church
'party. Since you have ftaid fo long at Windfor, I wifh now
'for your own fake, that you would ftay till after *my lord
'mayor's day*; for if you are in town, *you can't avoid going to
'the fhow*, and being in the country is a juft excufe; and,
'I think, one would be glad of any to avoid fo troublefom a
'bufinefs. I am at this time in great hafte, and therefore can
'fay no more to my dear dear Mrs. FREEMAN, but that I am
'moft paffionately her's.'

As my early zeal for the whigs is inconteftably manifeft
from what her majefty here fays to me, fo, I think, it will be
no lefs evident to any one who refleƈts on my fituation at that
time, that this zeal could proceed from nothing but conviƈtion
of the goodnefs of the caufe I efpoufed.

For, as to private intereft, the whigs could have done nothing for my advantage more than the tories. I needed not the
affiftance of either to ingratiate me with the QUEEN. She had
both before and fince her acceffion, given the moft unqueftion-
able proofs, that fhe confidered me, not only as a moft faithful
fervant, but as her dear friend. I have mentioned nothing of
her extreme goodnefs to me fince the breaking out of the
quarrel between her fifter and her, that I might not interrupt

the relation of that matter in which my chief aim was the juftification of my miftrefs's conduct and my own upon that occafion. Her letters to me afterwards (of which I have great numbers ftill by me) were in the fame ftrain of tendernefs as thofe you have read; and upon her coming to the crown, fhe had not only made me her groom of the ftole, and keeper of the privy purfe, but had given the command of the army to my lord MARLBOROUGH, and the treafurer's ftaff to my lord GODOLPHIN, to whofe fon my eldeft daughter was married.

It is plain therefore that I could have no motive of private intereft to biafs me to the whigs. Every body muft fee, that, had I confulted that oracle about the choice of a party, it would certainly have directed me to go with the ftream of my miftrefs's inclination and prejudices. This would have been the fureft way to fecure my favour with her.

* * * * * *

The QUEEN in her fpeech had declared her refolution to defend and maintain the church as by law eftablifhed. Of *this* they tell her they have no doubt, after her repeated affurances. But *this* was not enough. So illuftrious an ornament of the church muft not content herfelf with protecting it in it's *legal* rights, but fhe muft contribute to reftore it to it's *due* rights, that is, fhe muft reftore tories and high-churchmen to their *divine* rights and privileges of poffeffing all the civil offices in the ftate, and being the only men elected to ferve in parliament, to the exclufion of all whigs and low-churchmen, who being enemies of the church, and having a will to deftroy it, muft be divefted of the power to execute their malice.

That this was the meaning of the addrefs I believe no body doubts; and the *occafional conformity bill*, which, in confe-quence of this zeal for the church, was foon brought into parliament, did not aim at excluding from employments the *occafional* conformifts only, but all thofe *conftant* conformifts too, who could not relifh the high-church nonfenfe of pro-moting religion by perfecution. For as the tories were well acquainted with her MAJESTY's entire devotion to the church, they defigned this *bill*, as a *teft*, whereby fhe might certainly diftinguifh it's friends from it's foes; and they doubted not but she would reckon among the latter whoever should oppose so religious a scheme.

The bill, as every body knows, was carried triumphantly through the house of commons; and the PRINCE of Denmark (though himself an occasional conformist) was persuaded to vote for it, in the house of lords. However it miscarried there (I forget how) to the great disappointment and mortification of the party. Nay it began to be suspected that some of the chief men at court were not so zealous in the good cause as they should be. My lord ROCHESTER was, I think, the first of the tory leaders that discovered a deep discontent with the QUEEN and her administration. Before the end of the year he resigned the lieutenancy of Ireland in great wrath, upon her MAJESTY'S being so unreasonable as to press him to go thither to attend the affairs of that kingdom, which greatly needed his presence. For as the revenue, which had been formerly granted was out, it was necessary to call a parliament in order to another supply; and a parliament could not be held without a lord lieutenant. But when the QUEEN represented these things to him he told her with great insolence, that *he would not go into* Ireland, *though she would give the country to him and his son*; so that he seems to have accepted the post only that he might reign in Ireland by the ministry of his brother KEIGHTLEY, as he hoped to do in England, in person. Nor could he, after his resignation, overcome his anger so far as to wait upon the QUEEN or to go to council; which she observing ordered, after some time, that he should no more be summoned, 'saying, it was not reasonable my lord ROCHESTER 'should come to council only when he pleased.'

Perhaps his lordship's unwillingness to leave England might proceed from his zeal for the church, and from his fears left it should be betrayed in his absence. But it was generally thought, and I believe with good reason, that the true source of his dissatisfaction was the QUEEN'S not making him her sole governor and director, and my lord GODOLPHIN'S being preferred before him for the treasury: Which, if true, affords a remarkable instance, how much self-love and self-conceit can blind even a man of sense; for such, by his party at least, he was esteemed to be. I don't wonder that he should like power (it is what

moft people are fond of) or that being related to the QUEEN he
fhould expect a particular confideration. This was very natural
and very reafonable, if he had behaved himfelf to her as he
ought: But when one confiders, that his relation to her was
by fuch a fort of accident, and that his conduct had been fo very
extraordinary, 'tis an amazing thing that he fhould imagine,
he was to domineer over the QUEEN and every body elfe, as he
did over his own family.

Whether the church was in any danger or not *before*, it
could not be queftioned by any good churchman, but it *now*
began to be in fome peril when my lord ROCHESTER was no
longer in place, nor in the council.

The bill againft occafional conformity was revived by the
tories the next feffions of parliament; which proceeding, whatever regard it might fhow for the church, did certainly fhow
little refpect or gratitude to the QUEEN, who had hitherto
fhowered her favours upon the party. For her MAJESTY having
been informed, that this bill had alarmed a great part of her
fubjects, who were otherwife perfectly well affected to her
government, and no lefs able than zealous to affift her in
carrying on the war againft the common enemy, had endeavoured in her fpeech, by the warmeft expreffions, to dif-
fuade the parliament from this meafure, as it might prove a
fource of fatal divifions at home, where union and harmony
were fo neceffary in order to the fuccefs of our affairs abroad.

But the intereft of the *church*, that is, of *high-churchmen*,
was to be preferred before the intereft of the QUEEN or of the
nation, or the prefervation of the liberties of Europe. The bill
was therefore brought in again; but, though it had once more
an eafy paffage through the houfe of commons, it met with the
fame fate as the year before in the houfe of lords.

This new blow to the church was foon followed by another,
the removal of lord JERSEY and Sir EDWARD SEYMOUR from
their employments; and about the fame time lord NOTTING-
HAM refigned his place of fecretary of ftate, becaufe the whigs
were too much favoured.

The whigs did indeed begin to be favoured, and with good
reafon. For when they faw that my lord MARLBOROUGH
profecuted the common caufe with fuch hearty diligence and

fuch unexpected fuccefs, they, notwithftanding the partiality
which had been fhown to their oppofites, univerfally forgot
their refentments, and no longer confidering themfelves as an
oppreffed party, ran in with the loudeft acclamations, extolling
his merit and fervices: And as the trade and money of the
nation were chiefly in the hands of thofe, who efpoufed the
caufe in which the miniftry were then engaged, it is no
wonder that my lord GODOLPHIN began to pay them as much
regard as the times and the QUEEN's prejudices would permit
him to do.

The church in the mean while, it muft be confeffed, was in
a deplorable condition. The earls of ROCHESTER, JERSEY, and
NOTTINGHAM, and Sir EDWARD SEYMOUR out of place, and
the whigs coming into favour. It was refolved therefore the
next feffions of parliament to tack the occafional conformity
bill to the money bill, a refolution which fhowed the fpirit of
the party in it's true light. But it happened that my lord
MARLBOROUGH, in the fummer before the parliament met,
gained the battle of Blenheim. This was an unfortunate accident; and by the vifible diffatisfaction of fome people on the
news of it, one would have imagined, that inftead of beating
the French, he had beat the church. And I cannot here omit
one remarkable inftance of true party fpirit in the tories on
this occafion. My lord MARLBOROUGH, before he had had
fufficient opportunity of fhowing the greatnefs of the general,
had, for his firft fucceffes in the war, been complimented by
this very houfe of commons, as the *retriever of the glory of the
Englifh nation*, being then reputed a high churchman. But
now that he was thought to look towards the moderate party,
his *complete victory* at Blenheim was, in the addrefs of con-
gratulation to the QUEEN, ridiculoufly paired with Sir GEORGE
ROOK's *drawn battle* with the French at fea.

However, neither the glory of this victory, nor the important confequences of it, could be hid, even from the eyes of
thofe who would have been the moft willing not to fee them.
The power of France was broken by it to a great degree, and
the liberties and peace of Europe were in a fair way to be
eftablifhed upon firm and lafting foundations. The lefs violent
part of the tories therefore could not be prevailed with to

hazard thefe great and pleafing hopes, by tacking them to the fortune of the *occafional conformity bill*. The tack was rejeded by the majority of the members, even of this houfe of commons, fo rich in tories and high churchmen. And though the bill by itfelf was afterwards paffed in that houfe, it was again thrown out by the lords.

The laft great wound given to the church this year, was by the QUEEN's taking the privy feal from the duke of BUCKINGHAM.

And the next year I prevail'd with her MAJESTY to take the great feal from Sir NATHAN WRIGHT, a man defpifed by all parties, of no ufe to the crown, and whofe weak and wretched condud in the court of *chancery*, had almoft brought his very office into contempt. His removal however was a great lofs to the church, for which he had ever been a warm ftickler. And this lofs was the more fenfibly felt, as his fucceffor, my lord COWPER, was not only of the whig-party, but of fuch abilities and integrity, as brought a new credit to it in the nation.

But, what was worfe than all thefe misfortunes, the majority of the houfe of commons in the new parliament of 1705, proved to be whig.

No wonder if, in thefe fad circumftances, a loud and piteous cry was raifed upon the extreme danger of the poor church. A doleful piece, penn'd by fome of the zealots of the party, and called *the memorial of the church of England*, was printed and fpread abroad, fetting forth her melancholy condition and diftrefs; and much lamentation it occafioned. But what remedy? There could be no hope of getting an *occafional conformity bill* paffed in this parliament. One expedient ftill remained; and this was, to invite the princefs SOPHIA of Hanover, the prefent KING's grandmother, to come over and defend the church. Her prefence here, though fhe would not probably, as being a lutheran, be very zealous for a bill againft occafional conformifts, yet might happily prove a means to hinder the whigs from bringing in popery and the pretender. A motion was therefore made in the houfe of lords for this invitation; and the neceffity of it was urged with great ftrength of argument by the earls of ROCHESTER and NOTTINGHAM, and the other grave men of the party. Not that they had the leaſt hope or the leaſt deſire to carry their point, but being well aſſured that the QUEEN would never conſent to ſuch an invitation, nor pardon her miniſters if they encouraged the deſign, this was a notable ſtratagem to ruin them, either with her MAJESTY, or with the nation; for if in compliance with her prejudices they oppoſed this motion, it was to be hoped it would draw the publick odium upon them, as declared enemies to the proteſtant ſucceſſion.

This hopeful ſcheme however did not ſucceed. The whigs oppoſed the invitation, and yet preſerved their credit, to the great mortification of the other party. I know that my lord GODOLPHIN, and other great men, were much reflected upon by ſome well diſpoſed perſons, for not laying hold of this opportunity, which the tories put into their hands, of more effectually ſecuring the ſucceſſion to the crown in the houſe of Hanover. But thoſe of the whigs, whoſe anger againſt the miniſter was raiſed on this account, little knew how impracticable the project of *invitation* was, and that the attempt would have only ſerved to make the QUEEN diſcard her miniſtry, to the ruin of the common cauſe of theſe kingdoms, and of all Europe. I had often tried her MAJESTY upon this ſubject; and when I found that ſhe would not hear of the immediate ſucceſſor's coming over, had preſſed her that ſhe would at leaſt invite hither the young PRINCE of Hanover, who was not to be her immediate ſucceſſor, and that ſhe would let him live here as her ſon: but her MAJESTY would liſten to no propoſal of this kind in any ſhape whatſoever.

VI

SCOTLAND. THE UNION

SCOTLAND. THE UNION

THE DOCUMENTS in this section will be easily intelligible if studied with the excellent account of the events leading to the Union in Hume Brown's *History of Scotland*, vol. III, chap. III, pp. 75–153, or chap. v of Leadam's vol. IX of the *Political History of England* (Longman).

The first of the documents here printed is the account of the matter given by Sir John Clerk of Penicuik, one of the Scots Commissioners for the Union Treaty, a moderate Whig and convinced supporter of the policy of the Union. The second document is from vol. I of the *Papers* of George Lockhart, a Jacobite and convinced opponent of the Union. The third document consists of the most important clauses from the Union Treaty itself, as printed in Defoe's *History of the Union*, where much other information on the subject will be found.

I. *Clerk's Memoirs*

(Roxburghe Club publication, 1895)

I have throuen togither some observations on this session [1703] of Parliament in another Manuscript book, so shall say little here. It was divided in 3 factions, who, as they had different views, drove different ways. The first was what was called the Court party; they were for supporting the Crown and the Credite of the High Commissioner, consequently they were for giving moderat subsidies for supporting the Government against the insults of the French, with whom we were, at that time, in war. They had the union of the two nations in view, because they not only considered it as the happiest thing that cou'd be brought about for the Interest of Great Britain, but because it was expressly recommended to them by the Queen. The second faction was that of the Jacobites; they were to thwart and disturb the Administration at any rate. The third faction was what went under the name of the Squadrone Volante. These consisted of about fifeteen Lords and Gentlemen, all Whigs in their principles, but who herded together, and keept little or no communication with the Duke of Queensberry and his Friends. They were for opposing every thing which they durst oppose, but to keep firmly in their view the succession of the Crown in the House of Hanover. They pretented to be great Patriots, and to stand up chiefly in defence of the rights and privileges of the subjects; in a word, the publick good and the liberty of the subjects were still in their mouths, but in their Hearts they were known to have Court preferments and places in the chiefest degree of veneration. These were the springs and motives of all their Actions, which appeared in a hundred instances thereafter. However, by the bye, I must say that such a Squadrone Volante in any Parliament seems to be always a happy means in the hand of Providence to keep the several members of an Administration in their duty, for people in great power seldom fail to take more upon them than falls to their share.

The chiefs of the Squadrone Lords were the Dukes of Montrose and Roxburgh, the Earls of Rothess and Hadington, all these young men of about 24 years of Age; but the chief of all, at least the man under whose name they principally voted, was the Marquise of Twedale, a very good Man, but not perfectly qualified for Court intrigues.

Amongst their Gentlemen was one Mr. Fletcher of Saltoun, a Man of Republican principles, who had spent his youth in Holand, had been forfeited under the late King James, but afterwards restored under King William by Act of Parliament. He was a man a little untoward in his temper, and much inclined to Eloquence. He made many speeches in Parliament, which are all printed, but was not very dexterous in making extemporary replies. He was, however, a very Honest Man, and meant well in every thing he said and did, except in cases where his humure, passion, or prejudices were suffered to get the better of his reasone.

The above mentioned Factions rubb'd upon one another and with great severity, so that we were often in the form of a Polish diet, with our swords in our hands, or at least our hands at our swords. In all this struggle, therefore, there was no great good done, so that I am persuaded we had spent our time at home more to the benefite of the nation.

In this session, to silence the murmurs of some splenetick people, and those who were Ennemies to the last administration under King William, an Act past impowering certain Commissioners to enquire into the publick accompts and debts of the nation. I had the honour to be chosen one of them, I suppose by the Duke of Queensberry's recommendation. At this time, being in an humure of scribling, and debates rising very high about Limitations on the Crown to take place after her Majesty's decease, I took upon me to write two Pamphlets, one against diminishing the ancient prerogatives of the Crown, the other an Essay upon the intended Limitations. Both were well received by those of my own sentiments, others were pycked at them; but few ever discovered that I was the Author.

There was likeways a notable Act concerted this Session of parliament, intituled Act for Security of the Kingdom; but it was refused the Royal assent till the subsequent session of Parliament, of which hereafter.

By this Act all the people of Scotland were to be armed, and a provision made that on the event of the Queen's death the persone chosen in England to succeed her should not succeed to the Crown of Scotland, unless certain conditions should be granted by the English to the Scots, such as a free communication of Trade, and the Liberty of the Plantations, etc.

*   *   *   *   *   *

This session of Parliament met on the 6 of July 1704, the Marquise of Twedale being her Majesty's High Commissioner. He, it seems, had undertaken great things, and particularly to get the succession to the Crown of Scotland setled on the House of Hanover, with an oath of abjuration enacted against the Pretender, the son of the late King James the 7th, who had taken upon him the stile and tittle of King of Great Britain, or if these projects cou'd not succeed in parliament, he was at least to please those Members of the last session of parliament who had carried on the above mentioned Act of Security.

By these projects, the Duke of Queensberry and his Friends were laid aside, for as the Hannoverian interest prevail'd greatly in the Court at London, there was a necessity to give them all manner of satisfaction who pushed for the immediat settlement of the aforesaid succession.

The Queen her self, and some few about her, particularly her prime ministers, the Earl of Godolphin and the Duke of Marlebrugh, were far from approving of the sd measure, for tho they saw that there was no real security for the Revolution or Whig interest without such a settlement, yet they wanted to have it done by means of an Union of the two Kingdoms.

In the progress of the session of parliament a trial was made to settle the above mentioned succession with a great many limitations on the Crown, such as that no Officers of State should be created without consent of parliament, and, in a word, that all powers of any consequence should be taken out of the hands of the sovereign, according to what had been done in the last session of parliament in relation to peace and war.

These projects cou'd not take effect, so that the Act of Security formerly concerted and agreed to was passed, and had the Royal Assent.

* * * * * *

But to return to the affaires before the Parliament of Scotland, the chief business was to pave the way for the Treaty of Union. An Act for this purpose was concerted with great difficulty, for the main opposition was not only from the Jacobites, but from a party of Whigs of about 16 in number, who had for their chiefs the Dukes of Montrose and Roxbrugh and the Marquise of Twedale. These, as before mentioned, went under the name of the Squadrone Volante, their business being sometimes to joyn the Court party, sometimes the Jacobite party, as was most for their Interest. The Duke of Hamiltone was the head of the Jacobites, and, indeed, a man every way fitted to be the Head of a popular discontented party. He was a man of courage, and had a great deal of natural Eloquence, with much affability in his temper.

The reasonings on the Act for the above Treaty turn'd chiefly on Limitations and conditions to be put on the Commissioners, but the chief opposition proceeded from this, that both those of the Squadrone Volante and of the Jacobite party knew that when the States of Parliament came to choose their Commissioners all of them wou'd be excluded; however, at last, to put an end to Disputes, it was agreed that the nomination of these Commissioners should be left to the Queen. This was a proposal of the Duke of Hamiltone, who from that piece of independence expected the Honour of being appointed by the Queen, but in this he was disappointed, for the Ministry in England and Scotland found, by former miscarriages in Treaties of Union, no good cou'd be expected from Commissioners who were not sincerely disposed to drop minute things for the sake of attaining what was principally in view, the good of both nations, and the settlement of the Succession to the Crown in the Protestant Line, in the mean- time. I knew that this Duke was so unlucky in his privat circumstances that he wou'd have complied with any thing on a suitable encouragement. He was not only descended of the

Royal Family of the Stuarts, but under particular obligations to the Royal Brothers, King Charles and King James, however, he cou'd easily have been convinced that since the succession to the Crown of England had been for several years past, to wit, in the Regn of the late King William, setled on the Family of Hannover, it wou'd be next to madness to imagine that the Scots cou'd set up a seperat King, or force any King on England but the persone already chosen by that nation.

The nomination being left to the Queen to name Commissioners, she submitted this entirely to her Ministry, particularly to the Earl of Godolphin, her prime Minister, and to the Dukes of Queensberry and Argyle.

I hapned, therfor, to be one of those appointed by these noble Dukes, tho' at that time very young for so great a Trust. What moved them chiefly in my favours was the pains I had taken in the Commissions for examining the publick accompts, by which I had a thorough acquaintance with all the Finances of Scotland, and the whole management of the Lords of the Treasury and Exchequer of this Country, from the Revolution in 1688 down to the year 1706.

This choise, however honourable to me, was very far from giving me the least pleasure or satisfaction, for I had observed a great backwardness in the Parliament of Scotland for an union with England of any kind whatsoever, and therefor doubted not but, after a great deal of expense in attending a Treaty in England, I should be oblidged to return with the uneasy reflexion of having either done nothing, or nothing to the purpose, as had been the case of former Commissioners appointed for this end. I was, in short, upon the point of refusing the Honour conferred upon me, and the rather that my Father, whom I always considered as an Oracle seldom mistaken, seemed not to approve of it. However, as at last he grew passive, and that the Duke of Queensberry threatned to withdraw all friendship for me, I suffered my self to be prevailed upon, and to take journey for London with other Commissioners, and arrived there on the 13 of Aprile 1706.

I judge it needless for me here to narrate what was transacted by the Commissioners for both nations, every thing having been already published by the authority of the Parliaments of Scotland and England; however, I shall take notice of a few things relating to this great Transaction.

The Commissioners of both nations met in different apartments in the Royal palace of Westminster, which commonly goes under the name of the Cockpit. There was one great Room where they all met when they were called upon to attend the Queen, or were to exchange papers, but they never met to hold conferences together except once, when the number of the Scotch Representatives for the two Houses of the British Parliament came to be debated, all their transactions were reduced in writings concerted in seperat apartments. When proposals or Conditions of the union were to be made by the English Commissioners, the Scots were desired to meet them in the great Room, and their proposals were given in by the Lᵈ Chancellor, or the Keeper of the great seal, who was at that time the Lord Cooper, and when the Commissioners for Scotland had any thing to propose, or had answers to be made to the Commissioners of England, these were presented by the Lᵈ Seafield, then Chancellor for Scotland.

Sometimes the Scots Commissioners met at the Houses of the Secretaries of State for Scotland, who were then the Earls of Mar and Loudon, the first a most famous Man at the head of the Rebellion in Scotland in the year 1715. He was then very forward for the union and the settlement of his succession in the Protestant family of Hannover, but towards the end of Queen's Ann's Reign, in 1713, was as forward for the dissolution of the union, and being on that account and other reasons hated by King George the first, he turn'd Jacobite and Rebel, after he had taken the usual oaths to the Government and used all the subterfuges and subtilities of a Courtier to ingratiat himself with the Hannoverian Ministry in 1714.

The first grand point debated by the Commissioners for Scotland amongst themselves was whether they should propose to the English a Federal union between the two nations, or an Incorporating union. The first was most favoured by the people of Scotland, but all the Scots Commissioners, to a Man, considered it rediculous and impracticable, for that in all the Federal unions there behoved to be a supreme power lodged some where, and wherever this was lodged it hencefurth became the States General, or, in our way of speaking, the Parliament of Great Britain, under the same royal power and authority as the two nations are at present. And in things of the greatest consequence to the two nations, as in Councils relating to peace and war and subsidies, it was impossible that the Representatives or their suffrages in both nations cou'd be equal, but must be regulated in proportion to the power and richess of the several publick burdens or Taxations that cou'd affect them; in a word, the Scots Commissioners saw that no Union cou'd subsist between the two nations but an incorporating perpetual one. But after all the truble we gave ourselves to please the people of Scotland, we knew at the time that it was but losing our labour, for the English Commissioners were positively resolved to treat on no kind of union with us but what was to be incorporating and perpetual.

In the great Room above mentioned, was a long table, sufficient to hold all the Commissioners for both kingdoms, being about 50 feet in length. At the head of the Table, under a Canopy, was placed a large chaire, ornamented with gold lace and crimsone velvet, for the Queen, when she desired to come amongst us. On her left hand sat the Chancellor of Scotland, and on her right hand the keeper of the great seal, the Ld Cooper, afterwards Chancellor of England.

The Queen came amongst us three several times, once at our first or second meeting, to acquaint us of her intentions and ardent good wishes for our success and unanimity in this great Transaction. At about a month thereafter she came again to enquire of our success, and had most of our Minutes read to her; and for the last time to approve of what we had done. I endeavoured in all my conduct at this Treaty to acquit my self with the outmost duty to my Country, and for this end gave the greatest application possible to understand all the parts of the English Constitution, and particularly what related to their Debts and publick Taxes, to their Trade and all their Finances, comparing them with these of the people of Scotland, with which I was well acquainted, as having been for two full years a Commissioner of the public accompts in Scotland as above.

On these accounts, I was chosen by the Commissioners of Scotland for the Union to be one of four who were to conferr dayly with the like number of the English Commissioners in relation to the papers given in by both sides which were to be entered into our Minutes, for some of these papers needed some explications and alterations in order to be entered into these minutes agreeable to the sense of the respective Commissioners. I was likeways intrusted with another province by the Commissioners for Scotland, which was to review the Calculations made for the equivalent to be paid to Scotland for bearing their share of the Debt of England, which were afterwards to be considered as the Debts of Great Britain. These calculations were chiefly made by Doctor Gregory, professor of Mathematicks in the College of Oxford, and a certain great accomptant and projector, one Patersone, from Scotland, but bred in England from his infancy.

All this time I neglected not to cultivat that Friendship with the Duke of Queensberry, my Patron, which he had always shown me. I was frequently at Kensington with him, where the Queen keept her Court, and I twice saw her in her closet, to which the Duke was always admitted, being nominated Commissioner by her Majesty for representing her in the inseuing parliament of Scotland.

One day I had occasion to observe the Calamities which attend humane nature even in the greatest dignities of Life. Her majesty was labouring under a fit of the Gout, and in extream pain and agony, and on this occasion every thing about her was much in the same disorder as about the meanest of her subjects. Her face, which was red and spotted, was rendered something frightful by her negligent dress, and the foot affected was tied up with a pultis and some nasty bandages. I was much affected at this sight, and the more *when she had occasion to mention her people of Scotland,* which she did frequently to the Duke. What are you, poor mean like Mortal, thought I, who talks in the style of a Soveraign? Nature seems to be inverted when a poor infirm Woman becomes one of the Rulers of the World, but, as Tacitus observes, it is not the first time that Women have governed in Britain, and indeed they have sometimes done this to better purpose than the Men.

But to return to the Treaty of Union, the Articles were at last agreed to, sign'd, and sealed, by all the Commissioners, the 22 of July 1706. They were afterwards presented to the Queen at her palace of St. James, before a very numerous Assembley. The Lord Keeper of the Great Seal of England presented his copy to her Majesty, after making a handsome speech. That on the part of the Scots was presented by our Chancellor, Lord Seafield, whose speech excelled the other so far that it was spoken without Hesitation, whereas that of the Ld Keeper was miserably mangled in the delivery, and at last he was forced to draw it out of his pocket and read it. However, as he was a very eloquent man and a great Lawer, he was so conscious of his own merit that he never changed colloures at his accident, but first stopt a little, and then read his speech from a paper with great composure of mind, while all the Audience was in the outmost pain for him.

To these Speeches, and the Commissioners on both sides ranged on the Queen's right and left hand, her Majesty made a very handsome Return, with a very graceful pronountiation and tone of voice. After this great Transaction was brought to a conclusion the Commissioners on both sides left the Court, and I, with some of my country men, returned to Scotland. But before I left London I was advised to take my leave of the Queen which I did at Kensington. I was introduced to her by the Earl of Loudon, one of our Secretaries of State. She received me in her closet in the same homely way as before, for she had again fallen ill of the Gout. She spoke to me with great complacency, wished me a good journey, and in several warm expressions desired I might make it my business to recommend the Union to her people of Scotland.

I came down the Western Road and found my Father at Moffat. Here we had some Game on the moors for a few days, and at length I came to Edinburgh.

For the moneths of Septemb^r and October I staid for the most part with my Father at Pennicuik, always poring on Books, except sometimes when I followed my diversions of fouling and fishing.

The Duke of Queensberry having been appointed her

Majesty's Commissioner for the ensuing Parliament, he arrived in Scotland in November.

I need not narrate here what was done in this Parliament, there being a very exact History published of it by one Daniel Defoe, who was sent to Scotland by the prime minister of England, the Earl of Godolphin, on purpose to give a faithful account to him from time to time how every thing past here. He was therefor a Spy amongst us, but not known to be such, otherways the Mob of Edin. had pulled him to pieces.

The Commissioners, on their return to Scotland, fancied to themselves that as they had been doing great service to their Country in the matter of the Union, so they wou'd be acceptable to all ranks and degrees of people, but after the Articles of the Union were published by order of Parliament, such comments were made upon them, by those of the adverse party, that the Mob was almost universally set against them.

Under these hardships and misrepresentations the Articles of the Union were introduced into the Parliament of Scotland. The bulk of the nation seem'd altogether averse to them, nor indeed cou'd they expect a better usage, considering who they were who were determined at any rate to oppose them, for first there were a great many disoblidged Courtiers and self-conceited Men who cou'd relish nothing but what was of their own contrivance.

Next were a vast many of the Episcopal persuasion, who hated the Union meerly because of a first intention which many of the members of Parliament had of making the presbeterian Government and its security the basis of any Union between the two Nations, for tho there was no express Article concerted by the Commissioners of the Treaty to this effect, yet it had been commen'd upon, and agreed as the only Expedient to bring over the ministers of the church of Scotland, to give the Articles of the Union so much as a hearing; and, indeed, this was all they cou'd procure at first, for as the security of the church of England was to follow of consequence, many of the clergy of Scotland grew jealous of their neighbouring clergy, and endeavoured to instill notions in their Breatheren that such a security given to the church of England was contrary to the principles of their forefathers, who had strenuously supported the Solemn League and Covenant.

Another set of Enemies to the Union were the Jacobites, and as these were very numerous even in the Parliament of Scotland, they cou'd not think of imbracing a system for the union of the two kingdoms wherein the succession to the Crown was to be settled on the House of Hannover, to the perpetual exclusion of all the successors of the late King James.

I do believe that the generality of the members of the Parliament of Scotland had been of the same mind, if it had consisted with reasone to delay the settlement of the succession of Scotland on the same family on whom the English, before the death of the late King William, had settled their crown, for to all thinking Men it appeared evident that sooner or later the Scots behoved to come into the same succession, or expect to see their Country a schen of bloodshed and confusion, for it was impossible for the Scots to make choise of a different king from the persone who was to succeed to the Crown of England, but this I need not truble my self to explain here.

From the above mentioned differences amongst the several parties in Scotland nothing was left to the Commissioners of the Union and to the Ministry of Scotland, than firmly to resolve amongst themselves how to act and leave the event to the providence of God.

Honour, Honesty, and a firm persuasion that they had been acting a faithful part for the interest of their Country, left no room to doubt what they were to do, and therefor they resolved to adhere to the Transaction they had made with the Commissioners of England, and leave it to Members of Parliament to act such a part as they thought best for the interest of their Country.

With these Resolutions the Duke of Queensberry proceeded, and 'tho some additions were made to the Articles of Union, particularly what related to the Settlement of the Presbyterian Government, yet after much debate and opposition these Articles were approven of that seem'd to be best understood, others suffered some alterations, particularly that which related to the Excise, but in my opinion few or no alterations were made to the better.

I had discharged my duty in London, and so became entirely passive as to what should happen in the Parliament of Scotland; however, to vindicat the proceedings of the Commissioners as to things not well understood in Scotland, I wrote two pamphlets. One went under the Title of Some considerations on the Articles of the Union.

The other was for explaining the 15 Article in relation to the Equivalents to be paid to Scotland on account of subjecting ourselves to the payment of the debts of England [p. 238, below].

These pieces were known to be mine, but procured me no hatred from the other side who opposed the Union, and I had the thanks of those who were wellwishers to it.

Before the parliament ended I was chosen one of the 45 Members who were to represent Scotland in the first parliament of Great Britain. I had no hand in the honour conferred upon me, but the Duke of Queensberry insisted that I should be one on the List of those who were appointed, and as an incitement to me he offered me a place in one of his coaches to London, which I accepted of, and set out with his Grace on the 2d of Aprile 1707.

A very splendid Retinue accompanied his Grace to Dunbar, but except my self, and a few of his own family in two coaches, he allowed no body the favour of waiting on him to Berwick. I wished that the case had been otherways, for then his country men wou'd have been Witnesses to a quite different Reception which his Grace had in all the Towns of England situated on or near the Road to London than what he had in Scotland.

In Berwick he was received with great pomp and solemnity, as he was likeways at Newcastle, Durham, and other cities, for amidst the joyful acclamations of all the people he was received by all the Magistrates of the cities where he past, and by all the nobility and gentry of the several counties, with the same if not greater Honours than I believe had been paid to the Queen her self.

He was complimented and feasted wherever he went, and when he came within 20 miles of London the whole city turn'd out to meet him.

At Hartfoord his Grace was attended by above twenty Members of the parliament of Scotland, who had taken post before him on purpose to make their Court to the Queen and the Ministry of England, but Her Majesty refused to see or hear any body, 'till the arrival of his Grace. At Barnet he was met by the Ministry of England and most of the nobility then attending the two Houses of Parliament. Their Retinue consisted of 46 coaches and above 1000 Horsemen.

When the Duke arrived at his House in London, the Lord High Treasurer Godolphin, at the head of all the Queen's Ministry, waited upon him, and that same night he waited on her Majesty, by whom he was received with high acknowledgements of his great services.

I staid with the Duke in London about 2 months, in which time the Commissions for managing the Equivalent appointed by the 15 Article of the Treaty of Union, with the Commissions for managing the Customs and Excise in Scotland were concerted. I might have been a Commissioner in any of the two last, but the Affaire of the Equivalent requiring persons of known fidelity, I was in some measure compelled to accept of it, not without a positive promise from the Duke that I should be afterwards better provided for.

On the 1 of May 1707 the Union of the two Nations, as had been agreed to, took place. That day was solemnized by her Majesty and those who had been members of both Houses of Parliament with the greatest splendour. A very numerous procession accompanied the Queen to the Cathedral church of St. Paul, at least 3 or 400 coaches. The Bishops and Peers sat in Galleries on her Majesty's right hand, and the late members of the House of Commons of England, with such as had been chosen to represent the Commons of Scotland in the first British Parliament, were on her left hand. I think there were not above half a dussan of the Scots commoners then in London, and amongst these I had the happiness to be present at this solemn piece of Devotion.

A sermon was preached by the Bishope of London, and prayers of Thanksgiving were very heartily put up for the success of the Union, at least no body on this occasion appeared more sincerely devout and thankfull than the Queen her self. A fine piece of Musick closed the solemnity, and we return'd back to the Court at St. James's palace in the same order we came to the Cathedral.

On this occasion I observed a real joy and satisfaction in the Citizens of London, for they were terribly apprehensive of confusions from Scotland in case the Union had not taken place.

That whole day was spent in feastings, ringing of Bells, and illuminations, and I have reasone to believe that at no time Scotsmen were more acceptable to the English than on that day.

About the end of May I returned back to Scotland. Some time after this the equivalent stipulated to Scotland by the above mentioned 15 Article of the Union was sent down, viz. 398085 ℔. 10 sh. ster. 100,000 lib. str. came in specie, and the rest in Exchequer Bills, which was lodged in the Castle of Edin.

The Commissioners appointed for manadging the same, according to the 15 and 16 Acts of the last session of the Parliament of Scotland, immediately began to make the proper distributions, and particularly to refound the capital stock of the Indian and African Company in Scotland, the rest of the publick debts of Scotland succeeded, so that in a few months most of the Equivalent money was disposed of.

The first Parliament of Great Britain was appointed by her Majesty to meet at Westminster in —— —— thereafter. Thither all those who had been chosen to represent Scotland repaired, and I amongst the rest should have gone, but was oblidged to attend at Edin. for 2 months longer, to exchange above 100,000 ℔. in Exchequer Bills, which had fallen into a discount of 5 pr. cent. 3 other gentlemen were detained with me for the same purpose, being appointed by the Directors of the Bank of England to take in these Exchequer Bills and draw Bills on the sd Bank payable at sight.

This was an affaire of great trust, however it was manadged with the success that was necessary for the credite of the Bank. I carried up the retired notes with me to London in february 1708, and received the thanks of the Directors of the Bank.

I went up post, but near Anwick, the way being covered

with ice and snow, my Horse fell with me, by which I unfortunately brok my collar bone, however I recovered in a few days so as to be able to travel in a Coach, and got to London with much pain in two weeks.

I attended the House of Commons till the close of the session of Parliament in May, and observed with pleasure the Happy union that appeared between the Scotch and English members of parliament in both houses, happy presage of what I expected from the Union.

II. *Lockhart Papers*

Now we come to narrate what was done in relation to the Act of Treaty. The Earl of Mar, in the beginning of this session, had presented the draught of an Act, for appointing commissioners to treat with the commissioners from England, upon an union of the two kingdoms of Scotland and England, which lay upon the table till most of the overtures in relation to trade and the limitations were discussed; but these being now over, was reassumed. Both it and the English Act were much of the same nature, both empowering commissioners to meet and treat with one another of an union of the two kingdoms, and restricting them from treating of any alterations of the church-government and discipline, as established by law in the respective realms; only, as I said before, the English Act gave the nomination of their commissioners to the Queen, and even required the same of the Scots, without which they discharged their commissioners to meet and treat. But the draught presented by the Earl of Mar left the power of the nomination blank, and we shall see afterwards how that affair was managed. Mr. Fletcher of Salton, in a pathetick discourse, represented the scurrilous and haughty procedure of the English in this affair, and exhorted them to resent this treatment, as became Scotsmen, by throwing the motion of a treaty, until it were proposed in more civil and equal terms, out of the House, with indignation. But the House, rejecting the motion, called for the draught and the English Act, and both were read. The Cavaliers and Country parties, observing that there was a great inclination in the House to set a treaty on foot, thought it improper to oppose it any longer in general terms: and therefore resolved to endeavour to clog the commission with such restrictions and provisions as should retard the treaty's taking effect; and for that end the Duke of Hamilton presented a clause to be added to the Act, in these terms: viz. "That the Union to be treated on should no ways "derogate from any fundamental laws, ancient privileges, "offices, rights, liberties, and dignities of this nation." This the Court vigorously opposed, seeing it secluded them from treating on an entire or incorporating Union; of which the abolishing of our Parliaments, and subversion of our Constitution, was a necessary consequence. And it was this kind of union England designed and desired; because it rivetted the Scots in perpetual slavery, depriving them of any legal method to redress themselves of the injuries they might receive from them, by keeping them poor and under their chains. On the other hand, the Duke of Queensberry, Earl of Stair, and all that were thoroughly on a Revolution foot, were inclined the same way, because they were conscious of their own guilt, and afraid, some time or other, a Scots Parliament (if reserved even under a federal Union) might take them to task, and punish them as they deserv'd; whereas if it were out of their power, and the Scots representation stifled and suppressed by the much greater majority of the English representation in one and the same Parliament, they expected to be protected against the just resentments of an injured and exasperated nation. For these and such reasons, I say, the Court opposed this clause, and the arguments they adduced for rejecting it were to this purpose: That since Scotland and England were under the same sovereign, who did here mediate betwixt her two kingdoms, and that England had given ample powers to their commissioners, it would be unbecoming in Scotland to restrict their commissioners, and inferred a jealousy of Her Majesty: that it might occasion a stop to the treaty, since it was to be believed that England would expect our commissioners should meet and confer with as full powers as theirs: and lastly, There could be no hazard in not restricting our commissioners, since it was expressly provided, that no matter or point treated of, and agreed to, should take place, and be of force, unless it be first reported to, and obtain the apbrobation of, the Parliaments of both kingdoms; and that when this report was made, then was the proper time to consider whether they would agree to that scheme of Union which the commissioners had projected, or reject it. To this it was answer'd, That Scotland and England's being under one sovereign was the reason why this clause was necessary, since woful experience taught us, and it had been often complained of in this house, that our sovereign was under English influence, and subject to the councils of her English ministers, who regarded the interest and honour of Scotland no farther than was consistent with that of England; that the adding of this clause could never infer the least mistrust of the Queen's inclinations towards her ancient kingdom, since all that could be made of it was, that the Scots Parliament, being sensible that the Queen was not in a capacity to know the interest and circumstances of Scotland so well as that of England, had taken care to prevent any inconveniencies that might arise from thence: that there were some things so sacred, that the least innovation or alteration, far less abrogating or suspending of them, was never to be tampered with, or the subject of any treaty; and the particulars of this clause, such as the sovereignty, independency, and freedom of the nation, being of this nature, ought to be added: and that England could not take it amiss, seeing they themselves had, before they advised with us, restricted their own commissioners from treating on any alteration of the church government of that kingdom. But whether that had been or not, we were a free, independent people, and had a power to give what instructions, powers, and restrictions we pleased to our commissioners; neither was it to be imagin'd, that England, upon the account of this clause, would refuse to treat, because the very same clause, in the same express words, was inserted in the Act of Treaty, in the reign of King James VI. and to the same purpose in most of the subsequent Acts of Treaty; and yet neither that King (who would have had good reason to be offended at any disrespect or distrust shown toward him, who was known by the Scots, acquainted with their humours and constitutions, and had given signal proofs of his affection to his native country and subjects) nor his successors, nor the Parliament of England, made any scruple upon that account, to meet and treat with the commissioners of Scotland. These and many other arguments were adduced for and against this clause; and the question being put, "Add the clause or not," it carried in the negative by a plurality of two voices. And here I must observe and lament the woful fate of this nation; for though it was well known that the House was to be that day upon this grand affair, and the Court had mustered together every individual of their party; yet seven or eight of the Cavaliers and Country parties were absent, and thereby lost this clause, which, had it passed, would have proved a mortal stroke to the Court, they being resolved to have laid aside the Treaty of Union, and prorogued the Parliament; by which means the nation had been free of that fatal thraldom to which 'tis since subjected. Nor must I omit that the Earl of Aberdeen turned tail to the Cavaliers in this important affair: 'Tis not easy for me to determine the cause; but 'tis matter of fact, that His Lordship did not behave, on many occasions during this session, as might have been expected from one of his principles and circumstances, and (though this is not the proper place) could not be perswaded to be present at, and assisting against, the Union in the next sessions; nay, the Cavaliers at last, being informed of his inclinations towards it, were glad to compound with him to stay away.

This being over, another clause was presented in these terms: "Provided always, that the said commissioners shall "not go forth of this kingdom, to enter into any treaty with "those to be appointed for England, until there be an Act "passed by the Parliament of England, rescinding that clause "in the English Act, by which it is enacted, That the sub- "jects of Scotland shall be adjudged and taken as aliens after "the twenty-fifth of December 1705." The Cavaliers enlarged upon this clause, as necessary to vindicate the honour of the nation from the injustice of the English in that Act; believing, if it were added, the English would not comply with it, and so the treaty come to nothing. The Courtiers, upon the same grounds, opposed it; but observing it took with the House, they did not presume to do it openly, but by a consequential motion to this purpose: That the clause should be approven, though not, as was proposed, be engrossed into the body of the Act for a treaty, but a resolve of the House pass, that after the foresaid Act is finished, the House will immediately proceed to consider whether the clause should be by a particular Act, or by an order of the House; and the question being stated, "Add the clause to the Act, or by a "separate way;" the latter branch carry'd it. And now the Court thought themselves secure of having a treaty; for if the clause was turned into an Act at the close of the session, (when they had no more to require of the Parliament at this time) they might grant the Royal assent to the Act of Treaty, and refuse it to this, as they should be directed from England: and in case the clause was turned into an order of the House, then they might dissolve the Parliament, (their lawyers assuring them that no orders of a Parliament were valid and in force after its dissolution) by which means the Act impowering commissioners to treat remained, and the order ceased, and so the Treaty might go on, whether the Parliament of England did or did not repeal the Act, which was so unjust in relation to Scotland, and notwithstanding the Parliament of Scotland did so expressly require it. But before the vote was stated upon the Act for a treaty, the Duke of Athol entered his protestation in these terms: "In regard that by an English "Act of Parliament, made in the last sessions thereof, en- "tituled An Act for the effectual securing England from the "dangers that may arise from several Acts past lately in Scot- "land, the subjects of this kingdom are adjudged aliens, born "out of the allegiance of the Queen, as Queen of England, "after the twenty-fifth day of December 1705, I do therefore "protest for my self, and in the name and behalf of all such "as shall adhere to this my protestation, that, for saving the "honour and interest of Her Majesty, as Queen of this King- "dom, and maintaining and preserving the undoubted rights "and privileges of her subjects, no Act for a treaty with "England ought to pass in this House, unless a clause be ad- "jected thereto, prohibiting and discharging the commissioners "that may be nominated and appointed for carrying on the "said treaty, to depart the kingdom in order thereto, until "the said Act be repealed and rescinded in the Parliament of "England." To which most of the Cavalier and Country parties, and all the Squadrone, (these last, as I observed before, being inclined to go along with every motion that they thought would obstruct the Treaty's taking effect at that time) did adhere, making in all twenty-four Peers, thirty-seven Barons, and eighteen Burrows.

While the rolls were calling upon this vote, (it being by this time late, and having been a long *sederunt*) many of the members, after they had given their votes, went out of the House, expecting the Parliament would not have proceeded to any more business that night; when, instantly after the last name in the roll was called, the Duke of Hamilton, addressing himself to the Chancellor, moved, that the nomination of the commissioners for the treaty should be left wholly to the Queen.

This, you may be sure, was very surprizing to the Cavaliers and Country party; 'twas what they did not expect would have been moved that night, and never at any time from His Grace, who had, from the beginning of the Parliament to this day, roared and exclaimed against it on all occasions; and about twelve or fifteen of them ran out of the house in rage and despair, saying aloud 'twas to no purpose to stay any longer, since the Duke of Hamilton had deserted and so basely betray'd them. However, those that remained opposed it with all their might, and a hot debate arose upon it, wherein the Cavaliers used the very arguments that the Duke of Hamilton had often insisted on upon this and the like occasions. "What! leave "the nomination to the Queen! No; she is, in a manner, a "prisoner in England; and the Estates of Scotland had taught "us our duty in a case nearly related to this, during the captivity "of King James I. Our Queen knew none of us, but as intro-"duced by her English ministry, and recommended by our "inclinations to serve that kingdom. Our Queen never had an "opportunity to know the true interest of our country; and "though she did, yet, as she was circumstantiated, could not "show her regard for it; and who then so proper to nominate "Scots commissioners to treat on Scots affairs, as a Scots Parlia-"ment?" The Court, and the Duke of Hamilton, (though he well enough saw these and many other speeches and motions, such as, that no person that had any estate in England should be of the number of the commissioners, were levelled at him) made few or no answers to the arguments against the motion; but insisting that the sense of the House might be known upon it, a vote was stated at last in these terms: "Leave the nomina-"tion of the commissioners to the Queen, or to the Parliament:" And the former, by the unfortunate and unseasonable absence of the abovementioned twelve or fifteen members, did carry by a plurality of eight voices, of which His Grace the Duke of Hamilton had the honour to be one. Immediately after this was over, the whole Act impowering commissioners to meet and treat with England was voted and approven, the Duke of Athol having protested against it, in respect of the reasons contained in his former protestation, and being adhered to by twenty-one Noblemen, thirty-three Barons, and eighteen Burrows.

From this day may we date the commencement of Scotland's ruine; and any person that will be at the pains to reflect upon the management of this affair must be the more enraged, when he sees how easily it might have been, and yet was not prevented; for, if the first restricting clause (which was lost by the unaccountable neglect of some members) had been carried, we should not have had one word more of the Treaty; or had the nomination been left to the Parliament, (which was lost by the unreasonable humours of such members as left the house in a hurry) those of the commissioners that represented the Barons would have been so well chosen, that they might easily have obstructed the Treaty's being brought to such a conclusion as afterwards happened. For I may affirm, (it consisting with my certain knowledge) that the English, knowing the backwardness of the Scots nation to enter into an incorporating Union, would, if there had been but two or three members in the Scots commission that opposed it, been so far from pushing it as they did, that the treaty would have been advanced no further than those others that had been set on foot formerly.

But to consider the Duke of Hamilton's part in this affair a little more particularly: 'Tis true, some reports had been whisper'd about, from the beginning of the Parliament, that

His Grace's behaviour in this point would prove as it did, and many were uneasy at the great familiarity that appeared betwixt him and the Earl of Mar; but yet all were unwilling to believe any thing that was amiss of one who had stood so firm, and done such service to his country, especially in this point, whereupon he had so frequently, nay, not many days before it fell out, expressed and declared his opinion and resolution. But the following particular will make his conduct the more unaccountable: That very morning on which this affair was concluded, about forty or fifty of the Cavaliers being met together, had under consideration, whether it would be most proper to chuse the commissioners in a full House, or that every Estate should separate and chuse such as should represent themselves; and inclined to prefer the last, because they were sure to carry what Barons they pleased, but might run the hazard of losing all the other way. Yet such was their confidence in, and deference to, the Duke, that before they would determine themselves positively in it, they dispatched the Earl of Strathmore, George Lockhart of Carnwath, and George Home of Whitfield, to acquaint His Grace of what had passed amongst them, and desire his opinion: but His Grace being abroad when they came to wait upon him, the message was not communicated to him, till just as the Parliament sat down. Mr. Lockhart meeting him accidentally in the outer house, delivered his commission; to which he gave this answer: "Tell these gentlemen, 'twill be time enough for "us to consider on that affair; for it shall not be in this day." I never yet could hear of any reasonable excuse he made for this his behaviour. 'Tis true indeed, he endeavoured to vindicate himself, by alledging, that after the Parliament had rejected the several clauses that were proposed to be added to the Act, he thought it to no purpose to strive any longer; for since the Court would have had a majority to give the nomination to the Queen, he might be allowed to give her the compliment. And next, that he thought it better; because, if the commissioners that were named by the Queen did what was not approven of in the subsequent Parliament, we might better and more severely take them to task, than if we had named them ourselves. But, with His Grace's permission, this will not stand the test; for, to consider the last part of the argument first, it cannot be admitted, that the leaving the nomination to the Queen was preferable to the Parliament's having it; because it was obvious and plain, that if the Queen had the nomination, she would take care to pitch upon such as would be very pliable, and do what was desired of them: and since it was as plain, that there was too great an inclination in the House to have a Treaty, and accept of an Union, there was the greater need to have some well-chosen persons upon it, that would be an awe-band over others, and represent matters fairly and fully, both at the Treaty, and in the subsequent Parliament; and next, His Grace had no reason to imagine that the Court was able to carry it to the Queen. For he knew that the absence of some of the Cavaliers was the only reason of losing the restricting clause, and that there were several others that voted all along with the Court formerly, would have left them upon this occasion; and consequently, if those members I spoke of had not deserted the House, the Cavaliers, instead of the Court, had carried the vote by eight voices; and then he might have been sure of having had all the Barons, such as were his friends, and would have been faithful and useful to the country. But I am afraid the true matter was, His Grace had a great mind to be one of the treaters himself; and, foreseeing he would not be named by the Parliament, he resolved to rely upon the Commissioner's and the Earl of Mar's promise, of his being named by the Queen, and therefore (whether by capitulation with these noble Lords, or merely a thought of his own, the better to recommend him to the Queen on this occasion, I shall not determine) took upon him to make the motion, that it might appear he had indeed made the compliment, and been the promoter and advancer of leaving the nomination to the Queen. And to confirm what I advance, let us remember, that we never heard of any other reason for the Duke of Argyle's not being named upon the Treaty, than his having represented to the Queen, that he had engaged upon his honour to bring the Duke of Hamilton to be upon the Treaty, or else that he would not be concerned in it himself: And the Queen refusing to name the Duke of Hamilton as he had promised, he resented it so far, that he would not suffer himself to be named, and even threaten'd, at that time, to oppose the Union upon that account, though ways and means were fallen upon afterwards, to induce him to alter his mind. But to return back to His Grace's defences: Let us suppose them to be good; yet I would fain ask, whence he got that new light, and that so suddenly? and why did he not communicate the same to his friends, that, if they had been of the same mind, all might have gone on that way, and the compliment to the Queen been the greater? Little did he consider their differing this time encouraged the Court, and occasioned a thousand false reports, which did a great deal of harm, and, which was worst of all, was the foundation of that jealousy that, in some measure contributed much to the bad success that attended the country's affairs afterwards. I have dwelt the longer upon this subject, because, as I said before, this fatal Act was the first successful step towards Scotland's chains; and all I shall add concerning it, is an old Scots proverb, "That sitting betwixt two chairs often occasions a fall;" which was the Duke of Hamilton's case at this time.

III. *Treaty of Union.* (*Extracts*)

...MOST GRACIOUS SOVEREIGN, Whereas Articles of Union were agreed on the twenty-second day of July, in the fifth year of your Majesties reign, by the Commissioners nominated on behalf of the kingdom of England, under your Majesties Great Seal of England, bearing date at Westminster the tenth day of April then last past, in pursuance of an Act of Parliament made in England, in the third year of your Majesties reign; and the Commissioners nominated on the behalf of the kingdom of Scotland, under your Majesties Great Seal of Scotland, bearing date the twenty-seventh day of February, in the fourth year of your Majesties reign, in pursuance of the fourth Act of the third session of the present Parliament of Scotland, to treat of and concerning an Union of the said kingdoms: and whereas an Act hath passed in the Parliament of Scotland, at Edinburgh, the sixteenth day of January, in the fifth year of your Majesties reign, wherein 'tis mentioned, that the Eſtates of Parliament, conſidering the ſaid Articles of Union of the two kingdoms, had agreed to and approved of the ſaid Articles of Union, with ſome additions and explanations; and that your Majeſty, with advice and conſent of the Eſtates of Parliament, for eſtabliſhing the Proteſtant Religion, and Preſbyterian Church Government within the kingdom of Scotland, had paſſed in the ſame Seſſion of Parliament, an Act, intituled, "Act for ſecuring of the "Proteſtant Religion and Preſbyterian Church Government," which, by the tenor thereof, was appointed to be inſerted in an Act ratifying the Treaty, and expreſly declared to be a fundamental and eſſential condition of the ſaid Treaty or Union in all times coming, the tenor of which Articles, as ratified and approved of, with additions and explanations, by the ſaid Act of Parliament of Scotland, follows:

Article 1. That the two kingdoms of England and Scotland ſhall, upon the firſt day of May, which ſhall be in the year one thouſand ſeven hundred and ſeven, and for ever after, be united into one kingdom, by the name of GREAT-BRITAIN; and that the Enſigns Armorial of the ſaid United Kingdom be ſuch as her Majeſty ſhall appoint, and the Croſſes of St. George and St. Andrew be conjoined in ſuch manner as her Majeſty ſhall think fit, and uſed in all flaggs, banners, ſtandards, and enſigns, both at ſea and land.

Article 2. That the ſucceſſion to the Monarchy of the United Kingdom of Great Britain, and of the dominions thereto belonging, after her moſt ſacred Majeſty, and in default of iſſue of her Majeſty, be, remain, and continue, to the moſt excellent Princeſs Sophia, Electoreſs and Dutcheſs Dowager of Hanover, and the heirs of her body, being Proteſtants, upon whom the Crown of England is ſettled by an act of Parliament made in England, in the twelfth year of the reign of his late Majeſty King William the Third, intituled, "An act for the further limitation of the Crown, and better "ſecuring the rights and liberties of the ſubject:" and that all Papiſts, and perſons marrying Papiſts, ſhall be excluded from, and for ever incapable to inherit, poſſeſs, or enjoy the Imperial Crown of Great Britain, and the dominions thereunto belonging, or any part thereof; and, in every ſuch caſe, the

Crown and Government ſhall, from time to time, deſcend to, and be enjoyed by ſuch perſon, being a Proteſtant, as ſhould have inherited and enjoyed the ſame, in caſe ſuch Papiſt, or perſon marrying a Papiſt, was naturally dead, according to proviſion for the deſcent of the Crown of England, made by another act of Parliament in England, in the firſt year of the reign of their late Majeſties King William and Queen Mary, intituled, "An Act declaring the rights and liberties of the "ſubject, and ſettling the ſucceſſion of the Crown."

Article 3. That the United Kingdom of Great Britain be repreſented by one and the ſame Parliament, to be ſtyled "The Parliament of Great Britain."

Article 4. That all the ſubjects of the United Kingdom of Great Britain ſhall, from and after the Union, have full freedom and intercourſe of trade and navigation to and from any port or place within the ſaid United Kingdom, and the dominions and plantations thereunto belonging; and that there be a communication of all other rights, privileges and advantages, which do or may belong to the ſubjects of either kingdom, except where it is otherwiſe expreſly agreed in theſe Articles.

*   *   *   *   *   *

Article 6. That all parts of the United Kingdom for ever, from and after the Union, ſhall have the ſame allowances, encouragements, and drawbacks, and be under the ſame prohibitions, reſtrictions, and regulations of trade, and liable to the ſame cuſtoms and duties on import and export; and that the allowances, encouragements and drawbacks, prohibitions, reſtrictions and regulations of trade, and the cuſtoms and duties on import and export, ſettled in England, when the Union commences, ſhall, from and after the Union, take place throughout the whole United Kingdom, excepting and reſerving the duties upon export and import of ſuch particular commodities from which any perſons, the ſubjects of either kingdom, are ſpecially liberated and exempted by their private rights, which, after the Union, are to remain ſafe and intire to them, in all reſpects, as before the ſame; and that, from and after the Union, no Scots cattle carried into England ſhall be liable to any other duties, either on the publick or private accounts, than those duties to which the cattle of England are or shall be liable within the said kingdom....

*   *   *   *   *   *

Article 9. That, whensoever the sum of one million nine hundred ninety-seven thousand, seven hundred and sixty-three pounds, eight shillings and four-pence half-penny, shall be enacted by the Parliament of Great Britain, to be raised in that part of the united kingdom now called England, on land, and other things usually charged in acts of parliament there, for granting an aid to the Crown by a land tax, that part of the United Kingdom now called Scotland shall be charged, by the same act, with a further sum of forty-eight thousand pounds free of all charges, as the quota of Scotland to such tax, and so proportionally for any greater or lesser sum raised in England by any tax on land, and other things usually charged together with the land; and that such quota for Scotland, in the cases aforesaid, be raised and collected in the same manner as the cess now is in Scotland; but subject to such regulations, in the manner of collecting, as shall be made by the Parliament of Great Britain.

*   *   *   *   *   *

Article 14. That the kingdom of Scotland be not charged with any other duties laid on by the Parliament of England before the Union, except those consented to in this treaty, in regard it is agreed, that all necessary provision shall be made by the Parliament of Scotland for the publick charge and service of that kingdom, for the year one thousand seven hundred and seven; provided, nevertheless, that, if the Parliament of England shall think fit to lay any further impositions, by way of customs, or such excises, with which, by virtue of this treaty, Scotland is to be charged equally with England, in such case, Scotland shall be liable to the same customs and excises, and have an equivalent to be settled by the Parliament of Great Britain; with this further provision, that any malt, to be made and consumed in that part of the United Kingdom now called Scotland, shall not be charged with any imposition on malt during this present war....

Article 15. That whereas, by the terms of this treaty, the subjects of Scotland, for preserving an equality of trade throughout the United Kingdom, will be liable to several customs and excises now payable in England, which will be applicable towards payment of the debts of England, contracted before the Union; it is agreed, that Scotland shall have an equivalent for what the subjects thereof shall be so charged towards payment of the said debts of England in all particulars whatsoever, in manner following, viz. That, before the Union of the said kingdoms, the sum of three hundred ninety-eight thousand and eighty-five pounds ten shillings be granted to her Majesty, by the Parliament of England, for the uses after-mentioned, being the equivalent to be answered to Scotland, for such parts of the said customs and excises upon all exciseable liquors, with which that kingdom is to be charged upon the Union, as will be applicable to the payment of the said debts of England, according to the proportions which the present customs in Scotland, being thirty thousand pounds *per annum*, do bear to the customs in England, computed at one million three hundred forty-one thousand five hundred and fifty nine pounds *per annum*....

...it is agreed, that in the first place, out of the foresaid sum, what consideration shall be found necessary to be had for any losses which private persons may sustain, by reducing the coin of Scotland to the standart and value of the coin of England, may be made good: in the next place, that the capital stock or fund of the African and Indian Company of Scotland advanced, together with the interest for the said capital stock after the rate of five *per cent. per annum*, from the respective times of the payment thereof, shall be payed; upon payment of which capital stock and interest, it is agreed the said Company be dissolved and cease....

...and as to the overplus of the said sum of three hundred ninety-eight thousand eighty-five pounds ten shillings,...

...it is agreed, that the same be applied in manner following, viz. That all the publick debts of the kingdom of Scotland, as shall be adjusted by this present Parliament, shall be payed; and that two thousand pounds *per annum*, for the space of seven years, shall be applied towards encouraging and promoting the manufacture of coarfe wooll within thofe fhires which produce the wooll. . . .

Article 16. That, from and after the Union, the coin fhall be of the fame ftandart and value throughout the United Kingdom as now in England, and a mint fhall be continued in Scotland under the fame rules as the mint in England; and the prefent officers of the mint continued, fubject to fuch regulations and alterations as her Majefty, her heirs or fuc-ceffors, or the Parliament of Great Britain, fhall think fit.

Article 17. That, from and after the Union, the fame weights and meafures fhall be ufed throughout the United Kingdom, as are now eftablifhed in England; and ftandarts of weights and meafures fhall be kept by thofe burghs in Scotland, to whom the keeping the ftandarts of weights and meafures, now in ufe there, does of fpecial right belong; all which ftan-darts fhall be fent down to fuch refpective burghs, from the ftandarts kept in the Exchequer at Weftminfter, fubject never-thelefs to fuch regulations as the Parliament of Great Britain fhall think fit.

Article 18. That the laws concerning regulation of trade, cuftoms, and fuch excifes, to which Scotland is, by virtue of this treaty, to be liable, be the fame in Scotland, from and after the Union, as in England; and that all other laws, in ufe within the kingdom of Scotland, do, after the Union, and notwithftanding thereof, remain in the fame force as before (except fuch as are contrary to, or inconfiftent with this treaty), but alterable by the Parliament of Great Britain, with this difference betwixt the laws concerning publick right, policy, and civil government, and thofe which concern private right, that the laws which concern publick right, policy, and civil government, may be made the fame throughout the whole United Kingdom, but that no alteration be made in laws which concern private right, except for evident utility of the fubject within Scotland.

Article 19. That the Court of Seffion, or College of Juftice, do, after the Union, and notwithftanding thereof, remain in all time coming within Scotland as it is now con-ftituted by the laws of that kingdom, and with the fame authority and privileges as before the Union, fubject neverthelefs to fuch regulations, for the better adminiftration of juftice, as fhall be made by the Parliament of Great Britain. . . .

. . . And that the Court of Jufticiary do alfo, after the Union, and notwithftanding thereof, remain, in all time coming, within Scotland, as it is now conftituted by the laws of that kingdom, and with the fame authority and privileges as before the Union, fubject neverthelefs to fuch regulations as fhall be made by the Parliament of Great Britain, and without prejudice of other rights of jufticiary. . . .

. . . And that all other courts, now in being within the kingdom of Scotland, do remain, but fubject to alterations by the Parliament of Great Britain: And that all inferior courts within the faid limits do remain fubordinate, as they are now, to the fupreme courts of juftice within the fame, in all time coming; and that no caufes in Scotland be cognofcible by the Courts of Chancery, Queen's Bench, Common Pleas, or any other court in Weftminfter-hall; and that the faid courts, or any other of the like nature, after the Union, fhall have no power to cognofce, review, or alter the acts or fentences of the judicatures within Scotland, or ftop the execution of the fame; and that there be a Court of Exchequer in Scotland, after the Union, for deciding queftions concerning the revenues of Cuftoms and Excifes there, having the fame power and authority in fuch cafes as the Court of Exchequer has in England; and that the faid Court of Exchequer in Scotland have power of paffing fignatures, gifts, tutories, and in other things, as the Court of Exchequer at prefent in Scotland hath; and that the Court of Exchequer that now is in Scotland do remain, until a new Court of Exchequer be fettled by the Parliament of Great Britain in Scotland after the Union: And that, after the Union, the Queen's Majefty and her royal fucceffors may continue a Privy Council in Scotland, for preferving of publick peace and order, until the Parliament of Great Britain fhall think fit to alter it, or eftablifh any other effectual method for that end.

Article 20. That all heretable offices, fuperiorities, heretable jurifdictions, offices for life, and jurifdictions for life, be referved to the owners thereof, as rights of property, in the fame manner as they are now enjoyed by the laws of Scotland, notwithftanding this Treaty.

Article 21. That the rights and privileges of the royal burghs in Scotland, as they now are, do remain entire after the Union, and notwithſtanding thereof.

Article 22. That, by virtue of this Treaty, of the Peers of Scotland at the time of the Union, ſixteen ſhall be the number to ſit and vote in the Houſe of Lords, and forty-five the number of the repreſentatives of Scotland in the Houſe of Commons of the Parliament of Great Britain....

...And her Majeſty may, by her royal proclamation under the Great-ſeal of Great Britain, appoint the ſaid firſt Parliament of Great Britain to meet at ſuch time and place as her Majeſty ſhall think fit, which time ſhall not be leſs than fifty days after the date of ſuch proclamation; and the time and place of the meeting of ſuch Parliament being ſo appointed, a writ ſhall be immediately iſſued, under the Great-ſeal of Great Britain, directed to the Privy Council of Scotland, for the ſummoning the ſixteen Peers, and for electing forty-five Members, by whom Scotland is to be repreſented in the Parliament of Great Britain; and the Lords of Parliament of England, and the ſixteen Peers of Scotland, ſuch ſixteen Peers being ſummoned and returned in the manner agreed in this Treaty, and the Members of the Houſe of Commons of the ſaid Parliament of England, and the forty-five Members for Scotland, ſuch forty-five Members being elected and returned in the manner agreed in this Treaty, ſhall aſſemble and meet reſpectively in their reſpective Houſes of the Parliament of Great Britain, at ſuch time and place as ſhall be ſo appointed by her Majeſty, and ſhall be the two Houſes of the firſt Parliament of Great Britain; and that Parliament may continue for ſuch time only as the preſent Parliament of England might have continued, if the Union of the two kingdoms had not been made, unleſs ſooner diſſolved by her Majeſty. And that every one of the Lords of Parliament of Great Britain, and every Member of the Houſe of Commons of the Parliament of Great Britain, in the firſt and all ſucceeding Parliaments of Great Britain, until the Parliament of Great Britain ſhall otherways direct, ſhall take the reſpective oaths appointed to be taken, inſtead of the oaths of Allegiance and Supremacy, by an act of Parliament made in England, in the firſt year of

the reign of the late King William and Queen Mary, intituled, "An act for the abrogating of the oaths of Supremacy
"and Allegiance, and appointing other oaths;" and make,
subscribe, and audibly repeat, the declaration mentioned in an
act of Parliament made in England, in the thirtieth year of
the reign of King Charles the Second, intituled, "An act
"for the more effectual preserving the King's person and
"government, by disabling Papists from sitting in either House
"of Parliament;" and shall take and subscribe the oath mentioned in an act of Parliament made in England, in the first
year of her Majesty's reign, intituled, "An act to declare the
"alterations in the oath appointed to be taken by the act, in-
"tituled, An act for the further security of his Majesty's per-
"son, and the succession of the Crown in the Protestant line,
"and for extinguishing the hopes of the pretended Prince of
"Wales, and all other pretenders, and their open and secret
"abettors, and for declaring the Association to be determined;"
at such time, and in such manner, as the members of both
Houses of Parliament of England are, by the said respective
acts, directed to take, make, and subscribe the same, upon the
penalties and disabilities in the said respective acts contained.
And it is declared and agreed, that these words, "This realm,
"the crown of this realm, and the Queen of this realm,"
mentioned in the oaths and declaration contained in the aforesaid acts, which were intended to signify the crown and realm
of England, shall be understood of the crown and realm of
Great Britain; and that, in that sense, the said oaths and
declaration be taken and subscribed by the Members of both
Houses of the Parliament of Great Britain.

* * * * * *

Article 24. That, from and after the Union, there be one
Great-seal for the United Kingdom of Great Britain, which
shall be different from the Great-seal now used in either
kingdom; and that the quartering the arms, and the rank and
precedency of the Lyon King of Arms of the kingdom of
Scotland, as may best suit the Union, be left to her Majesty....
Article 25. That all laws and statutes in either kingdom,
so far as they are contrary to, or inconsistent with, the terms

of thefe articles, or any one of them, fhall, from and after the Union, ceafe and become void, and fhall be fo declared to be by the refpective Parliaments of the faid kingdoms, as by the faid Articles of Union ratified and approved by the faid act of Parliament of Scotland, relation thereunto being had, may appear; and the tenor of the aforefaid act, for fecuring the Proteftant religion and Prefbyterian Church Government within the kingdom of Scotland, is as follows.

    OUR SOVEREIGN LADY, and the Eftates of Parliament, confidering, that, by the late Act of Parliament for a Treaty with England, for an Union of both kingdoms, it is provided, that the Commiffioners for that Treaty fhould not treat of or concerning any alteration of the Worfhip, Difcipline, and Government of the Church of this kingdom, as now by law eftablifhed, which Treaty being now reported to the Parliament, and it being reafonable and neceffary, that the true Proteftant Religion, as prefently profeffed within this kingdom, with the Worfhip, Difcipline, and Government of this Church, fhould be effectually and unalterably fecured; therefore her Majefty, with advice and confent of the faid Eftates of Parliament, doth hereby eftablifh and confirm the faid true Proteftant Religion, and the Worfhip, Difcipline, and Government of this Church, to continue without any alteration to the people of this land in all fucceeding generations; and more efpecially, her Majefty, with advice and confent aforefaid, ratifies, approves, and for ever confirms, the fifth Act of the firft Parliament of King William and Queen Mary, intituled, "Act ratifying the Confeffion of Faith, and "fettling Prefbyterian Church Government," with all other Acts of Parliament relating thereto, in profecution of the declaration of the Eftates of this kingdom, containing the claim of right, bearing date the eleventh of April, one thoufand fix hundred and eighty-nine; and her Majefty, with advice and confent aforefaid, exprefly provides and declares, that the forefaid true Proteftant Religion, contained in the above-mentioned Confeffion of Faith, with the form and purity of Worfhip prefently in ufe within this Church, and its Prefbyterian Church Government and Difcipline, that is to fay, the Government of the Church by Kirk Seffions, Prefbyteries,

Provincial Synods, and General Assemblies, all established by the foresaid Acts of Parliament, pursuant to the claim of right, shall remain and continue unalterable; and that the said Presbyterian Government shall be the only Government of the Church within the kingdom of Scotland. And further, for the greater security of the foresaid Protestant Religion, and of the Worship, Discipline, and Government of this Church as above established, her Majesty, with advice and consent foresaid, statutes and ordains, that the Universities and Colleges of St. Andrew's, Glasgow, Aberdeen, and Edinburgh, as now established by law, shall continue within this kingdom for ever. And that, in all time coming, no Professors, Principals, Regents, Masters, or others, bearing office in any University, College or School, within this kingdom, be capable, or be admitted or allowed to continue in the exercise of their said functions, but such as shall own and acknowledge the Civil Government in manner prescribed, or to be prescribed by the Acts of Parliament. As also, that before, or at their admissions, they do and shall acknowledge and profess, and shall subscribe to the foresaid Confession of Faith, as the Confession of their Faith; and that they will practise and conform themselves to the Worship presently in use in this Church, and submit themselves to the Government and Discipline thereof, and never endeavour, directly or indirectly, the prejudice or subversion of the same; and that before the respective Presbyteries of their bounds, by whatsoever gift, presentation, or provision, they may be thereto provided. And further, her Majesty, with advice aforesaid, expresly declares and statutes, that none of the subjects of this kingdom shall be liable to, but all and every one of them for ever free of any oath, test, or subscription, within this kingdom, contrary to, or inconsistent with, the foresaid true Protestant Religion and Presbyterian Church Government, Worship, and Discipline, as above established; and that the same, within the bounds of this Church and Kingdom, shall never be imposed upon, or required of them in any sort. And, lastly, that, after the decease of her present Majesty (whom God long preserve!) the Sovereign succeeding to her in the Royal Government of the kingdom of Great-Britain shall, in all time coming, at his or her accession to the

Crown, fwear and fubfcribe, that they fhall inviolably maintain and preferve the forefaid Settlement of the true Proteftant
Religion, with the Government, Worfhip, Difcipline, Right,
and Privileges of this Church, as above eftablifhed by the laws
of this kingdom, in profecution of the claim of right. And it
is hereby ftatute and ordained, that this Act of Parliament,
with the eftablifhment therein contained, fhall be held and
obferved, in all times coming, as a fundamental and effential
condition of any Treaty or Union to be concluded betwixt the
two kingdoms, without any alteration thereof, or derogation
thereto, in any fort, for ever. As alfo, that this Act of Parliament, and Settlement therein contained, fhall be infert and
repeated in any Act of Parliament that fhall pafs, for agreeing
and concluding the forefaid Treaty or Union betwixt the two
kingdoms; and that the fame fhall be therein exprefly declared to be a fundamental and effential condition of the faid
Treaty or Union, in all time coming....

AND WHEREAS an act hath paffed in this prefent
feffion of Parliament, intituled, "An act for fecuring the
"Church of England as by law eftablifhed," the tenor whereof
follows,...

...whereas certain Commiffioners appointed by her
Majefty, in purfuance of the faid act, and alfo other Commiffioners, nominated by her Majefty, by the authority of the
Parliament of Scotland, have met and agreed upon a Treaty
of Union of the faid kingdoms, which treaty is now under the
confideration of this prefent Parliament; and whereas the
faid Treaty, with fome alterations therein made, is ratified and
approved by act of Parliament in Scotland, and the faid act
of ratification is by her Majefty's royal command laid before
the Parliament of this kingdom; and whereas it is reafonable
and neceffary that the true Proteftant religion profeffed and
eftablifhed by law in the church of England, and the doctrine,
worfhip, difcipline, and government thereof, fhould be effectually and unalterably fecured; Be it enacted by the Queen's moft
Excellent Majefty, by and with the advice and confent of
the Lords Spiritual and Temporal, and the Commons in this
prefent Parliament affembled, and by authority of the fame,
that an act made in the thirteenth year of the reign of Queen

Elizabeth of famous memory, intituled, "An act for the "Minifters of the Church to be of found religion;" and alfo another act made in the thirteenth year of the reign of the late King Charles the fecond, intituled, "An act for the uniformity "of publick prayers and adminiftration of facraments, and other "rites and ceremonies, and for eftablifhing the form of making, "ordaining, and confecrating Bifhops, Priefts, and Deacons, in "the Church of England" (other than fuch claufes in the faid acts, or either of them, as have been repealed or altered by any fubfequent act or acts of Parliament), and all and fingular other acts of Parliament now in force, for the eftablifhment and prefervation of the Church of England, and the doctrine, worfhip, difcipline, and government thereof, fhall remain and be in full force for ever. And be it further enacted, by the authority aforefaid, that after the demife of her Majefty (whom God long preferve!) the Sovereign next fucceeding to her Majefty in the royal government of the Kingdom of Great Britain, and fo for ever hereafter every King or Queen fucceeding and coming to the royal government of the king-dom of Great Britain, at his or her coronation, fhall in the prefence of all perfons who fhall be attending, affifting, or otherways then and there prefent, take and fubfcribe an oath to maintain and preferve inviolably the faid fettlement of the Church of England, and the doctrine, worfhip, difcipline, and government thereof, as by law eftablifhed within the king-doms of England and Ireland, the dominion of Wales, and town of Berwick upon Tweed, and the territories thereunto belonging. And be it further enacted, by the authority afore-faid, that this act, and all and every the matters and things therein contained, be, and fhall for ever be, holden and ad-judged to be a fundamental and effential part of any Treaty of Union to be concluded between the faid two kingdoms; and alfo that this act fhall be inferted in exprefs terms in any act of Parliament which fhall be made for fettling and ratifying any fuch Treaty of Union, and fhall be therein declared to be an effential and fundamental part thereof....

...OUR SOVEREIGN LADY confidering that, by the twenty-fecond article of the Treaty of Union, as the fame is ratified by an act paffed in this feffion of Parliament, upon the fixteenth of January laft, it is provided, that, by virtue of the faid Treaty, of the Peers of Scotland, at the time of the Union, fixteen fhall be the number to fit and vote in the Houfe of Lords, and forty-five the number of the reprefentatives of Scotland in the Houfe of Commons, of the Parliament of Great Britain; and that the faid fixteen Peers, and forty-five members in the Houfe of Commons, be named and chofen in fuch manner as by a fubfequent act in this prefent feffion of Parliament in Scotland fhould be fettled; which act is thereby declared to be as valid, as if it were a part of, and ingroffed in, the faid Treaty; therefore, her Majefty, with advice and confent of the Eftates of Parliament, ftatutes, enacts, and ordains, that the faid fixteen Peers, who fhall have right to fit in the houfe of Peers in the Parliament of Great Britain on the part of Scotland, by virtue of this Treaty, fhall be named by the faid Peers of Scotland whom they reprefent, their heirs, or fucceffors to their dignities and honours, out of their own number, and that by open election and plurality of voices of the peers prefent, and of the proxies for fuch as fhall be abfent, the faid proxies being Peers, and producing a mandate in writing duly figned before witneffes, and both the conftituent and proxy being qualified according to law; declaring alfo, that fuch peers as are abfent, being qualified as aforefaid, may fend to all fuch meetings lifts of the Peers whom they judge fitteft, validly figned by the faid abfent Peers, which fhall be reckoned in the fame manner as if the parties had been prefent, and given in the faid lift: And in cafe of the death, or legal incapacity, of any of the faid fixteen Peers, that the aforefaid Peers of Scotland fhall nominate another of their own number in place of the faid Peer or Peers in manner before and after mentioned. And that of the faid forty-five reprefentatives of Scotland in the Houfe of Commons in the Parliament of Great Britain, thirty fhall be chofen by the fhires or ftewartries, and fifteen by the royal burrows, as follows, *videlicet*, one for every fhire and ftewartry, excepting the fhires of Bute and Caithnefs, which fhall choofe one by turns, Bute having the firft election; the fhires of Nairn and Cromarty, which fhall alfo choofe by turns, Nairn having the firft election; and in like manner the fhires of Clackmannan and Kinrofs fhall choofe by turns,

Clackmannan having the first election: And in case of the death or legal incapacity of any of the said members from the respective shires or stewartries above-mentioned, to sit in the house of Commons; it is enacted and ordained, that the shire or stewartry who elected the said member shall elect another member in his place. And that the said fifteen representatives for the royal burrows be chosen as follows, *videlicet*, That the town of Edinburgh shall have right to elect and send one member to the Parliament of Great Britain; and that each of the other burghs shall elect a Commissioner in the same manner as they are now in use to elect Commissioners to the Parliament of Scotland; which Commissioners and burghs (Edinburgh excepted), being divided in fourteen classes or districts, shall meet at such time and burghs within their respective districts as her Majesty, her heirs or successors, shall appoint, and elect one for each district, *videlicet*, the burghs of Kirkwal, Week, Dornock, Dingwall and Tayne, one; the burghs of Fortrose, Invernefs, Nairn and Forrefs, one; the burghs of Elgine, Cullen, Banff, Inverury and Kintore, one; the burghs of Aberdeen, Inverbervie, Montrose, Aberbrothock and Brichen, one; the burghs of Forfar, Perth, Dundee, Cowper and St. Andrews, one; the burghs of Crail, Kilrennie, Anstruther Easter, Anstruther Wester, and Pittenweem, one; the burghs of Dysart, Kirkcaldie, Kinghorn and Bruntisland, one; the burghs of Innerkeithing, Dumfermline, Queensferry, Culrofs and Stirling, one; the burghs of Glasgow, Renfrew, Ruglen and Dumbarton, one; the burghs of Haddington, Dunbar, North Berwick, Lawder and Jedburgh, one; the burghs of Selkirk, Peebles, Linlithgow and Lanerk, one; the burghs of Dumfreis, Sanquhar, Annan, Lochmaben and Kirkcudbright, one; the burghs of Wigtoun, New Galloway, Stranrawer and Whitehern, one; and the burghs of Air, Irvine, Rothefay, Campbeltoun and Inverary, one. And it is hereby declared and ordained, that where the votes of the Commissioners for the said burghs, met to choose representatives from their several districts to the Parliament of Great Britain, shall be equal, in that case the President of the meeting shall have a casting or decisive vote, and that by and according to his vote as a Commissioner from the burgh from

which he is fent, the Commiffioner from the eldeft burgh
prefiding in the firft meeting, and the Commiffioners from the
other burghs in their refpective diftricts prefiding afterwards
by turns, in the order as the faid burghs are now called in the
Rolls of the Parliament of Scotland. And that in cafe any of
the faid fifteen Commiffioners from burghs fhall deceafe, or
become legally incapable to fit in the Houfe of Commons, then
the town of Edinburgh, or the diftrict which chofe the faid
member, fhall elect a member in his or their place: It is
always hereby exprefsly provided and declared, that none fhall
be capable to elect or be elected for any of the faid eftates but
fuch as are twenty-one years of age compleat, and Proteftant,
excluding all Papifts, or fuch who, being fufpect of Popery and
required, refufe to fwear and fubfcribe the *formula* contained
in the third act, made in the eighth and ninth feffions of King
William's Parliament, intituled, "Act for preventing the
"growth of Popery;" and alfo declaring, that none fhall be
capable to elect or be elected to reprefent a fhire or burgh in
the Parliament of Great Britain for this part of the United
Kingdom, except fuch as are now capable by the laws of this
kingdom to elect or be elected as Commiffioners for fhires or
burghs to the Parliament of Scotland.

QUEEN ANNE'S PRINCIPAL MINISTERS
1702–7

LORD TREASURER — Sidney, Lord Godolphin.

LORD CHANCELLOR — Sir Nathan Wright (High Tory), removed 1705; Sir William Cowper (Whig), Lord Keeper 1705; cr. Lord Cowper 1706; becomes Lord Chancellor May 1707.

SECRETARY OF STATE (Northern Department) — Sir Charles Hedges; succeeded May 1704 by Robert Harley.

SECRETARY OF STATE (Southern Department) — Daniel Finch, Earl of Nottingham (High Tory); succeeded May 1704 by Sir Charles Hedges from Northern Department; succeeded Dec. 1706 by Charles Spencer, Earl of Sunderland (Whig).

LORD-LIEUTENANT OF IRELAND — Laurence Hyde, Earl of Rochester (High Tory); succeeded Feb. 1703 by Jas. Butler, Duke of Ormonde (High Tory); succeeded 1707 by Thos. Herbert, Earl of Pembroke (Moderate Tory).

LORD HIGH ADMIRAL — Prince George of Denmark. Died Oct. 1708.

SECRETARY AT WAR — William Blathwayt; succeeded 1704 by Henry St John.

MASTER GENERAL OF ORDNANCE — John Churchill, Duke of Marlborough.

PARLIAMENTS OF ANNE'S REIGN

1. William's last Parliament, elected December 1701, Tory and Whig, strong for war, continued sitting on Anne's accession and took first Parliamentary steps of her reign. Dissolved in summer.

2. August 1702. Newly-elected Tory Parliament meets, and sits for three winters.

3. June 1705. New Parliament meets, Whig and Moderate Tory. Strong for the Ministerial war policy.

   In April 1707 this Parliament becomes first Parliament of Great Britain by addition of Scottish members.

4. 1708. Whig Parliament.

5. 1710. Tory Parliament.

6. 1713. Tory Parliament.

   [1715 George I. Whig Parliament.]